Last Man In

The End of Empire
in Northern Nigeria

Other titles by the same author:
The Lost Camels of Tartary
Shadows across the Sahara
The Mysteries of the Gobi
Kawndolawa and Itinate: Ritual Pottery of the Cham and Mwana

For children:
Rhino's Horn
Leopard's Coat
Elephant's Tusk
The Dragons of Tiananmen Square
Letters for a Spy
Ticket to Tallinn
The Fearless Four
The Fearless Four, Hijack!
The Fearless Four and the Smugglers
The Fearless Four and the Graveyard Ghost

Last Man In

The End of Empire
in Northern Nigeria

John Hare

Neville & Harding

A Village Head in his grandfather's
German Imperial Government uniform

For Bobboi and DVM – two of the very best

Contents

Maps

Preface

They tolerate us because they need us. They do not look upon us resentfully as conquerors but complacently as stepping stones. What will happen when they can, or think they can, mount alone and have no further use for the stepping stones, no one can tell.

Sylvia Leith-Ross, *Stepping Stones*

On 19th July 1884, the German explorer Dr Gustav Nachtigal took possession of a vast tract of land in West Africa in the name of the German Emperor, Kaiser Wilhelm II, in furtherance of Chancellor Otto von Bismarck's colonial policy of developing a *Mittelafrica* empire. It later became known to the outside world as the German Cameroons.

During the First World War the territory was overrun by British, French and Belgian troops and was seized from the German government. It was partitioned by the British and French, the British taking the western sector – divided into two parts by the Benue valley – and the French taking the eastern sector.

In 1922 this partition of the Cameroons was confirmed by the recently formed League of Nations which awarded the sectors as mandates to Britain and France.

The northern portion of the British mandate was placed under the jurisdiction of the regional government of Northern Nigeria, and Eastern Nigeria's regional government administered the southern section. This mandate continued when the League of Nations became the United Nations after the Second World War.

In the early 1960s, when independence came to Nigeria, a plebiscite was held which asked the people in the mandated territory whether they wished to join an independent Nigeria or remain a British colony. Much to the consternation of Whitehall and the anger of the Northern Nigerian government they voted to remain a colony.

This book attempts to explain the reasons behind this unexpected vote and how a fortunate few administrators, myself included, ruled a new British colony in the early 1960s for 18 volatile months, headed by a governor who was directly answerable to Whitehall and who could do almost anything except declare war.

At the end of 18 months a second plebiscite was held. This time there was to be no further embarrassment for a British government that was trying to relinquish colonial responsibility as quickly as possible. The citizens could join either an independent Nigeria or an independent Cameroon Republic.

The first section of the book describes my personal experiences in isolated parts of Northern Nigeria prior to my involvement with the fate of the former German Cameroons.

The second part describes my connection with the plebiscites in some of the remotest parts of the territory and how I came into contact with cultures and customs that were fast disappearing. At the same time I had become caught up in political events which merit, I believe, a footnote in African history.

I was the last recruit into the Colonial Administrative Service in Northern Nigeria – hence the title of this book. The years 1957 to 1964, during which I worked for both the British and Nigerian governments, coincided with a time of momentous political change in Nigeria – from a colony to an independent state – and ended just prior to the onset of a military coup and the Biafran war.

I have used language that was in current usage at the time, and have quoted some opinions which today are not held to be politically correct, in particular the use of the words 'native', 'boy' and 'pagan'. Today, for example, 'pagans' are referred to as 'animists'. But this book is a record of the past and no offence is meant to anyone whatsoever.

I have used italics for quoted text and foreign words. When pounds are mentioned these are Nigerian pounds (£N), which were used before the introduction of the present Nigerian currency, the *naira*.

For those who are mystified why I enlisted in a service which was quite clearly entering its death throes, there is a brief explanation and autobiography in Appendix I.

NORTHERN NIGERIA
Areas in which I served

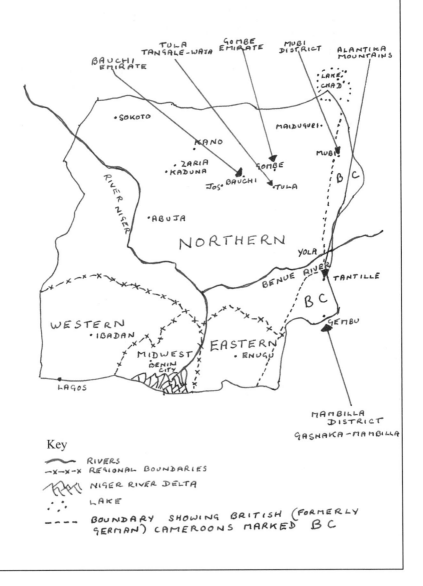

BAUCHI
EMIRATE

TULA
TANGALE-WAJA

GOMBE
EMIRATE

MUBI
DISTRICT

ALANTIKA
MOUNTAINS

LAKE
CHAD

•SOKOTO

MAIDUGURI•

•KANO

•ZARIA
•KADUNA

GOMBE

MUBI

RIVER NIGER

JOS• •BAUCHI

•TULA

B C

•ABUJA

NORTHERN

YOLA

BENUE RIVER

TANTILLE

B C

WESTERN
•IBADAN

EASTERN

GEMBU

MIDWEST
BENIN
CITY

•ENUGU

LAGOS

MAMBILLA
DISTRICT
GASHAKA-MAMBILLA

Key

~~~~ RIVERS

-x-x-x REGIONAL BOUNDARIES

NIGER RIVER DELTA

LAKE

- - - - BOUNDARY SHOWING BRITISH (FORMERLY GERMAN) CAMEROONS MARKED B C

1

The Tricks of Time

And finding you again I find
The tricks of time all thrown away.
The recollected turns to here and now.
                    Edmund Blunden, 'Recognition'

The telephone rang for the third time in as many minutes. A quiet, slightly hesitant voice with a West African accent asked whether he was speaking to John Hare.

'Yes.'

'I'm Bobboi, sir.' The speaker sounded nervous, 'Bobboi from Mambilla. Do you remember me?'

'Bobboi – Bobboi Jauro? '

'Yes, Abubakar Bobboi Jauro.'

'Bobboi. What a surprise. Where are you?'

'In Tangiers.'

'Tangiers? What on earth are you doing there?'

'I've been representing Nigeria on the African Electoral Commission. I am on my way home but if you are free next Sunday I can fly to England to see you.'

And that was how in 2008, after a gap of 48 years, I renewed my acquaintance with Abubakar B. Jauro, alias Bobboi, by then a retired Federal Permanent Secretary with the Nigerian Government.

I had first met Bobboi in another world, on the remote Mambilla plateau on the Nigerian–Cameroon border. A young District Officer, I had been seconded from the British Government to the newly independent Northern Nigerian Government and charged with administrating the Gashaka-Mambilla District.

In March 1962, a young Fulani secondary school student peered round my office door. Bobboi must have been about 14 years old then and unlike most of the fair-skinned Mambilla Fulani his complexion was quite dark. His clothes were clean and neat and his eyes sparkled.

'Hello, sir,' he said, 'can I help you? I am on my long summer vacation and would like something to do.'

Bobboi had appeared at an opportune moment: my clerk was about to go on annual leave and I needed help in the office. Although Bobboi couldn't type, he soon progressed with two fingers. I gave him some tidying up to do and he did it well. He was clearly intelligent and there was something rather special about him.

'Come back if you want more things to do.'

The Fulani roam from the Gambia to the Cameroon with their white and red *zebu*, long-horned and humped-back cattle. However, on Mambilla, a steep-sided plateau with first-rate grazing, they were confined in a *cul-de-sac* and had lost the true nomad's freedom. Fulani fathers were resistant to change and wanted their sons to look after and inherit cattle, not waste their time on Western education. Things are different today, except for the views of the current terrorist organisation Boko Haram,[1] but at that time antipathy to education among the Fulani was strong.

Bobboi did so well and proved so capable that whenever my

---

1 Boko Haram ('Western education is forbidden or a sin') is a Muslim fundamentalist terrorist organisation which wants the full imposition of Islamic Law throughout Nigeria and the creation of an Islamic State. In 2009 the sect committed atrocities in Maiduguri in the far north-east of Nigeria and in 2010 a series of car bomb outrages in Abuja during the 50th anniversary celebrations of independence from British rule. In 2011, Boko Haram employed suicide bombers for the first time, an indication that they may be falling under the control of Al-Qaeda. In January 2012 outrages were committed in Mubi and Gombe, two towns which are described in detail in this book.

clerk went on leave, he always stood in as his replacement. In 1963 I left Nigeria as an administrator but Bobboi kept in touch with me long after and it was no surprise when he proudly wrote to tell me that he had graduated from Ahmadu Bello University in Zaria, Northern Nigeria. He had become the first person from the Mambilla plateau ever to obtain a university degree.

Over the ensuing years I lost track of him, although I did learn he had been appointed Executive Secretary of the Lake Chad River Basin Authority, a regional organisation based in Ndjamena, Chad. Then all contact faded apart from a chance meeting when I was working in Nairobi for the United Nations Environment Programme.

It was only in the autumn of 2007, during a visit to my home by some Northern Nigerians who worked with the BBC Hausa Service in London, that it emerged in conversation one of them knew Bobboi who, he said, was alive and well and living in Abuja, Nigeria's capital city. This man, an eminent physician, was returning home in a week's time and I asked him if he would take some books and a letter to Bobboi.

A few months later, I received the phone call.

The following Sunday, Bobboi flew from Tangiers and came to my home in Kent. Beneath the lined face and a sprinkling of grey, the same intelligent eyes twinkled. His sense of humour had not dimmed. We reminisced for hours and the intervening years fell away.

His visit affected me greatly and set me thinking. Fifty years after Nigeria's independence the attitude of the current generation to colonial administrators who served the British Empire is one of embarrassment at best and downright hostility at worst. We are seen as oppressors who annexed land for white settlement and subjugated unwilling subjects to foreign rule.

So it struck me, as I mused about Bobboi and his selfless journey to meet me, that my youthful idealism and desire to try to do some good in Africa was exactly the same clutch of ideals that inspires today's 21-year-olds to go out with Médecins sans Frontières, Oxfam or any other worthwhile NGO. We are idealistic brothers and sisters under the skin, only our times and ages are different. And if Bobboi had made such an effort to meet up with me after an interval of almost 50 years, then all colonial administrators could not have left a wholly negative impression on their 'subject' races.

My own experience was that colonial administrators were, for the most part, deeply appreciated, because they were impartial, had no tribal loyalty, had the utmost integrity, were not working in a colony to enrich themselves and were energetic and hard-working. And above all, they cared – sometimes too much so – for the people who had been placed under their tutelage and guidance. They never owned land – Africa's perennial and contentious issue – and in the end were birds of passage who, as all the locals knew, would one day go home.

And when they left and African District Officers replaced them inevitably things changed. The black administrators were constantly under pressure to place tribal loyalty above allegiance to a newly fledged nation. Sometimes those pressures were too great and they administered with a judgement clouded by tribal and religious loyalties. With no permanent stake in the country, no tribal allegiance, no religious intolerance, white colonial administrators were subjected to none of these formidable internal pressures and were able to remain impartial.

After Nigerian independence in 1960, the Premier of Northern Nigeria, Ahmadu Bello the Sardauna of Sokoto, wrote to me saying that the Northern government felt the need to retain the expertise of some of their erstwhile colonial administrators and would I remain in Mambilla for at least a further two years. These approaches to expatriate officers by an independent Nigeria are something that greatly surprises today's generation of Western idealists.

During the ensuing 50 years, a civil war, military coups and numerous internal scandals have strained Nigeria's cohesion as a single entity – hardly surprising for a country cobbled hastily together by the British government at the beginning of the 20th century. Yet somehow, in spite of its vast diversity of over 140 tribes and languages and a population approaching 150 million, Nigeria has held together. Whenever, during those 50 years, the north of Nigeria, with its religious and cultural differences strained to break away, the final decision was tempered by the stark fact that the oil, the ports and the country's overwhelming potential wealth, lay in the south.

2

In the Beginning

You are only an amateur? That's no matter as long as you are sincere.
Professor C G Seligman

The journey that led me to Mambilla began in 1956, when I found myself standing at Waterloo Station in London on an overcast February morning. As grim, grey hordes of commuters streamed off their over-crowded, early morning trains with their rolled brollies and tense faces I vowed I would never join them. I would not spend my life straining through crowds to get to a desk in some crowded office in the City. I made another vow: I would make every attempt to return to the Africa I loved (*see Appendix I*). And so, having enquired whether they were still seeking recruits into the Colonial Administrative Service and having received the answer that they were, I applied to join.

At my interview for the service – quaintly renamed 'Her Majesty's Overseas Civil Service' in the interests of 1950s political correctness – in Church Hall, Great Smith Street, Westminster, they had put it bluntly: 'You will be lucky if your career takes you beyond the age of 30.' However, 30 to a 21-year-old, especially a 21-year-old who had never looked too far ahead and who never worried about long-term job security, seemed to be one foot in the grave territory. In retrospect, it amuses me that the one question which the interviewing panel put to me, and treated with the utmost seriousness, was a query aimed at extracting my views on a controversial Oxford by-pass scheme. Its relevance to administrating Africans completely eluded me at the time, and still does.

However, I must have given those grey-beards the right answer because after a two-month delay I was appointed to serve in the Northern Nigerian administration as an Assistant District Officer (ADO). Colonial Secretary Alan Lennox-Boyd signed the letter of appointment personally.

Papers and official documentation soon arrived together with a *Handbook of Health in the Tropics*. The book's green cover had been treated to render it 'impervious to white ants' and its main purpose seemed to be to warn of the dangers of local women, malaria (one Paludrine a day) and bilharzia (don't swim in stagnant water). Alcohol was best left until after six o'clock and one was encouraged to ensure ankles were covered and sleeves rolled down before the sun set, the mosquitoes started buzzing and the right arm was raised, glass in hand.

Kitted-up with, among other items, a tin bath, a camp bed, a folding table, mosquito boots and long and short puttees by Griffith McCallister in Soho's Golden Square, the long-since defunct suppliers of equipment and clothing for service in the tropics, I left for Nigeria from Liverpool aboard the Elder Dempster passenger vessel, MV *Aureol* on 10th January 1957.

For decades, Elder Dempster had monopolised the passenger run to West Africa, but with air services operating regularly to Nigeria from Heathrow, passenger services by sea were falling off and by 1960 were defunct. However, the Westminster sages decided that the last recruit should take the route to the 'coast' in traditional style.

The only government administrator on board was M, of vast girth, appetite and self-regard. Larger than life and too clever to be the blimp he looked, M was intrigued to learn on making my acquaintance that 'his' service was still recruiting. M held trenchant views which echoed round the decks and soon made it known to me and the rest of the passenger list that 'bleeding hearts' – a term embracing *Manchester Guardian* readers, the BBC and most of the 'time-servers' in the Secretariat in Kaduna, the headquarters of Northern Nigeria – were anathema to him. So too were missionaries, especially American, with the notable exception of bush-based Irish Roman Catholic fathers.

M had an extraordinary scar on his upper lip. Before we finally docked in Lagos he explained that a bullet had winged him when he was, according to his account, leading an assault at Monte Cassino during the Second World War. He fought on and, according to M, personally scattered the Germans. 'They patched me with skin taken from my bottom,' he proclaimed, and then made the rather startling assertion that, 'I am the only man in Nigeria who wears his bum on his face.'

On arrival in Lagos, I lost track of M. Unbeknown to me, I was to see a great deal more of him during my Nigeria days.

Lagos had not yet acquired its current reputation for chaos, thuggery and violence; nevertheless as I disembarked I was challenged by the port Customs Officer, a wily Yoruba in peaked black cap and khaki uniform, to pay duty on my collection of 78 r.p.m. gramophone records in my kit. They were old and worn and I refused. The customs officer was startled, indignant and extremely annoyed when, to close our argument, I tipped them all into the sea. He threatened me with 'water pollution', which given the state of the waters around Lagos harbour was a joke. However, a Hausa customs officer at Kano airport exacted revenge on behalf of the Customs Service many years later when he confiscated apples I was bringing into the country and proceeded to 'destroy' them by eating them one by one in front of me.

I was to catch a train that would take me to Jos, a township on a plateau of the same name in the centre of Northern Nigeria. At Iddo railway station, in the heart of noisy, dirty, hectic Lagos, the hour of departure of the Up-Limited train to Jos drew close and the atmosphere became increasingly frenetic. People with huge bundles on their heads rushed up and down the platform amid a deafening hubbub of farewells. Wooden and cardboard boxes were thrust up at the last minute through windows to passengers within. Men in long-flowing gowns and fleshy, brassy women in colourful blue wrappers and head scarves struggled and sometimes fought to board the train. It was overwhelmingly humid as I strained and sweated to get into the first-class coach with its crisp clean sheets, iced water and comfortable fold-away bed.

Once outside the vast sprawl of urban Lagos, the train passed due north through the homeland of the Yoruba people – steaming, green vegetation, with an occasional forest-clad hill rising in the distance and tall palms standing high above the bush. Then, after almost 300 miles, we crossed the River Niger, the forest dwindling and the landscape gradually changing to rolling savannah. Finally and abruptly the land rose to form the beginnings of the Jos Plateau.

As the train climbed up to the plateau to its final destination we passed Africans working on the land, big muscular women, naked but for a covering of leaves fore and aft, some adorned with brass rings and girls with ears strung with strange ornaments. Streaming with sweat in the hot sunshine, they hacked at the soil with short hoes or mattocks. Their villages of close-clustered round thatched huts stood upon rocky outcrops.

Jos is situated on a plateau which rises to about 4,000 feet above sea level. It is a grassy, rocky landscape, reminiscent of downland and dominated by flat-topped, isolated hills and escarpments with commanding views. The climate is much drier than further south, with a marked difference between night and day temperatures.

The centre of the Nigerian tin-mining industry, Jos in 1957 was an untidy sprawl of concrete, mud and rusty tin roofing. Along its bustling streets, leaf-clad girls from the pagan Birom and Bokkos tribes jostled with robed Muslim Hausa traders, nomadic Fulani in short white gowns and Christian Yoruba and Ibo shopkeepers in Western dress.

In 2011 and 2012 I read of riots in Jos. The descendants of these Birom, Bokkos and other tribal groups, their women no longer adorned in leaves, had bonded together to deny Hausa and Fulani intruders any local governmental and residential rights. This led to the riots and as a result a considerable number of people were killed. The riots and killings are always reported as being between Muslim and Christian; however, the origins go back much further in history to the antagonism between native tribesmen and alien Muslim intruders, people who came onto the plateau from lands further north, first in an attempt to catch slaves, and then as pastoralists, seeking out the rich grassland on the plateau to graze their cattle. As will be seen, there is a similarity to this situation and the one that developed many years later on the Mambilla plateau in the Northern Cameroons, in which I was deeply involved.

I spent one night in the quaintly old-fashioned hill station, run with military precision by a dour ex-miner called Pop Bowler, where barefoot staff with black boot-polished feet, were dressed in long white brass-buttoned coats. Next day I was driven through the cool *harmattan*[1] mist along a narrow strip of tarmac to Bauchi, 66 miles to the east.

The tarmac road wound out of Jos down a steep escarpment with the crude workings of open-cast tin-mining on either side. Mechanical diggers had left behind mountainous piles of red earth beside seemingly random excavations. It was ironic that the technological onslaught and depredations of open-cast mining should have taken place among some of the most primitive people in Nigeria, who had successfully repulsed Hausa and Fulani[2] Muslim slave-raiders from their mountain stronghold. I noted for the first time that high cactus walls protected some of the tiny Birom huts and that they had beehives lodged over the

---

1   The *harmattan* is a dry, cool wind, which blows south from the Sahara Desert from November to January carrying clouds of dusty sand. It sucks the moisture out of everything, even causing furniture to crack and fall apart.
2   There are two kinds of Fulani: town Fulani, *Fulanin gida* and nomadic Fulani or Mbororo, *Fulanin daji*. The town or settled Fulani were Muslim scholars and administrators. The nomadic Fulani who are cattle owners were part Muslim, part pagan and were true nomads, within clearly defined limits. Fulani of both kinds extend throughout West Africa and although their origins are disputed, they are clearly of non-Bantu descent.

10

entrances. A stir in the hive activated the immensely fierce species of African bee into action against all invaders.

After 30 miles we reached the great bare slope of the massive Panshanu Rock, which falls at a steep angle down to the plains 400 feet below. The road here, built by the colonial government, was an engineering feat, running diagonally down and across the rocky slope, and built up with concrete walls, the gradient steep but practicable.

Ben, the cheerful government driver who had met me in Jos, stopped the car and pointed to the east towards Boule Mountain, 55 miles away, overshadowing the town of our destination, Bauchi. He showed me the jagged hills of Dass, and further to the east, the king of all, Zaranda, a mighty isolated mass rising 4,200 feet above sea level. I felt a growing sense of excitement as we drove towards this wonderful mountainous panorama. Once we had descended the slope of Panshanu, the road followed a straight course through acacia scrub. This was inhabited by Fulani nomads and their cattle, Jarawa pagans and the remnants of a small tribe whose lips were distended with large wooden plugs that could reach the size of dinner plates.

On arriving at Bauchi, the Emirate township and capital of Bauchi Province, I was welcomed by Derek Hooper, a contract District Officer (DO) brought out of retirement to boost the ranks of the rapidly depleting administration. These contract men were called, appropriately enough, 're-treads'. Hooper, who must have been approaching 60, had worked with the Chinese Customs Service and had been based for 20 years smuggler-catching on the border between China and Tibet. At one time he had seen no white person for nine months. 'When that happens,' he told me, 'it marks you for life.' One day I was to realise for myself the truth of his words – and I carry the mark to this day.

Derek Hooper introduced me to a young Nigeria police officer called P who loved horses more than policing and whom I was to come across many times in my subsequent time in Nigeria.

Bauchi, like the other old Emirate towns of Northern Nigeria, consisted of three distinct parts. The largest was the Muslim area, containing the ancient mud-walled palace of the Emir and his numerous household, a mosque or two, and the various buildings of the Native or Local Authority: the treasury, the court, the police and prison, the works department, health and education. There was a rambling street market, and hundreds of round huts with circular roofs where the Muslims lived.

The second area was called the *Sabon Gari* or 'new town', inhabited by non-Muslim people from the southern parts of Nigeria such as the Ibo and the Yoruba. These included a large proportion of clerical workers, mechanics and artisans of many kinds. Here also were shops belonging to Lebanese, Syrian and Indian traders.

Lastly, there was the government area containing the administrative offices of the government of the North and the European residential area. Here were bungalows with shady verandahs, gardens with flowers and vegetables and decorative trees.

There were stylistic differences between the architecture of the buildings and the appearance of the people in the Muslim parts of the town and the *Sabon Gari*. In the former there was little colour in the men's clothing, which consisted of long white *riguna* or gowns, occasionally heavily embroidered. There was an austere slowness of movement and reserve in the whole way of life. Only very young girls and old women were seen. In the *Sabon Gari*, however, things were different. Buildings were rectangular, quasi-European in shape and frequently constructed from concrete blocks or mud bricks. Men dressed in Western style, in trousers or shorts and brightly coloured shirts. Gaily dressed women could be seen everywhere; their flamboyance and assertiveness were accompanied by physical skill and vigour. The contrast with the Muslim township could not have been more marked.

Each Northern province was administered by a Resident, and shortly after my arrival I was sent away by the then Bauchi Resident, Ian Gunn, on a three-week intensive course at the Institute of Administration in Zaria, 500 miles to the west of Bauchi, to study Native Law and Custom, Common Law and, the financial bible of all Native (Local) Authorities, the Financial Memoranda. We were also required to become fully acquainted with the Native Authority Act, which outlined the powers and limitations of Northern Local Authorities.

In the past, cadet administrative officers had been sent on a much longer course, the Devonshire Course at Oxford University, but in these times of rapid change this had been abandoned in favour of the intensive course in Zaria.

All the other participants on my intake were Northern Nigerians, as the Northern government planned to retain this system of administration after independence and recruit bright young Africans to an Africanised former colonial administrative service working directly under the control of the Premier of Northern Nigeria's office in the headquarter town of Kaduna. Many, such as Yusufu Gobir and Joseph Gomwalk, were to become brief leading lights in subsequent military or civilian regimes. One of them, Ibrahim Dasuki, became the leader of all Nigerian Muslims and the Sultan of Sokoto.

Having managed to pass the course and been wished well by the retiring British Governor of the North, Sir Bryan Sharwood-Smith, I was sent back to Bauchi. My ambition was to work in one of the remotest parts of the North. Bauchi, the headquarters of one of the Northern Emirates, was within easy reach of Jos, and with its 30 or 40 Europeans, much too glamorous and civilised to qualify as remote. Luckily for me, the pressures of impending self-government and officers taking early retirement made vacancies in the remote out-stations hard to fill.

After a few weeks in Bauchi, and having sat in on meetings of the Emir and his council, and visited dispensaries, veterinary stations and native courts, I was told to my delight that I was to be posted to Gombe, 90 miles to the east.

3

The Apprentice

Apprentices their craft must learn.
E C Adams, *Lyra Nigeriae*

'You will have to learn Fulani in Gombe,' the Emir of Bauchi had said as we made our farewells, 'that is all they understand there.'

This was not strictly true, as all the local government officials spoke fluent Hausa. But Gombe was a very Fulani town, faithful to Islam and retaining a pure-spoken form of the Fulani language. It was most unlike the town of Bauchi with its multi-tribal and religious mixture of Hausa and Fulani Muslims and its Christian/ pagan hill tribesmen from Dass and Jarawa.

Gombe was the headquarters of the Emir of Gombe, who, like the Emir of Bauchi, was one of seven Fulani Emirs imposed on an existing Hausa ruling structure by the great 19th-century Fulani Islamic reformer, Uthman dan Fodio. Built as a new town in the 1920s, Gombe was systematically laid out on a grid pattern. The original site of Gombe town was at a place called Gombe Aba, 60 miles to the north on the River Gongola, but it had been condemned as unhealthy due to its proximity to a swamp and so an entirely new town had been constructed. The baked mud houses were large and well built.

In the centre of Gombe were the government and local authority offices. These faced a formidable prison with high surrounding mud walls. One of my first duties was to make a weekly inspection of this prison to check on food and general cleanliness, and to listen to any of the prisoners' grievances. The most distressing part of this inspection was the visit to the quarter where insane prisoners were incarcerated. These poor howling creatures were manacled to rings in the wall. On one horrific occasion, just prior to one of my inspections, a mad prisoner had managed to free himself and disembowel a fellow inmate.

The District Officer (DO) or Assistant District Officer (ADO) was also required to be present when the court decreed a beating for punishment. The prisoners were not stoic, frequently wriggled and yelled and the whole procedure was most unpleasant. On the plus side, the prisoners' food ration, which included goat meat, was in most cases far superior to the food they ate at home, and old lags would welcome a return visit as a means of improving their diet; some even treated prison as a second home.

In those days Gombe was 'dry' in deference to Islamic susceptibilities. To drink alcohol, an addict's licence had to be obtained and the liquor had to be brought down from 'pagan' Jos. So I became a registered alcoholic at the age of 22 and also had to issue addicts' licences to the 12 other expatriate Europeans in Gombe. There cannot have been many towns in the world where the total expatriate community was registered as alcoholics. On returning to Gombe in the 1980s, I was surprised to find that in spite of the rise of Islamic fundamentalism there were bars serving alcohol everywhere. Dancing was discouraged but the drinking of beer was rife, and the bars were crowded with local prostitutes. Boko Haram has, in 2012, killed six people with AK47s drinking in a crowded bar.

In 1957 there was no electricity or piped water in Gombe. I lived in a large, round, thatched mud house which was impossible to lock, but in those halcyon days there were no problems with thieves. Giant kapok trees surrounded the house, and the downy cotton from their large cylindrical seed pods was used locally to stuff mattresses and pillows. When these pods burst open each year, a cloud of white down would drift into the house and stick to everything.

My boss Alan Martin, an ex-Indian Army colonel, was the senior administrator in Gombe Emirate. He patrolled his administrative area in a Rolls-Royce that had been converted to a open pick-up and must have been the most up-market pick-up in the world. He was extremely efficient and held in high regard by the Emir and his councillors.

Another highly regarded character, was a volatile Pole called Tony Krzywon, who worked as a cotton seed multiplication officer in the agricultural department. Krzywon transformed the Gombe economy by encouraging and cajoling the farmers into growing high-quality cotton on their rich black soil. He was an overtly sentimental Pole and on party nights played Polish folk music on a prized accordion with tears rolling down his cheeks.

Apart from a handful of other government officials, the rest of the white community comprised representatives of commercial firms that had trading stores in Gombe, dealing in everything from haggis to hatchets. These stores were quaintly called 'canteens', a legacy from early trading days when every major outlying station had, up until the outbreak of the First World War in 1914, a military cantonment.

Within weeks I managed to acquire a chestnut stallion in the 'Horses for Sale' section of Gombe market. Horses in Nigeria were all ungelded and it was considered unbecoming for a man to ride a mare. Every morning I rode to work from my mud house to Gombe town, a distance of five miles, tethering the stallion to a rail, cowboy-fashion, outside the District Office.

Three weeks after my arrival, Alan Martin suggested it was time for me to undertake my first tour into the bush. Touring in areas within a division was part of a DO's job; it was intended to show goodwill and concern on our part. Even if there was no practical business to deal with, it was important to keep the Africans aware of a benign administration. If we remained in our offices surrounded by files and petitions, talking only among ourselves, with African clerks or with the Emir and his men, villagers would have ceased to be aware of our presence. They would have felt that we had become irrelevant to their lives and indifferent to their welfare. When there was no specific business to discuss, conversation would range around farming and crops, adult education classes and the need to prevent school children from drifting away from work on the farm to the alluring lights of the local township. The DO would visit the school, talk with a teacher, inspect the local lock-up, check court records or decide the fate of some harmless lunatic.

I was instructed that this specific tour was instigated to check on the state of tax collection at the district headquarters at Malam Sidi. Finance was an obsession with the administration. Native Authority treasuries and honest accounting were supposed to be the keystone of the first Northern Colonial Governor Lugard's theory of Indirect Rule – ruling through the established native administration. As a result, a DO spent long, sweaty hours poring over dusty ledgers in crowded treasuries or counting dirty shillings under a thorn tree. One usually became quite good at adding up but it was a long and tedious business.

The obsession reached its zenith when the harvest was in and tax had to be collected. There were two sorts: General Tax (*Haraji*), paid by the farmers; and Cattle Tax (*Jangali*), paid by the cattle-owning Fulani. The theory was simple. When *Jangali* was due for collection, the District Head summoned the Fulani leaders in their areas at the time and told them that it was time to collect the tax. In theory, at this point, the Fulani would admit to having so many hundreds, or more likely thousands of cattle; this was then multiplied at the rate per head laid down for that year. The Village Head would have his scribe write a receipt for the said amount and it would be duly entered. To make sure, the District Head would make a check. Finally, Indirect Rule would creak into action as the DO went round the country checking that the treasury was not being defrauded.

The chance of a Fulani being defrauded where his own cattle were concerned was small, and the end result often differed wildly from the government's accounting theory.

C L Temple, writing in *Native Races and Their Rulers* sums it all up:

> I have known the possessor of hundreds and even thousands of herds of cattle not only to deny such possession but also the very existence of such an animal on the face of the earth. When pressed, to admit that he had heard of such animals running wild, when further pressed, to admit he had seen such animals, when further pressed, to admit that he had friends who owned cattle, when further pressed again, to admit that he had one cow in his possession, bought from a friend (but not yet paid for), for the sake of its milk, which was to be given to one of his children, who lay at the point of death.

No one likes paying tax and many will do their utmost to avoid it. I was a total novice in the hands of the wily farmers and cattle-owning taxpayers. With my inadequate Hausa, I had been thrown into a very deep, deep end. So, it was with some apprehension I set out with newly recruited carriers on my first trek. I was the very last ADO to ride out of Gombe on tour, although later I was to cover thousands of miles on foot, on camel or on horse elsewhere in Africa and Central Asia. All the district headquarters in Gombe Emirate, including Malam Sidi, could by then be reached by car in the dry season. Lacking a car and the desire to obtain one, I could only set out to check the district tax collection in old-fashioned style, on horseback.

4

Gombe Emirate – First Treks

There was a chill in the air as we rode through the trading area and out of Gombe town on my first trek into the African bush. The suffused light of a waning moon reflected on the corrugated-iron roofs of the canteens and illuminated pools of water in the riverbed. Great trees of tamarind, locust bean and baobab were scattered upon a sward that looked like a lawn in the moonlight.

Dawn broke with a rapidly reddening glow as the sun rose over the sugar-loaf-shaped Bima hill far to our right. It was a dawn of rosy sun-gilded rocks, dappled earth and sparkling dew-dropped bushes and fronds. As the sun rose higher in the bright blue sky, the dew vaporised and wisps of mist faded in quick succession. For about 40 minutes, the vigour of the fresh new day filled my lungs, then the freshness evaporated and the air became stagnant in the shimmering heat of an unremitting sun.

We moved off the motor road and followed a dusty track winding through maize, guinea-corn and other crops grown on the farms surrounding Gombe.

Cocks began crowing, people stirred in their huts and the blue smoke of cooking fires drifted up into the early morning haze. Greetings were shouted back and forth. As we slowly moved away, the farms gave way to scrubby acacia bush with bold hills outlined on either side. I cantered on ahead, pausing to let the

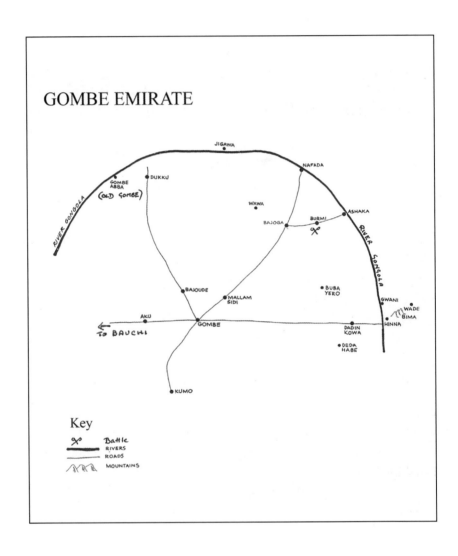

carriers catch up and then pushed on again over gullies and dried-up riverbeds savouring for the very first time the liberating feeling of riding into the vast empty space of Africa.

Professional carriers, a long-since vanished breed, bore 44 pounds plus on their heads for up to 20 miles a day; consequently their foreheads were rutted and their lives short. Their time in the trade could be measured by the depths of their brow-ridges and the thickness of the soles of their feet. Rutted brows kept sweat out of their eyes and thick soles kept jiggers – a skin-burrowing flea – out of their toes. Once carriers were welded together as a team under a good headman they were capable of covering vast distances and climbing steep hills. Cheerful and enduring, they would troop into a village, streaming with sweat after a hot and weary march, lift their loads into the air at arm's length to ease their straining necks and shout to the gawping villagers '*Muna zuwa*' ('We are coming') in defiance of fatigue and thirst.

They were by choice drifters who had cut themselves loose from tribal customs and constraints: most of them were scallywags and sinners. They knew they were as free as air to leave and go their own way at the end of the trek. At the outset, I was not regarded with much respect or enthusiasm. However, if they were treated fairly and protected from outside interference, they would follow you to the ends of the earth.

We headed north-east from the farms surrounding Gombe and for an hour travelled over open grassy plain, passing so close to a feeding flock of great crested crane that we could have touched them with a long stick. With its long neck and golden crown of stiff feathers, it was obvious why the bird had been incorporated into the regimental crest of the Royal West African Frontier Force.

After ascending a steep slope to a skyline dotted with formidable boulders, we dropped down into a river valley patchwork of still, green-crusted pools and patches of dry, sandy riverbed. From the waterline, marked by dry vegetation high up on the bank, I knew this must be a tributary of the River Gongola, which encompassed Gombe Emirate in a great sweeping curve.

It was February and only two months of the dry season were

left. Some of the tinder-dry grass had been burnt off leaving blackened stubble. Bush-turkey, large, portly birds, 30 pounds of white tender meat, had arrived in flocks of ten to 20 and were walking through the stubble feeding on grasshoppers rendered wingless by the heat of the bush fires. Arriving lean and strong, these big birds fattened so rapidly that by the end of a few weeks their wings would no longer lift them off the ground. They scuttled along in ungainly hops and leaps, easy targets for my carriers who would drop their loads and give chase.

Messenger Malam Adamu taught me to recognise the wild paw-paw and the bitter-sweet yellow cherry. He also taught me to beware of acacia thorns. There are many varieties of acacia bushes and trees in sub-Saharan and East Africa, some with thorns as long as six inches; their foliage is rich in protein and only a hungry camel is able to feed on the branches by crunching up the sharp thorns in its cast-iron mouth.

A government messenger[1] invariably went with a District Officer on tour. He was there to advise and explain and, unofficially, to report back to the Emir. Malam Adamu, a dark-skinned, long-faced, devout Muslim had trekked out with young administrators for over 30 years. He was cautious, discreet and knowledgeable; his badge of office, a small, square, black and gold cloth crown, was pinned on the upper left side of his flowing white, embroidered gown. If the DO was a non-Hausa speaker the messenger doubled as an interpreter. This gave an unscrupulous messenger immense power, as he could easily pass on to a naive DO information that he wanted him to hear or that he thought the DO would like to hear.

---

1 One trusted messenger of mine was Malam Ibrahim Aliyu, a Fulani from Gombe who worked with me later in Tangale-Waja and who had previously been the youngest Regimental Sergeant Major in the Nigerian Army. Another strict Muslim, immaculate in his dress and meticulous in his manner, he became a reliable mentor, particularly in the area of elementary security. He once removed the keys from the top of my desk where I had carelessly left them on leaving the office. I searched and sweated before he confessed to having taken them to teach me a lesson – a lesson I have never forgotten. After independence, Malam Ibrahim Aliyu became chief warder of Gombe prison. I learnt later, much to my distress, that a prisoner had assaulted him with an axe and murdered him.

Another messenger, this time when I was posted to Mambilla in 1960, was Malam Abba. He had begun working with me in the lowly position of headman of my carriers. His promotion from the rank of headman was only achieved after much battling with the bureaucrats in Kaduna – the Northern Nigerian capital city – who refused to believe that a lowly headman could become a trusted and loyal government messenger. As it turned out, ex-headman Abba was an outstanding success.

After trekking for 17 miles we reached the district headquarters of Malam Sidi at noon. The District Head, Maina, had waited with his retainers about a mile outside Malam Sidi so that he could escort our party into his town. This was an old-fashioned, polite custom, now long out-dated.

Maina was a freed slave who had been caught by the Fulani 60 years previously from the pagan Tera tribe whose homeland was 120 miles due east of Gombe. He was scarified with Tera tribal markings, long vertical lines covering the whole of his face meeting at the top of his head; in addition, two short horizontal lines were etched over his cheekbones. These markings were very similar to those of another tribe, the Waja, who bordered the Tera to the south. Tribal markings were common to the pagan tribes and dated from the days of inter-tribal slave raiding. Gouged onto the face at a very early age, a child slave growing up with an alien tribe would always be aware of his true background by these incised marks.

Maina was well over 80 but proudly told me that his umpteenth wife had just produced a son. 'How many children do you have?' I asked through Messenger Adamu. 'Oh, I lost count long ago,' the toothless, greybeard replied. Malam Adamu whispered that it was much more likely that some young buck had breached the security of the high mud walls, which protected the chastity of his wives and concubines.

Later that day I listened helplessly as the Village Heads crowded into Maina's house to discuss the state of the tax collection which was overdue. Not only did I not understand what they were saying but I had little idea of the workings of the system itself.

I acted out a part with the help of Malam Adamu, but the wise old chiefs soon realised I knew nothing and was easy game for distorted truths. I listened to complaints, visited the school and dispensary, then, desperate to say something useful, I suggested to Maina that perhaps he should tidy up the market area where piles of rubbish had accumulated.

I was housed in the entrance hut, the *zaure*, of a well-built compound comprising a number of mud and thatched circular huts. For privacy the *zaure* had been surrounded by five-foot-high grass matting. On arrival, Maina sent over a bowl of eggs, some rice and onions as a gift and my cook suggested a tomato and onion omelette to which I readily agreed. At that time the local people didn't eat eggs but they were aware that Europeans valued them as food. Maina had clearly kept the eggs for weeks so that he could offer them to his next foreign visitor. I was the victim. My cook duly produced a completely inedible toxic mixture of pink and green slime.

It had been a very hot day, and in the comparative cool of the evening I listened to the sounds of Northern Nigerian village life around me, sounds that are unchanged down the years – the faithful being called to prayer; the rhythmic pounding of grain in a wooden mortar, accompanied by a soft song; the shrill-tongued voice of a woman bending over a clay cooking-pot, her husband grumbling a reply; a drum beat. A slim shadowy female shape passed the open door of my hut as the household settled to an evening meal – women and girls in one hut, men and boys in another.

A dog began to bark. Another dog took up the chorus and I lay silently perspiring, the mosquitoes buzzing greedily around my head. I tossed and turned and finally fell asleep. Later, my restless horse broke loose from his stake and cantered off into the blackness of the night.

Two days later we returned to Gombe along the same track. The first trek into the bush, the forerunner of many more, was over.

Not long after I was again sent on tour, this time into the Wawa bush, some 70 miles north of Gombe. This was a vast, waterless tract of thick scrub and thorn, uninhabited except for sporadic visits from nomadic Fulani and some of Nigeria's last remaining lion. It was infested with tsetse fly and to encourage the Fulani to settle there an intensive campaign of tsetse eradication was in progress. To further encourage settlement, reservoirs had been bulldozed in the red clay soil. I was instructed to tour these reservoirs, or *tapkuna*, to see if they had caught any rainwater and to assess whether they would provide a year-round source of water for the Fulani cattle. *Wawa* means 'fool' in Hausa and this is what the local people thought of anyone who was stupid enough to enter the barren, tsetse-fly ridden wasteland of the Wawa bush.

I had been given a small ex-United Nations water filter which was supposed to convert any brackish puddle into drinkable liquid by hand-pumping it through a filter candle. However, the makers had not reckoned on the Wawa bush. I quickly discovered that the thick, muddy water that had collected in the *tapkuna* would not filter through the candle. Being inexperienced, foolhardy and romantically determined to live off the land, I had brought with me only a minimum of food and drink. Soon, my only liquid was the sticky sweet juice from a tin of grapefruit and some rancid Fulani milk. My throat clogged on both until I could drink no more. After three days of trekking more than 15 miles a day from *tapki* to *tapki* I was thoroughly dehydrated. The carriers had just managed to drink the thick muddy *tapki* water, but I couldn't, and my messenger, headman and the Fulani chief who accompanied us were showing signs of concern.

It was April, the hottest time of year, just before the rains were due. The Wawa bush jumped and shimmered in the waves of heat, the blue of the sky was veiled in a hot white haze, and a fierce sun evaporated sweat before it left the pores. Occasionally a dust devil would form. A tiny spiral of chaff would rise up beside the track, dance along a yard or two, and then die down, before springing up again and whirling off into the bush with widening coils; once more it would collapse, then suddenly rear up again and come swirling down on us. From a rustling murmur it would grow to a rushing, crackling roar, hurling up leaves, twigs and small stones amid a thick cloud of dust and sand. Down it would descend, filling our ears and eyes and nose with prickling sand, before dancing off into the bush again, swaying and thrashing among the dried grass, leaving us parched and gasping for breath. These whirling columns of sand give the impression of an invisible living thing wrapped in a layer of dust. Some whirl to the left – a male – and others to the right – a female – or so it is thought. In Central Asia, as in Africa, many people consider dust devils to be the home of lost souls, eternally restless spirits who agitate the desert in their endless search for rest and peace of mind.

On the fourth morning of the tour I watched the sunrise with dismay, feeling threatened by its red and angry face. Finally, at the end of the day we managed to find some water that could be forced to drip through the filter. Half an hour's desperate pumping produced barely a tumblerful but down it went in one gulp. Then I blacked out for over two hours, the after-effect of dehydration.

The Wawa bush reservoir scheme came to nothing. The *tapkuna* dried up and the tsetse returned. The Fulani continued on their nomadic way and Africa acquired another white elephant. But all the lions in the Wawa bush have gone; the 'caterpillar' tractors brought in to dig the *tapkuna* and the poachers who followed them saw to that.

We made other treks into the bush during my five months in Gombe. One took me to the ruined town of Burmi where Buba Yero, the first Emir of Gombe, had established a Fulani outpost for the Fulani reformer, Uthman dan Fodio. It was here in 1903 that Malam Geni, a fanatical Fulani Muslim, put up a tremendous fight against the advancing British. Geni had gathered round him not only the Gombe people, but also malcontents from other quarters, among them the deposed Sarkin Musulmi (Chief of all the Muslims) of Sokoto, Attahiru. It was not a long battle and was decided by the power of the Maxim machine-gun, but it was sharp while it lasted. Attahiru and many others were killed but the British also had their casualties, notably one Major Marsh who was struck down by a poisoned arrow and whose grave we saw. Burmi was subsequently razed to the ground and the British prevented renewed settlement there.

On that occasion we trekked on to Ashaka, later to become the site of a railway bridge across the River Gongola, then but a tiny and delightful hamlet of the Bolewa people, whose round thatched houses were topped with ostrich eggs. On to Jigawa with its locally dug well-shafts that reached deep into the ground. From there to another old township on the River Gongola, Nafada. Many of the towns and villages in Gombe Emirate were enclosed by crumbling walls of mud, witness to more turbulent days of tribal fighting and slave-raiding.

Another trek took us due east of Gombe to the land of the Tera with their dramatically scarified faces. This particular trek took me through Dadin Kowa, Wade, Hinna and Deba Habe where I was entertained under the stars to my first authentic pagan dancing, the forerunner of many more nights of drums, dust, sweat and frenzied activity. Trekking through the hills near Wade, we discovered fascinating traces of old iron ore workings amid long-abandoned Tera settlements. But there was much more to this particular trek than showing the flag, checking on tax, explaining the implications of independence, hearing local grievances or relaxing with the dancers.

Bordering this Tera country was the large sugar-loaf shape of Bima. This great hill held, and still does, strong religious connotations for Muslims all over Nigeria, as followers of the defeated Malam Geni had fled to Bima after the battle of Burmi in 1903. It was also at Bima, in 1948, that a Muslim from Sokoto proclaimed himself to be a religious Mahdi – one who was appointed by Allah to mount a holy war against non-Muslims – and thousands acknowledged his claim, flocking to his standard from all over Nigeria. He vowed to oust the infidel British, but he and his followers were eventually routed by policemen under the command of an officer called Papas. However, the Mahdi was never captured and legend had it that he climbed Bima and was taken directly up to heaven in a great white cloud. It was said that a huge white horse, the renowned steed of Malam Geni, was seen on the top of the hill before he disappeared.

By 1957, people had once again started to flock to Bima, especially members of the Islamic sect the Tijjaniya, who mostly came from Sokoto. The administration was worried that Islamic fanaticism might once again break out at Bima, where it was believed that a quick exit to heaven was assured when the end of the world finally came.

Thus the real purpose of this trek was to gather intelligence on the reason for the new migration to the hill. We discovered that the movement of people was linked to a belief that at independence, which was imminent, the world would end, but not before the true Mahdi had reappeared to lead his people up into heaven. It was also rumoured that once again the great white horse had been sighted.

Although their numbers grew and new settlements flourished at the foot of Bima, the world did not end and no Mahdi appeared. Government Messenger Malam Adamu and I climbed Bima and saw no white horse or gateway to the world beyond, though the mist that suddenly enveloped us on the summit certainly tested our nerve. Although Boko Haram is a 21st-century phenomenon, religious fanaticism in the north of Nigeria is not new and has erupted spasmodically over the centuries.

Trekking through the bush was not always interesting. There could be monotony in following long sandy tracks, a kind of on-and-on-forever feeling that sapped the spirit as much as did the glaring heat and dust. Camp life too had its disadvantages: dusty floors full of jiggers, sand flies, white ants and scorpions, bad water, the lack of fresh food, spilt whisky, supplies ruined by rain, wet clothes and bedding and the rain pouring through leaky thatch. Torrential rain and hail are dispiriting to even the keenest recruit.

But for me, trekking was the soul of life and I couldn't get enough of it. Every new tract of country was an exploration, every new village an adventure. It kept you in touch with life in the remotest hamlet and with the true aspirations of the villagers and their chiefs. Three weeks' travelling on foot or horse was worth six months' office work.

As for discomforts, they vanished quickly enough. A long trek in furnace heat ended with a bath and breakfast. Drowned like a rat in an hour's heavy rainstorm you dried out before a roaring fire and laughed at earlier misery. For if you had the love of it, the joy of early mornings in rain-washed air, the evening cool when the sun had gone, and all the incidents that the day had brought, gave you a feeling of great satisfaction. And at night, tucked up under a mosquito net, surrounded by the sounds of Africa and staring up at the brilliant stars above, you dozed off totally at peace with the world.

It was obvious that Gombe was on the verge of dramatic change. Thanks to the efforts of Tony Krzywon, cotton was starting to boom and a railway extension from Bauchi to Maiduguri would pass through the town.

We did not realise at the time just how quickly Gombe would change from being a sleepy Fulani backwater, where alcohol was banned and outsiders were rigorously confined to the *sabon gari*, to a rough, dirty boom town. When I re-visited Gombe in the 1980s and saw the dirt and squalor, it was clear the place had changed a great deal during its 20 years of chaotic and haphazard development. It had gained a railway outlet for its cotton and the people had obviously prospered, but something of value had gone, and it showed in their faces. My old mud house had long since disappeared. The giant kapok trees had been cut down and in their place were a roundabout and a dilapidated petrol station. The nightly rattle of stick on calabash and drum and the cheerful cries of the dancers were to be heard no more. Islamic fundamentalism and television had seen to that. Yet the bars and brothels were flourishing.

In 1957, Abdullahi, the Fulani Emir of Gombe, was literate only in Arabic but he was blessed with wisdom and common sense. Seated in council, wearing his great white turban, he would listen attentively to the views of his literate and highly intelligent councillors: Wazirin Jalo, later to become a Federal Member of Parliament; Malam Jauro, the lively educational spokesman; the Ubandoma who looked after town affairs; Mohammadu Kumo who managed works; and Malam Pella whose responsibility was for police and prisons. As I became more experienced I would sit in on these deliberations, occasionally offering a tentative word of advice. The Emir would listen attentively to all the views expressed, saying little and allowing the discussion to flow. Then raising a hand he would say, *'Za mu yi haka'* (This is what we will do) and proceed to outline a course of action. Just prior to independence in 1960, the Emir had Grade 'A' legal responsibilities, which even gave him the power to impose the death sentence on murderers. After independence the status of Emirs was greatly reduced and many of their legal powers were abolished.

It was in Gombe I saw the first of many a *salla* (festival) to celebrate the end of Ramadan. Seated beside the Emir, the DO Gombe Alan Martin was wearing his starched, white uniform crowned with a white topee (soon to be replaced by a Pakistan woolly forage cap which was thought more suitable for an African DO). As I was not yet been confirmed in my appointment and had not been given a uniform, I sat on the other side of the Emir, dressed in an unromantic, brown tropical suit, feeling and looking ridiculous under a trilby. Behind us sat the Emir's councillors and personal retainers, the latter gaudily dressed in a bold red and green uniform.

After prayers had been said at the central mosque, horsemen, who had trekked into Gombe from outlying districts within the Emirate, galloped down the wide central thoroughfare in front of the Emir's palace, shouting loyal greetings and firing off their flint-lock muskets. Some of these Gombe horsemen wore armour of chain-mail, which, it was said, was copied from patterns handed down from the crusades. Others wore flowing white gowns and turbans of deep blue material that had been dyed in the town dye-pits and beaten until it developed a dazzling sheen.

Red dust swirled about us as, amid a crescendo of drumming, wave after wave of charging horsemen pulled up sharply in front of our seats, shouted their loyal greetings to the Emir then wheeled back to begin another dust-laden charge. Cruel spiked bits dug deep into the roof of their horse's mouth ensuring their horses stopped abruptly and the riders did not end up in the lap of the Emir; but the horses' blood-flecked mouths showed the pain these bits inflicted. We were later to try to persuade the Gombe horsemen to adopt the 'pelham', a mild, unspiked bit, handing them out free in exchange for the spiked horrors. They willingly took them, but their own bits were soon back in their horses mouths.

Alan Martin ceremoniously presented the Emir with a large basket of kola nuts when this wild display of horsemanship was over. These nuts, beloved as a mild stimulant throughout the North and a supposed ingredient of Coca-Cola, were the traditional present from the government on such occasions.

With independence fast approaching we were instructed by Kaduna to burn the Gombe district historical files on the grounds that the language used and the comments made on individuals might prove too sensitive for our African administrative successors. This instruction seemed to me to be very short sighted, for much of the meticulously recorded information in the files would be of great future anthropological interest and importance. They contained the reports and sometimes the diaries, dating from 1907, of the first administrators who visited both Gombe Emirate and the pagans living in the wild Tangale-Waja area to the south. Their observations of the people and their traditions, customs and beliefs were a unique record of the time when whites and blacks met for the first time. To burn these hand-written reports seemed an act of unpardonable folly.

After reading these fascinating Tangale-Waja files I resolved to do my utmost to travel to that wild and hilly country. This wish was granted. Five months after my arrival in Gombe I was told that I was to be posted to the headquarter town of Tula in the Independent District of Tangale-Waja.

5

Tangale-Waja – Treks and Palavers 1

Gombe Emirate boundary extends about 30 miles due south of Gombe town to just outside the thriving cotton town of Kumo. Beyond Kumo you enter the jurisdiction of the Tangale-Waja Native Authority (local government), known colloquially as Tangale-Waja after the two dominant tribes who lived there. This fascinating mountainous area contained, in 1958, 17 pagan tribes who had in pre-colonial days spent centuries fighting each other or resisting the Muslim Fulani as they swept across the plains from Gombe raiding for slaves. The tribes were never conquered.

Some, such as the Awak and the Piri, were tiny minorities who clung to their rocky fortresses. The fact that they had developed their own customs and language showed how long they had been there. When not fighting the Fulani these tribes had fought each other, sometimes for food, sometimes for sport. Tribes developed alliances with their neighbours and would undertake joint attacks on common enemies. After the harvest was over and the corn beer was flowing this 'silly season' of sport began. But this had changed and ancient inter-tribal rivalries when I was there were conducted in the council chamber and not on former tribal battlefields.

On the road heading south from Gombe you first entered the territory of the Tangale. They had been forcibly resettled from their hilly fortress by the colonial government in the late 1940s

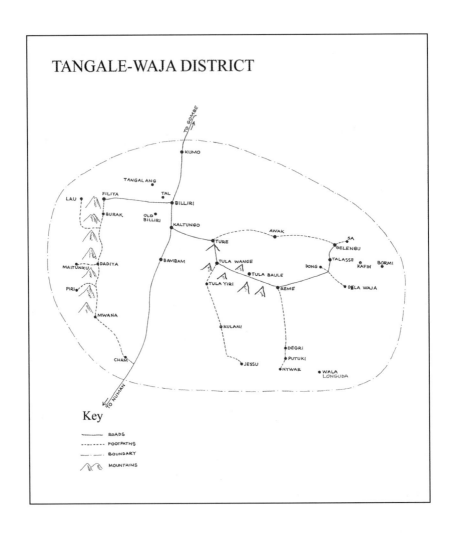

TANGALE-WAJA DISTRICT

Key

—————— ROADS
- - - - - - FOOTPATHS
· — · — · BOUNDARY
/ꞏ\ MOUNTAINS

alongside a single-track, laterite[1] motor road which ran through Tangale-Waja from north to south. A traveller going south then reached the Kaltungo tribe, kinsmen to the Tangale and savage pagans in the past.

The Kaltungo were rapidly acquiring religious education from the fundamentalist Sudan Interior Mission, an American mission of Bible Belt origins which by government decree had never been allowed to penetrate the Islamic Emirates further north. Just to the east of Kaltungo township, Tangale Peak pointed spectacularly to the sky.

The small Ture and Awak tribes lived on or at the foot of two prominent hills that bordered the northern part of a central range which advanced to the Tula escarpment. To the west of these central tribal areas lay a great massif stretching for over 40 miles and along which lived the Pero, Burak, Dadiya, Cham, Mwana, Piri and Lau tribes, small groupings but each with a different language, customs and dress. On the plains to the east of the Tula hills lived the peaceful Waja, partly Islamised and kinsmen of the Tera to the north in Gombe Emirate.

Besides the elaborate facial markings, which were similar to their Tera cousins, the Waja shared another characteristic: easy laughter and a capacity to enjoy life. The amount of drink consumed on market days clearly suggested that Islam had not, at that time, taken too firm a hold.

Finally, south-west of the Tula escarpment, lived the hill Waja on another great range of hills which they shared with their kinsmen, the Longuda. These two tribes, who also shared kinship with the Waja on the plains, were tucked away in a terrain which could only be reached after much hard trekking.

My house and the Native Authority headquarters were in Tula. At 60 miles from Gombe, a mud track branched off the main laterite road heading south and wound its way up into the Tula hills. After reaching Tula township, the road left the hills and

---

1   A laterite road is made from a red clay soil. It is used all over Africa to surface minor roads and in East Africa is called 'maram' in Swahili. It is also used to construct the surface of tennis courts.

ran in an easterly direction into Waja tribal country These two roads were the only all-weather connecting links in 600 square miles of mountainous country. I arrived in Tula with all my kit and two dogs in a government truck. My two horses had been ridden down from Gombe in advance, and for the next 18 months I travelled around the mountainous district either on foot or on horse.

The Tula tribe, whose huts surrounded the Native Authority offices and my thatched house, practised remarkably advanced terraced farming on their rocky hills with a skill that amazed Western agricultural experts. These terraces, formed by stones and rocks freely available on the slopes, followed the contours of the land and enabled the Tula to grow corn on the steepest inclines. Intermingled with these terraced farms were their tiny mud and thatch huts, the gaps between them filled with piles of rocks as a barrier against intruders.

The Tula were divided into three fractious clans: the Tula Yiri, the Tula Baule and the Tula Wange. Internecine feuding between the three clans usually arose through the machinations of the Chief of Tula Wange. All the government and local authority buildings were situated in his territory – the council chamber, the DO's office, the councillors' offices, the public works yard and the prison. Although the three clan chiefs were supposed to be equal in status, not unnaturally the ambitious Chief of Tula Wange took the lead and provoked trouble.

These then were the inhabitants of Tangale-Waja. With politics, education, missions and a host of European ideas causing flux and change, the tribal ties of kinship had been replaced by political alliances. Five chiefs of the major tribes – the Dadiya, Kaltungo, Tangale, Waja and Cham – rotated authority on a bi-monthly basis and tried to influence, by fair means or foul, major decisions during their brief tenure of office. In short, the area was full of intrigue and sometimes violence, based on age-old feuds and tribal alliances. Before one could attempt to administer Tangale-Waja, one had to understand it – and this took time and effort.

Fortunately, a young ADO was greatly helped in this acquisition of vital knowledge by a daily diary that had been kept, with great regularity, ever since the days when the first British administrators came to the area. This diary was required reading during a newly posted officer's first few weeks and had not yet fallen foul of the colonial government's policy of destroying historical records which might cause offence. Consequently, one appeared a fount of wisdom before flabbergasted tribesmen who were either trying to revive ancient and long-since settled disputes or generally attempting to mislead. It was also possible from reading them to assess the character and ability of a predecessor, another valuable insight.

These diaries were particularly valuable because the jealousies between the five rotating chiefs were great and in particular there was a concerted move by the Kaltungo chief to have the district headquarters moved off the Tula escarpment and down to his township. Lobbying on this issue was taken to Kaduna, the capital of Northern Nigeria, and the Northern Elements Progressive Union (NEPU), the political opposition to the ruling Northern People's Congress (NPC), took up this and other divisive causes with political relish. The NPC represented conservative interests and the Emirate system, whereas NEPU were radicals who wanted to introduce radical reform and change to the whole political structure in the North. In pursuit of this strategy, NEPU was adept at aligning itself with minority interests especially when they clashed with the interests of the Hausa/Fulani establishment in Kaduna. Any embarrassment that could be caused by stirring up potential pagan hornets' nests was quickly exploited. Malam Aminu Kano, the leader of NEPU, paid a personal visit to Tula as Tangale-Waja was fertile recruiting ground for creating a volatile opposition to the NPC, the party of the Premier of Northern Nigeria, Alhaji Sir Ahmadu Bello, the Sardauna of Sokoto – a province that was not only identified locally with Hausa/Fulani dominance but with Uthman dan Fodio, Islam and slave-raiding.

Malam Aminu, or 'Malam' as he was called, gave me no trouble. We talked for a short while and he made one or two specific complaints of alleged injustice. His bodyguards and companions were a tough-looking bunch and, like political hangers-on all over the world, seemed to be spoiling for trouble.

The political pressure from NEPU added to the tension and intrigue of the inter-tribal council disputes. Corruption was never far from the surface of debate, and a particularly productive environment for intrigue was the contracts committee, especially when building contracts were debated.

As I was chairman of the contracts committee it was usually patently obvious to me when a committee member had received an inducement to influence a decision in a certain contractor's favour. The individual concerned would pursue his client's cause with unnatural fervour and, if the favoured bid was ousted when the tender was awarded, his anger was all too apparent.

In those days, being full of an idealism untempered by realism, I priggishly made mistakes. In particular I made one big mistake in the pursuit of righteousness, which I very much regretted. The Chief of Dadiya (Sarkin Dadiya) was, after Sarkin Kaltungo, easily the most respected and competent of the five Tangale-Waja chiefs. A tall man with a ready smile, his common sense was widely respected. One day, when inspecting his court records as part of a periodic check, I came across indisputable evidence that he had misappropriated a paltry sum, not more than £N20, which by the standards of Nigerian corruption, even in those days, was ludicrously small. Instead of having a quiet word at an appropriate time, I stupidly pursued this petty crime with misguided self-righteousness. It ended with his being summoned to court in Tula. But his case was never heard. On the way to the trial the lorry carrying him crashed and he was killed. His people said that his tribal gods had protected him from unnecessary shame. But the shame was wholly mine.

However, corruption practised by successive chiefs of Cham was on a different level. They had a particular penchant for dipping into the tax extorted from their own people. The Cham chiefs changed with startling regularity. Before my arrival one had recently been dismissed so the chieftainship was vacant.

One of my first tasks was to organise an election for a new

chief, for unlike the chieftainships in the Muslim areas to the north which were based on the principle of male succession, these pagan tribes selected their chiefs by balloted election. Unfortunately the method of selection was often suspect. Having organised a fully democratic secret ballot between three aspirants for the chieftainship, I discovered to my horror that the count had resulted in a tie between the two leading contenders. When the result was announced I nearly had a riot on my hands. Had I been older and wiser no doubt I would have quietly exercised the right of a casting vote, but tiresome idealism once again got in the way. Justice had to be seen to be done.

The truculent Cham tribesmen, some drunk and dangerous, called for a second ballot, insisting that they line up in the open behind their chosen candidate. In my inexperience I unwisely agreed to this although I postponed the election date to allow tempers to cool. On the day of the second election, as the long lines formed behind the two contestants, intimidation was blatant and obvious. Beer had flowed and tempers flared. I only had one policeman armed with a truncheon and I could see the whole fiasco deteriorating into mob violence – with me in the centre. I therefore told everyone to go home and declared the exercise null and void. Gradually, the crowd dispersed, but not without grim muttering and furious glances in my direction.

Three months later we organised another ballot-box election. This time Tsabar Kudi, not our favoured candidate, won by two votes. It was an unnecessarily long and drawn-out saga but I had learned a great deal about African politics and behaviour just as I was soon to learn more through my legal work.

The tribal courts in Tangale-Waja did not follow Islamic Shari'a and were based on Common Law and on Native Law and Custom and although presided over by the chief of the area, the mainly illiterate tribal elders also sat in as advisers. While on tour, part of my job was to inspect these court records and if necessary order a re-trial. The same applied during the weekly prison inspection if a prisoner objected to his sentence. What was revealed in court was often startling as the following two cases show.

The first involved the phrase *cin maita* which means literally 'eating the spirit'. When I first heard this phrase my Hausa was still very basic. I knew that *ci* meant 'eat' and was told that *maita* meant 'body'. I suppose 'spirit' and 'body' could be thought to be synonymous, but I thought, to my great alarm, that I had stumbled across a case of cannibalism, a practice long since outlawed. Fortunately, the ever-reliable Government Messenger Malam Ibrahim explained that *cin maita* meant spirit-eating or witchcraft. In this unfortunate case a man had died as a result of a presumed 'spell' that had been put on him.

Later, on Mambilla I was to witness the power of witchcraft when an educated Fulani friend in his 30s and in perfect health died in spite of my efforts to convince him that there was nothing the matter with him. He was adamant that he had been bewitched and that nothing could save him from death unless the 'spell' was removed. The 'spell' remained and he died, totally convinced that his death was inevitable.

The second case was more bizarre. A Tula woman had complained to her husband that he was not satisfying her sexually and had told him that she would seek out a lover to obtain satisfaction. The husband decided to teach her a lesson and placed a small red pepper on the end of his penis, at the same time skilfully protecting his own foreskin from irritation by covering it with a small leaf. He then deposited this red-hot object in the seat of his desire. The complainant spent days in agony before finally taking her husband to court.

As his wife had threatened adultery, the husband was deemed to have been unduly provoked. The woman's plea of cruelty was dismissed and she spent a week on remand in the local prison.

The prison wardress who was in charge of the female prisoners in the stone and cement Tula prison when I was there had been a mistress of T F Carlyle, the first British administrator sent to Tangale-Waja in 1910. His handwritten letters and notes were particularly fascinating as he had single-handedly subdued the wild Tula tribe who were then human flesh-eaters and whose ferocious reputation extended far beyond the Gombe area.

Indeed, their epithet '*maza ba tsoro*' (the men without fear) is well known to this day. Carlyle frequently disobeyed orders from a headquarters whose lack of understanding of his dangerous environment was all too apparent from the documents. One of the letters from the Governor's office expressed more concern over the fact that Carlyle had lost a spade, than his having to set fire to a Tula village to 'impress the natives'.

His Fulani mistress must have been very young when she aligned herself with him because, 50 years later, she was still full of vigour, had retained her sharp wit and was held in high esteem. I soon discovered that Tula womenfolk were equally formidable.

In Tula, my large, mud, thatched house, with walls three foot thick, had been well sited by one of my predecessors. To the north-west on a fine day one could see the large conical Tangale peak, not only a hill of mystic power, but the centre of a rain-making cult for the Kaltungo tribe. Tragedy was said to befall anyone who attempted to climb it.

Captain Phillips, an administrative officer, made the first known solo attempt in the 1920s. How and why he fell to his death have not been recorded and the touring officer in Tula was allocated £10 a year to tend his grave at the foot of Ture hill. But the gods must have been appeased by his death, for a few adventurers have since climbed it unscathed. My Muslim government messenger, Malam Ibrahim, became the first known Nigerian to climb it when we reached the top together. Ibrahim had no fear of the gods of the Kaltungo.

Beyond the peak a shimmering plain of black cotton soil stretched to Gombe township, 66 miles away, and on a clear day the holy Bima hill could be seen over 70 miles away. To the south, at the back of the house, the rolling terraced hills were covered with clusters of the Tula tribe's tiny houses. Next to my house, also overlooking the escarpment, was another substantial thatched, mud house which served as a resthouse for visitors.

The thatch on my house extended over a narrow veranda, which encircled the house three feet from the ground. In order to enter, a visitor had to bend double. I managed to construct a not too smoky fireplace by building a chimney up one corner of the sitting-room and poking it through the thatch. It leaked but it was worth it, for during *harmattan* nights, when the cold, dry wind blows dust-laden air from the desert, it could be very cold.

The wood from the *giginiya* palm is impervious to white ants and prized by builders of mud and thatch houses. The palm had been used as a frame for thatching my house and a colony of bats had decided that the palm and thatch made an excellent home for them too. Their squeaking and droppings together with the pungent smell of their urine did not make for comfortable nights. Lying on the bed and blazing away with a .22 rifle failed to dislodge them; even lighting a fire on the bedroom floor to smoke them out only drove them away until the fire died down. Eventually I was forced to retreat to a camp bed and a matted zone on the verandah. The bedroom became a bat sanctuary where the occupants led an untroubled existence behind a firmly locked door.

One morning, I was roused from my camp bed at six o'clock by the shrill, angry voices of a large group of Tula women. I emerged from behind the matting surrounding my bedroom to be confronted with a multitude of chanting semi-naked females of all shapes, sizes and ages. They were wild eyed and distraught.

Due north of my house, at the end of a paved garden, was a long drop down a steep escarpment, where before Carlyle had set foot in Tula land, custom decreed that the old, sick and inedible (the Tula had formerly eaten their own kind if they were young, tender and had died in battle) were disposed of. The women were wittingly or unwittingly edging me towards this drop until I spotted, much to my relief, the tall figure of Messenger Ibrahim elbowing his way towards me through the crowd.

'It's to do with their costume, sir,' he shouted to me in Hausa above the hubbub.

I was mystified. 'Their what?'

'Their costume, their dress – their leaves.'

Ibrahim was choosing his words carefully. As a devout Muslim he was highly disdainful of the semi-naked Tula ladies.

'They have been prevented from collecting their leaves.'

Except for those under the sway of my one white neighbour, the Reverend Silas Hilker, a Sudan Interior Mission missionary from the Bible Belt of America, the Tula women wore leaves. A bushy bunch covered their bottoms and a more modest tuft concealed the essentials to the fore – except in the case of unmarried girls where nothing was worn in front at all. However, the women were fastidious – they did not use any old leaf but one plucked from a species that grew in a particular area.

Just before my arrival, a Forestry Officer had arrived in Tula and designated a new Federal Government Forest Reserve, and it was in this spot that the sartorial tree of the Tula women grew. They had been barred from collecting their verdant knickers. Their dresses were wilting and withering. They needed a new outfit and their situation was desperate. No wonder they were angry.

The prevailing mood was rapidly deteriorating, a firm decision had to be made. I took a deep breath, 'Tell them, Malam Ibrahim, that they can collect their leaves, provided they touch no other tree and bring no firewood out of the reserve – only their leaves.'

With the help of a Tula interpreter who had come with Malam Ibrahim, the mood of the Tula abruptly changed. They dispersed, ululating and giving vent to joyful whoops of satisfaction.

And that is how the official *Nigerian Government Gazette*, which was published in Lagos three months later, contained an addendum to the Tula Forestry Reserve in the Independent Districts of Tangale-Waja allowing the leaves, and only the leaves, of a designated tree to be collected by the womenfolk of the Tula tribe.

Missionary and Western influences have today ensured that all the Tula women, young or old, married or unmarried, wear blouses over their tops and cloths wrapped around their waists. But the statute remains in force.

My decision won me short-term popularity with the Chief of Tula Wange, and shortly after the confrontation with his wild women he came to say that the Tula would like to dance at my house to thank me for placating his womenfolk .

'Now we can at last get some sleep,' he added.

Two days later, at about nine o'clock at night drumming started up in the hills behind the township. It gradually grew louder, and interspersed with the drums I heard the booming of the two eight-foot-long wood and leather 'male and female' horns which were brought out on every Tula festive occasion. After an hour of practice and the downing of many calabashes of corn beer, a huge crowd of some 60 male and female dancers advanced noisily towards my house. On arrival they formed a large circle in my courtyard and with shouts, yells and ululations began to dance.

The drums beat out a compulsive rhythm. All the youths had strapped bells on the back of their waists and as they suggestively thrust their pelvises backwards and forwards their bells jingled in unison with the drums. The girls circled around the men, also gyrating in time to the pulsating music. Firelight threw into relief the swaying figures and flickered on the oiled bodies of the girls. The young girls' rounded breasts bobbed up and down like corks on wind-whipped water. Their elder sisters' more pendulous attachments swayed sedately from side to side. All shapes and sizes were well represented.

The men's bells jingled in unison with the swish, swish of the girls' leaves, bunched out specially for the occasion. Even the girls from the nearby mission could not resist the call of the drums. They too wore leaves, but over the cloth wraps that proclaimed their religious separation from their pagan sisters. At first they were shy, no doubt expecting fire and brimstone from the Reverend Hilker, but soon they too were whirling about with the best of them, shedding their inhibitions and sometimes their cloths.

On the far perimeter of the gyrating dancers, small wide-eyed children and nervous-looking, skinny pi-dogs gathered, scattered and then reformed in little groups. In the half-dark of the surrounding trees the children watched and chattered. At one stage a small group clustered around my chair and I could see the look of wonder in their eyes.

At about 2am, the dancers' energies dissipated, I thanked them and tipped the music makers. One or two of the more lusty pagans chased after their favourite girls until their shouts and shrieks of laughter faded into the darkness.

During my two-year stay in Tula the dancers came with increasing frequency. Reverend Hilker was often away for long periods and the dancing helped to keep me both amused and sane. If there was a good sweeping of leaves on the paving stones outside my house the next morning, it was a clear sign that the *wasa* had been a good one.

Reverend Hilker and his wife lived in a tin-roofed house some distance from the ADO's house; they generated their own electricity, the only such power source in Tula. Silas Hilker had been there for many years and was somewhat suspicious of the administration. His aged mission colleague in Kaltungo, the Reverend Harling, was thought to have been a German sympathiser during the Second World War, which no doubt accounted for the name Hitler Kaltungo appearing with some frequency on the Kaltungo tax register. Dinner with the Hilkers was memorable not only for the lack of alcohol but also because of a microphone fixed underneath the dining-room table with which the minister used to talk to his cook in the outside kitchen. The cook would reply through a loudspeaker fixed to the wall and in this way a kitchen crisis could be overheard by all the Hilkers' guests. A do-it-yourself Coca-Cola machine was also fixed to the dining-room wall, and into this the teetotal Hilker would pour copious packets of brown powder.

The only other missionary in the area was a cheerful New Zealander called Nicholson who lived in Waja country near a town called Talasse. He was fluent in Waja and a source of much local knowledge, having been in the area since 1928. He told a revealing story of how, when an anthropologist came to the area, he had been called in to interpret for a Waja greybeard. The anthropologist proceeded to ask all sorts of searching questions and finally came to one about the burial of the dead.

'Do you bury your dead in an upright position?'

'Yes,' was the response.

'Like this?' asked the anthropologist sitting down on the ground and putting his legs straight out in front of him?

'Yes, just like that,' replied the weary Waja man.

The anthropologist noted down this fact with great interest. After he had left, Nicholson turned to the Waja man and asked, 'Why did you tell him that? Your burial customs are not like that at all.'

'He wanted to be told something interesting and so I let him believe what he wanted to hear,' came the reply. 'If I had told him that we just buried them in the ground lying down he would not have been nearly so interested and I would not have got such a good tip.'

Shortly after my arrival in Tula, an instruction came to go to Kaltungo to represent the colonial government at the opening of a new mission hospital. It was a two-day ride and when I got there, much to my embarrassment, the assembled brethren rose from their seats and started to applaud. As he was about to cut the ceremonial red ribbon with scissors to open the hospital, the visiting American evangelical turned towards me and pronounced, 'We are proud to welcome here today, the messenger of Queen Elizabeth Two.'

However, these Bible Belt missionaries did not display much Christian virtue when it came to acknowledging their rivals in soul-catching. In Billiri in Tangale country I asked the Roman Catholic, Father Carroll, if he could provide mission labour for the construction of a dam that was to benefit the whole of Billiri township. 'Sure,' replied this jovial Irishman. I then went to the Sudan Interior Mission at the other end of the town and posed the same question adding unwittingly, 'Father Carroll has agreed to help, too.'

'As far as we are concerned,' came the immediate retort, 'Father Carroll and his mission do not exist.'

Pity the poor African caught up in this religious turmoil.

I had started out with different and indifferent cooks and houseboys. My inexperienced but clean and easily trainable Fulani from Gombe soon tired of pagan Tula and left for home. Two Waja boys quickly departed and an ex-Tula cook displayed too many characteristics of his warrior tribe. Then one day Luttu Cham appeared. Luttu had started work as a tax collector for the Native Authority in the 1930s. He had subsequently been taught to cook by the wife of an English engineer who had just left the country.

Unlike the boy who answered an advertisement in a local newspaper for a paraffin refrigerator by writing to say that he had passed educational standard six and was therefore in every way qualified to be a paraffin refrigerator, Luttu did know how to cook. But more importantly he was a bush cook who could bake bread in an empty kerosene tin over a fire of wet wood and turn out a tasty stew in surroundings where only a pagan warrior was truly at home. In short he was ideal. Unlike his tribal rulers he was also honest and he stayed with me for the rest of my time in Nigeria.

Although called Cham, Luttu really came from the smaller, closely related Cham tribe, the Mwana. As these tribal cousins were much smaller numerically than the Cham, Luttu, standing four square at six foot two, was looked upon as the Father of the Mwana which, with his 40 plus children, he certainly was.

Luttu saved my life when I had a bad bout of malaria. He followed me from Tangale-Waja to the even harsher environment of Mambilla where the trekking was constant and the rain incessant. Together we pioneered the Alantika Mountains and walked the length of the hills bordering Cameroon from Mubi to Madagali. He was a true bush DO's cook, able, as in the case of Alantika, to rustle up a meal even when we were surrounded by hostile Koma spoiling for an excuse to eject us from their village.

Normally, one man to clean and another to cook were employed.

However, for a bachelor bush DO who spent the best part of his time on tour, a good cook was invaluable. Turning unpalatable foodstuffs into an edible meal was a rare art form at which Luttu excelled. He also had a very wise head on his massive shoulders.

A servant who left employment or was sacked would always ask for a chitty – a recommendation to a future employer. One day a prospective applicant for employment came to me with this recommendation. The hopeful aspirant handed over a piece of paper which read: 'Bulus came to me fired with enthusiasm. He left me fired with enthusiasm.'

On another occasion, a crafty-looking individual, posing as a cook, showed me a dirty piece of paper on which was written, 'This cook leaves me owing to illness – mine.'

6

Tangale-Waja – Treks and Palavers 2

When it was the turn of Tangale-Waja to host, at Tula, the bi-monthly meeting of the rotating Provincial Council, the Emir of Misau was its chairman (Misau Emirate, like Gombe Emirate and Tangale-Waja, was in Bauchi Province). Now, the Emir of Misau's grandfather had been eaten by the Tula when he was captured during a slave raid in 1900. Normally the Emir, a Fulani, would have had no cause to visit such a wild place, especially one that carried such emotional undertones for his family. In fact, no Misau man, let alone the Emir, had visited Tula in the 58 years since the family catastrophe.

The Emir arrived for the meeting in a car covered in dust, and as he slowly emerged from the backseat his face was ashen. He was a tall, lean Fulani with a very pale skin and finely crafted features. He wore a blue gown, heavily embroidered with gold thread. Like all Fulani Emirs in the North, he moved at a stately pace befitting his dignity, but he hardly uttered a word during the whole of the three-hour meeting, remaining an aloof figure, his face grey with fear and anxiety.

The Tula had arranged a dance at the end of the proceedings in honour of the Provincial Council members. Sitting under a hastily erected mat enclosure, the Emir of Misau looked on in utter disdain at the gyrating Tula. All the girls had been instructed to wear cloth, but even this nod to modesty could not assuage the Emir. As soon as the dancing was over he spurned the offer of a meal and was last seen hurtling away from the Tula hills in a cloud of dust. And who can blame him? It must have been the most unwelcome journey of his life.

When I later asked the Chief of Tula Wange whether the skull of the late Emir was still kept in one of the numerous stone shrines that dotted the hills, he proudly answered, 'We built one specially for it. Come, let me show it to you. It is one of our most sacred relics.'

I trooped after him up to a cairn overlooking a large, overhanging rock, where a wizened old man in a dirty loincloth appeared and gave me a toothless grin. This was the guardian of the shrine. One by one, he carefully removed the rocks forming the cairn. After a few moments the skull of the Emir's ancestor was proudly displayed.

'It brings great good fortune to our people,' exclaimed the Chief. 'We are very proud of it.'

The old man, squatting on his haunches, grinned up at me and held out his hand, not for a shake but for a tip. '*Nwalame*,' I said, using one of the few Tula words of greeting that I had learnt. The old man beamed up at me.

'Good, very good,' he said in English to my great surprise.

As I trudged down the hill after the Chief, I mused to myself that it was not often in life that one meets a man whose grandfather had been eaten – by human beings.

A few weeks later Alan Martin sent a message from Gombe letting me know that Sir Gawain Bell, the newly appointed and very last colonial Governor of the Northern Region of Nigeria, was to visit Tangale-Waja together with Lady Bell. A governor had never before ventured into Tangale-Waja and Martin told me to make Tula look smart.

'Can the Tula dancers entertain him?' I queried.

'Of course,' was the reply, 'but keep it decent. Remember, his wife is coming too.'

Money was sent for repairs and paint. Even the stones leading to the ADO's house were whitewashed. When the great day arrived Tula was looking at its best.

Peas were growing in my vegetable garden, a difficult feat in a dry climate, and they had been cordoned off with a piece of red tape to preserve them for our important guests. A roast duck and a raspberry flan were being sent from Gombe 60 miles away.

Governor Bell arrived at my house and changed into his dazzling white uniform, complete with his ostrich-plumed cockade hat.

The Tangale-Waja chiefs were decked out like Islamic peacocks and all the people were wearing their best finery. We had placed the Tula dancing girls down the long drive to my house, their bottoms lavishly leafy and their breasts well oiled for the occasion. The red-flowering Flame of the Forest trees lining the drive were in full bloom. The sky was a brilliant blue. The perfect picture of colonial pomp and native pageantry.

The Governor walked slowly down the two rows of our 20-strong local authority police force armed with First World War .303 rifles, burnished for the occasion. The 'Governor Salute – Present Arms' ritual proceeded without a hitch.

Then the Governor and his lady followed by Alan Martin and myself walked slowly into the council chamber where the five senior chiefs were seated in splendour.

'It gives me great pleasure … ,' began the Chief of Kaltungo who was the current president of the Provincial Council. Governor Bell inclined his head and smiled. As the Chief continued his oration, heads slowly turned to the open window directly behind him. In full view of councillors, guests and the Governor, a long line of prisoners filed past with brimming buckets of raw sewage carefully balanced on their heads. An acrid smell wafted into the chamber but the Chief of Kaltungo did not falter in his speech of welcome. I glanced at the rather austere and upright Lady Bell, but she was well trained and not an eyelid was batted.

The speeches finally over, we retired to lunch at my house, driving slowly through the pulsating Tula dancers.

I had unwisely told Alan Martin about the home-grown peas

and he had told Bell. Unfortunately, when the gardener had gone to the kitchen garden to pick them he found hardly enough to fill a small coffee cup. Luckily, I had a can of peas and quickly instructed Luttu to open them. In his haste, he cut his finger on the tin and blood dripped on to the tin's contents. Inspiration. 'Add a little ketchup,' I said to Luttu.

'Remarkable, remarkable,' murmured the Governor. 'Delicious,' echoed his wife. 'How clever of your gardener to have grown them in this climate. He must have green fingers.'

I smiled bleakly and mumbled thanks. The meal finished, coffee was to be served, when through the door Luttu made his entrance dressed in his smartest whites and proudly bearing no more than a dozen tiny peas. These he placed with great ceremony before the Governor of Northern Nigeria. Bell, carefully and with irreproachable aplomb, consumed the tiny offering.

VIP visits and Provincial Council meetings occurred infrequently and I have often been asked what I did while I was in Tula and not touring the district.

The short answer is I was busy day and night. The duties of a DO were endless. He was judge, policeman, tax collector, election officer, census official and interpreter of political change. He delineated boundaries, settled feuds and accounted for cash. The list did not end there, for the bush DO was doctor of himself and others, sanitary officer, road builder and town planner. He collected tsetse flies, and samples of local produce. He answered such taxing questions as how best to segregate lepers or lunatics; why a person should be vaccinated or, indeed, educated. He assessed taxes on cattle and people and oversaw their collection. He stamped out witchcraft and other unpleasant practices such as trial by ordeal.

Let us imagine that as a District Officer I am just back from touring in Tangale-Waja. I see the crowd that waits outside the little thatched office and I know that the sun will go down before the paper and palaver are finished. I enter the bare, mud-walled room. Upon the walls are hung a map or two and a board for notices. Some shelves made from old boxes hold the record books and in one corner stands my table covered with a locally woven blanket, ink-spotted and stained with muddy drippings from the old and leaky thatch roof above my head. In a corner lie some confiscated weaponry.

My clerk greets me with a wide grin. He is glad that I have returned. His smile hides his misery and many complaints. I settle behind the table and an office day begins. The mail is in and there are letters from DO Alan Martin and the Resident in Bauchi. There is a query from the audit office, a request for the Tangale-Waja estimates (they are late), and an explanation required for a situation that was handled by my predecessor and about which I know nothing (it was not recorded in the invaluable touring diary). I deal with a query from the High Court about a murder case which had earlier been the subject of a Preliminary Inquiry. The paperwork is finished.

One by one, I see the patient individuals squatting in the sun outside. Their patience, especially in cases of litigation, is inexhaustible. They will wait all day outside a DO's office or a court and, if their case cannot be heard, will go away quite cheerfully and return the next day. Time is no object to them and there is always tomorrow. Most are complaining about cattle damage or farm boundary problems. Some about disputed womenfolk.

The sun is due to set in an hour. There are people still waiting. The last one leaves and my head is aching from the prolonged contact with the African mind. The sun has gone and dusk comes shadowing down as I lock the office door to the sound of the *kurcia*, the ever-cooing dove. Smoke rises from the Tula houses as I go solitary to my house and to my evening meal.

But of course there was spare time to fill. I didn't fly-fish for lizards like one of my predecessors in Tula, or shoot at empty beer bottles like another. A public works department well-digger and I tried to find out whether Nigerian cocks would fight each other and we fashioned a cock-pit out of baked mud and spurs out of flattened nails. But even though the two cocks had been well fattened and kept away from the hens in a dark hut, they both fled at the first sight of each other, so this diversion was very short lived.

Living on one's own could make you forgetful. I once sat eating in front of guests invited to lunch in Tula, totally oblivious of the fact that they had been invited at all. And so accustomed had I become to teetotal American missionaries that when a non-missionary arrived, he was given soft drink after soft drink in my mistaken conviction that Americans drank no alcohol.

Visitors sometimes provided their own diversions. An auditor's wife set us pushing an upturned tumbler on a polished table top so that it knocked against Scrabble letters. When it started to move of its own accord and spelled out the message 'send for police' we hurriedly packed the Scrabble away and threw water over our 'medium' who was having a hysterical fit.

Life in Tangale-Waja was full of contrast – a day of dancing or ceremonial could end up with a report of murder and sudden death. Blood did not just flow onto peas set before a governor. Life was cheap and the situation never constant when surrounded by these volatile and hot-headed pagans. Not long after the Governor's visit, a report came that the Village Head of Tur, a Tangale minor chief, had been murdered while tax-collecting. The remote hamlet of Tur was near Kaltungo and I immediately set out in the local authority pick-up van with two policemen.

When we reached Tur, we found the Chief's naked and uncared-for body stretched out in the sun. Someone had chopped him in the neck with a machete. There was no difficulty in identifying or even having to catch the murderer. He was standing quietly near the body.

'He was asking me to pay too much, so I killed him,' was all the man was prepared to say. We took him back to Tula prison and he was later sent for trial in Jos where murder cases were heard. I was told later that he had been hanged.

On another occasion, when returning from Gombe late at night,

Luttu and I came across a road accident near Billiri, about 15 miles from the hamlet of Tur. A lorry carrying sacks of groundnuts had overturned and the poor unfortunates seated on top had drowned in a tiny stream under the weight of the sacks. There must have been about 12 of them, but because they were strangers the pagan Tangale would not touch them. No amount of threats and insults would shake the villagers from their paralysis, and the Tangale chief was nowhere to be found. In the end Luttu and I buried the victims in shallow graves by the roadside using tools that the unwilling villagers had brought us.

When based in Tula one was actively concerned with the local government administration. I was helped in this by the delightful Magajin Gari, the councillor for local administration; Umaru Kulani, who looked after education; Shehu Awak, the treasurer who later became Nigeria's High Commissioner in Britain and was the son of the pagan chief of the tiny Awak tribe; Sarkin Daji, the forestry officer; and the young and energetic Malam Pilipo, the mission-educated Ture, who acted as Native Authority secretary.

But as the name Touring Officer implied, a prime task was to tour the district, and in this fractious and rebellious area touring was very important. Apart from specific duties such as supervising the election of a chief or preparing the people for federal or Northern regional elections, the imminent approach of independence in a primitive and politically unsophisticated area left much difficult explaining to be done. Also, there was always the matter of constant intelligence gathering so one could keep a finger on the political pulse and tabs on potential trouble-makers. As a consequence I was frequently on tour, and in this richly diverse area the rewards were great, and they were not just scenic.

For example, quite by chance, we arrived in Nyuwar as a Longuda initiation ceremony was taking place. This only occurred once every ten years to coincide with the coming-of-age of a new generation, and has long since been abandoned. The Longuda initiates were dressed in leather loincloths and carried on their backs a kind of hump-shaped pack covered in netting. Many had porcupine quills through their noses. They were

chased over the hills from one shrine to another by the youth of
the previous generation and on reaching each shrine a dance was
performed. Two long 'male' and 'female' horns were blown at
each dancing session. Leaf-clad girls, some with babies slung in
leather carriers, danced with elderly pipe-smoking women. The
dancing was slow and tightly controlled until, at a given signal,
the initiates would flee to the safety of the next shrine pursued by
the male dancers. If they were caught they were savagely beaten.
If they survived they continued in the next round of the dancing.

On another occasion we arrived at the village of Lau behind
the great Dadiya mountain range and found the tiny Lau tribe
participating in spirit possession. The whole tribe were talking
in a language that was not their own and totally unintelligible
to an outsider. They were literally speaking in tongues and, led
by an evil-looking witch-doctor, they danced in pairs facing him,
occasionally falling to the ground, writhing and gibbering in a
strange ecstasy. The men here, too, wore a peculiar white fish
netting like the Longuda and from time to time broke off from the
dance to enter the *tsafi* (shrine) hut and refresh themselves with
beer. The girls were almost totally naked except for the scantiest
of leaves, and the dancing was spectacular, involving violent
shoulder blade rotation.

By contrast, the Dadiya, neighbours of the Lau, contorted their
bellies and danced sedately and slowly. We chanced upon another
ceremony high up on the Dadiya range with spectacular views of
the surrounding countryside where, decked out in bird and other
animal skulls, Dadiya youth rolled their stomachs backwards and
forwards and up and down, while standing on the edge of the
ridge.

Their neighbours the Cham, whose women and girls did not
wear leaves but beaten shredded cactus fore and aft, were also
spectacular dancers. Their dancing was very sedate and rhythmic
and they carried a ceremonial axe as they circled around inside
a larger circle composed of the leather loin-clothed youth. Again
by chance we arrived in Cham when a youth had killed a leopard
with a bow and arrow, a very rare feat. A seldom-performed

leopard dance was underway in his honour. The hero was carried shoulder high and by the time we arrived was quite drunk. The village girls were making their sedate way behind him to the sound of the throbbing drums. I was told that any girl was his for the taking.

In common with the Waja and the Longuda to the east of them, the Cham and the Mwana built figurative terracotta pots for divination, the curing of disease in both humans and animals, the protection of the foetus during gestation and the well-being of the child until puberty. In their local language these pots were called *itinate*; the Longuda pots were collectively known as *kwandalowa*.

One day when touring in the Mwana/Cham area we came across a discarded pile of these *itinate*. I took some of them back to Tula, and Luttu, who came from Mwana, was able to identify them and explain how and why they were used. Apparently, the practice of constructing these intricate pots had almost died out. Only the very old knew their uses and many of the younger generation (mainly mission-educated) were totally ignorant of the existence of the craft. Luttu explained that this terracotta work was produced entirely by male potters, in contrast to the normal domestic pots, which held food or water and were the work of females.

Anyone who was sick or felt in need of protection against forces outside his control consulted the tribal diviner (Sarkin Tsafi). This man was regarded with great respect in Cham and Mwana and formerly had great authority. He lived in a compound separate from the rest of the village and received his visitors in a hut without windows. Inside this dark, circular mud hut stood two terracotta figures, one male and one female. When the villager's problem had been put to the diviner, he would consult either the male or the female pot according to the sex of the petitioner.

When Sarkin Tsafi received his response from the pot, he advised the petitioner to go to a particular craftsman who had the skill to make the pot that suited his or her need. On payment of an agreed fee the pot would be made – payment used to be in the form of either chickens or tobacco although when we visited

Cham and discovered the discarded pots, it was in cash. The new pot was then taken to the diviner who invested it with magical power, usually with an incantation accompanied by the spilling of a cock's blood, but in certain rare cases with water from a pool high up in the mountains. The diviner was then paid and the pot taken back to the villager's own hut where it was kept until their request had been answered or the particular sickness cured.

During important festivals, notably the November harvest festival of Jitum, the pots were filled with locally brewed guinea-corn beer as a means of general thanksgiving to all the benign household spirits. Occasionally the beer was drunk by the householders as a protection against evil and sickness.

The male and female pots consulted by Sarkin Tsafi were in some cases supplied to householders as an additional protection for the home. However, they could not be consulted by the villager – this power rested with Sarkin Tsafi alone. Pots that had served their purpose were discarded as useless and it was these that we had stumbled across. Even after they were discarded, superstitious villagers preferred not to look at them too closely nor handle them with disrespect, for it was widely believed that the affliction which had originally affected the sick person had been transferred from the person to the pot. The pots varied artistically depending on the skill of the person who made them, but some were beautifully constructed, a testimony to the latent artistic talent of the Cham and the Mwana. One or two examples are with me still.

I never saw Waja 'medicine' potters or pots and assume the craft had died out under the pressure of Islam, which the Waja were enthusiastically embracing. But it was in Waja country that we watched a hunter dressed in black cloth and with a great hornbill's skull on his head stalking a flock of hornbill which were completely unaware of his presence. In the same area, one daybreak, my messenger, the Village Head and I blew down a hole in a deep depression in a rock reputed in local Islamic legend to have been left by Mohammed when he walked across the area. A true Waja pagan would no doubt have a different explanation, but as we each blew, a noise like a fog-horn sounded through another opening some hundred yards away.

We saw dancers in Longuda with monkey skulls strapped to their heads, sedate dances for chiefs among the friendly Waja, and the graceful dancing of Sarkin Kulani of the hill Waja tribe. And in Burak there was a shrine full of the skulls of former enemies, each marked with a great red cross. In Tula Yiri I once stumbled across a litter of puppies being cooked for supper in a pot.

Age-old customs and the demands of the mid-20th century were often in conflict. We once came upon the Chief of the Tangale tribe performing a pagan ritual in an abandoned settlement high up in the hills. For many years he had dressed in flowing gowns and worn a turban to identify himself as a staunch Muslim. When we saw him, he was, much to his embarrassment, dressed only in a loincloth and was leading his people in some ancient ritual that would have been total anathema to Islam. It was difficult not to feel sorry for these erstwhile pagans, caught in an Islamic/Christian cultural crossfire not of their making.

I once saw the Tula perform a dance to appease the spirit who protected them from smallpox. Huge leafy branches were held high by both the Tula girls and youths. There was none of the usual carefree excitement on this occasion. They were dancing at dusk on the top of a great cliff overlooking the plains that stretched to Gombe in the north. The cliff had formerly been used by the Sarkin Tsafi as a place of execution, from where murderers and malefactors would be hurled to their deaths on the jagged rocks below. It was an eerie spectacle; the sun had set and in the twilight the swaying branches, some the size of small trees, gave the unearthly impression of a whole forest on the move. Two long male and female horns accompanied a low mournful song with loud, low-pitched blasts sounding out one after the other. The Tula were so preoccupied as to be completely unaware of my presence and I watched until darkness fell before returning home, but they continued well into the night in a determined effort to appease the spirit who had the power to drive the dreaded spectre of smallpox out of their village.

One night, bored and aimless, I wandered up into the hills behind my house to where the drums and horns were playing. This time it was the turn of the old men of the tribe, the wizened old pensioners who had been lusty youths when Carlyle suddenly appeared among them like a great white god. They were circling round and round in time to the drumming, each holding the head of a baboon in his hand. I kept in the shadows not wanting to be seen, for I had chanced on a forbidden ceremony, the dance reserved for the heads of the bodies of enemies that were about to be eaten. The old ones were re-living their warlike past, the baboon head taking the place of a human skull. The Tula had been cannibals, observing the unusual practice of not only eating their slain enemies but also their own young men who had been killed in battle.

In 1906, A C C Hastings, a District Officer based in Gombe, described the cannibal habits of the Tula as follows:

The countless huts were built of mud and grass thatch within a few feet of each other in and out among the rocks, fifteen and twenty together all linked up by joining walls of piled up rock and stone, thus forming a fortified group of houses occupied by a family. Little mud grain bins were dotted about inside the area, and small goats and fowls wandered in and out of the huts, which had low open doorways three feet high. Hundreds of these hut groups were dotted about the sides of the ridge, not only on the flat spaces, but on the rocky slopes, so steep that the base of many huts stood higher than the roofs of others.

The condition inside was indescribably filthy. The huts were pitch dark and evil-smelling. Upon the wall top in the larger ones numerous skulls were ranged, some stained a terracotta colour, others a bleaching white – the horrid relics of killings and feasts. Large smoke-black pots of earthenware held cold gruesome masses which we dare not investigate. The light of grass torches showed us half-gnawed human bones, flung into a corner, the flesh yet adhering to some of them, and upon the walls hung quivers of freshly-poisoned arrows with the gummy concoction of strophanthus and other horrid mixtures scarcely dry upon the barbs. Other ghastly bundles too hung there, dried human skin and finger bones, with other horrors wrapped in coarse woven cloth. A horrible stench clung to every hut, and disgusting filth lay everywhere, the odour of blood and excrement and animal matter rising from every quarter.

The Tula were of a fine physique, taller and stouter than most of the neighbouring tribes. They were stark naked, and armed themselves with long spears pointed with iron and barbed-like fish hooks. They carried large round shields of bush cowhide. They do not belie the reputation for ferocity and the cannibal tendencies of which I have heard so much. As I came to know them later, they ate their kind from a real pleasure in human meat, and not, as some other tribes told me they did, because men were easier to get than game!

Hastings continued:

… I was sitting on a rock above the valley, looking down upon our camp and the ground beyond, when to my amazement I saw through my glasses the ocular confirmation of the man-eating customs of the Tula. Two old ladies were wandering on the battlefield, each with a basket on her head, and presently, to my horror, they set these down near to the body of a warrior who had fallen in our skirmish that morning, and calmly began to dismember him! I could see their arms rising and falling as they hacked away, or tugged at a joint, and put it in a basket. I made for camp to have the old ghouls driven off.

In addition to their individual characteristics, the tribes of Tangale-Waja built their houses and corn bins in a variety of architectural styles. The Tula houses were constructed of stone and mud. Like most pagan houses they were very small and, for security, the spaces between the round huts that formed the little clusters of an individual's compound were infilled with rocks and stones, a single gap being left for entry. The Tula also used larger stones to construct platforms round trees for use as sitting and meeting places. Old men would squat on these all day, watching the world go by.

The Waja of the plains built houses with walled compounds

and larger huts based on Hausa styles. The houses of their cousins in the hills were similar to those of the Tula but their corn bins sported tall conical hats made of woven grass. All the different tribal corn bins had this woven matting to cover the stored millet or guinea-corn, but the hill Waja weave was particularly striking. Sometimes I had to stay in some of these pagan huts, there being no other accommodation available, and they were so small that my camp bed would scarcely fit in. They were often smoke blackened, full of animal skulls, cocks' feathers, mysteriously woven objects and other items of juju.

The annual agricultural show was one of the highlights of the year. Stalls were erected for the judging of the farmers' produce; goats and sheep were paraded and awarded prizes; a speech was made; and Tony Krzywon was much in evidence. But the highlights of the show were the dances and competitions afterwards. Most of the tribes sent in their dancers, the Tula and Cham girls holding pride of place. Even on alien ground no attempt was made by the Cham to display any modesty. I am sure Hilker totally disapproved, dedicated as he was to wrapping the girls up in cloth. There was a game for the old men too. A chicken was released and the greybeards flung themselves about in their effort to catch it, much to the amusement of the crowd. Finally the wrestlers would come on to the sound of drums. There was a great deal of ferocious grimacing at opponents. Bets were laid. Inevitably Paulo, our small stocky Tula mechanic, who serviced and drove the Native Authority truck, would win, much to the delight of the crowd.

Apart from excelling at wrestling, Paulo performed other duties, some of which were unconventional. One Sunday morning, a Tula came to my house accompanied by his pregnant wife who was in great agony as she could not give birth. Her heaving belly bulged above her leaves and I was at my wits' end to know what should be done. Hilker was on leave and there was no one to give medical advice. In desperation, I suggested she be put in the Native Authority lorry and driven over the roughest possible roads. As the dilapidated vehicle disappeared into the distance trailing a cloud of dust I wondered whether I would shortly be sued for murder. An hour later the lorry returned empty but with little Paulo grinning from ear to ear. 'It worked,' he said, 'it's a boy!' Apparently the woman had given birth halfway through the journey, with our mechanic, who was usually covered in motor oil, acting as mid-wife.

In fact, these pagan women used to go to their farms to plant or hoe, have a baby in the field as they paused from work and then continue their work later that day. To them, childbirth was as natural as the performance of their other bodily functions and occurred with regularity nearly every year. They hoed with rigidly straight legs though I never discovered if this had anything to do with natural childbirth.

During my second year in Tula, the May rains suddenly failed and by mid-June the crops were withered and dying. The worried Tula villagers had consulted their traditional rainmaker who had demanded the usual tribute of chickens, goats and corn before he brought the rain. This payment was made, but ten days later when rain had still not fallen the people began to accuse the ancient one of fraud. A riot was brewing and the young chief of Tula Wange came to my house and begged me to intervene. 'How can one intervene in such circumstances unless one has the power to make rain fall oneself?' I asked myself. The chief told me that the Reverend Hilker had been responsible for the rainmaker's appearance in court some years earlier on a related charge of defrauding the people. As I didn't want my fundamentalist neighbour to score religious points off the pagan Tula, Ali Sikkam, the Chief of the Native Authority police was sent for.

'Just how serious is this situation?'

'If it doesn't rain soon, there will be a big riot,' came the prompt reply.

He was asked to let me know if the mood of the villagers deteriorated further, and I decided to visit the rainmaker myself.

It is often thought that witch doctors, rainmakers and the keepers of tribal secrets are exotic figures dressed in feathers and war-paint. More often than not they are tired, ragged old men with rheumy eyes. The Tula Wange rainmaker was no exception. Old, dirty and ragged, he was the very picture of wronged humanity. But when questioned his ancient frame twitched into vehement life.

'They were told that I needed another week,' he proclaimed, stabbing a forefinger into the dusty earth to emphasise his point. 'They are too impatient, they will not give me enough time. Give me a few more days and I will show you all just how well I can make rain.' He looked up in despair. 'These mission people give me too much trouble,' he said. 'The world is too impatient.'

It was odds on that in a few more days the much-needed rain would arrive anyway, but in order to try to induce a sense of urgency he was allowed just one more week. If there was no rain after that, then the court would decide whether or not he was what he claimed or just an old charlatan. He looked at me as though I were an heretic and I retreated with relief from his tumbledown mud hut with its smoke-blackened monkey skulls hanging from the wall and pots smeared with dried chicken blood and feathers littering the floor.

The days passed. The sun shone and the sky remained cloudless. It had to rain soon, not to save the old man's skin but to avert a serious food shortage. On the seventh day after my visit to the rainmaker, the morning sun rose in a cloudless sky.

In desperation, I took some sandwiches and a bottle of beer and picnicked on top of one of Tula's larger peaks. This crazy notion was prompted by my upbringing in a country where it invariably rained when a picnic was attempted. Sitting there in solitary and stupid splendour, I waited in vain for the heavens to open. The sun shone harshly out of a bright blue sky. Tula shimmered in the heat. Cicadas' wings beat hectically all around me. The big red ants discovered unconcealed flesh and my spirits sank.

I dozed off, awaking to find a small black cloud overhead – not a big cloud, but big enough to release a tiny shower of rain that, for a moment, flattened the Tula dust. It had worked. The picnic juju was stronger that the rainmaker's and I laughed out loud to the amazement of three naked, dust-covered Tula children who were staring at me from behind a large boulder.

The spell was broken. It rained hard the next day, and the next and the next. The rains had come and the old man's honour and prestige had been restored. He and his family were supplied by the villagers with enough food to last them for the next six months.

7

The Self-Government Durbar and the Chamba

'Make your number, when you go on leave. Go and see them in Church House, it's always useful to get yourself known.'

I had not returned to Church House, Westminster, since my initial interview and I went back there with some trepidation in order to meet the man on the West Africa desk.

A door marked 'Africa West' opened on to a small untidy office where I was introduced to a paunchy, middle-aged civil servant wearing rimless spectacles, the bridge of which had been repaired with Sellotape. He held out a limp hand of greeting.

'I understand you are from Northern Nigeria,' he said rising to his feet. 'Like it there?'

'Very much.'

'Excellent.'

The three walls of his room were covered with maps of Nigeria, the Gold Coast, Sierra Leone and the Gambia.

'Show me where you have been working,' he continued as he stubbed a chubby finger on the map of Nigeria, '

I pointed to where Gombe and Tula were clearly marked on the map.

'Have we built any roads in those parts recently? We like to keep things up to date.'

'Yes, there are one or two which are not on your map,' I replied, noting that the map was dated 1946.

'Care to put them in for me?' said Her Majesty's West African expert, handing me a red marker pen.

I marked the road between Bauchi and Gombe and the road to Tangale-Waja as best I could.

'Keeping busy in the bush?'

'Yes, thank you, Sir.'

'Good.'

He gave me a watery smile, thanked me for coming and as I walked briskly into Great Smith Street, in an attempt to put as great a distance between myself and Church House as quickly as possible, I determined never again to attempt to make my 'number'.

On return from leave, I was told I had been chosen to be the Bauchi Province Provincial Marshal at Northern Nigeria's celebratory self-government Durbar to be staged in Kaduna. A Durbar, as understood in Northern terms, is a parade of horse and men in honour of rulers, important visitors or a significant event. For example, a Durbar had been held when the Queen visited the North in 1956. It had been spectacular and so successful that a repeat was now being planned for the 1959 self-government celebrations when the royal visitors would be the Duke and Duchess of Gloucester. Each of the 13 provinces that made up Northern Nigeria was to send a contingent of horsemen, drummers and dancers to represent the tribes and culture of the province. It was to be a tremendous undertaking and one that would never be repeated. Old cultures and traditions were rapidly crumbling, new roads were under construction, and the idea that a younger generation would ever again trek hundreds of miles on horseback to Kaduna was unrealistic.

Each Native Authority from the Emirates and Independent Districts within Bauchi Province was instructed to send a contingent to the headquarters at Bauchi. There they would gather and march on Kaduna, arriving two days before the planned full dress rehearsal. In practice, the organisation of the

Bauchi contingent, which would eventually comprise over 1,000 participants and camp-followers, 300 horses and 20 camels, was a tough exercise. The Native Authorities had to work out their own routes and forage as far as Bauchi, then it was up to the Provincial Marshal to plan the route to Kaduna some 220 miles away. Each stage would comprise a march of about 15 miles and the journey was estimated to take just over two weeks. The camels were to be sent by lorry and most of the horses by train from Jos, but the cross-country journey had to be carefully planned well in advance to ensure that food and forage for both men and animals were available all along the route.

I wanted to trek all the way with the men, but was told to oversee the complicated task of loading and unloading the horses, which were to travel by train, and the camels, which were to go by road. A whole day was spent trying to load the fractious camels into three ten-ton lorries. They bit, spat and snarled. They lay down and refused to budge. In moments of extreme vexation they regurgitated their food and blew half-digested vegetable matter into our faces. In the end we resorted to digging a large hole under one lorry until the tail-board, when extended, was level with the ground outside, for the camels would not walk up a wooden tail-board and no amount of inducement would persuade them to do so. Eventually, after reversing each lorry into the hole, and with further cursing and cajoling we managed to load them and send them on their way – still, quite understandably, grumbling and protesting at their fate.

Having finalised the route and forage for the main contingent and their remaining 100 horses, and having seen them off, I set out ten days later with 200 horses and their grooms on the 90-mile route to Jos. We completed the journey in three days and then spent another difficult five hours loading stallions into railway wagons. Not a mare or gelding was to be seen and these animals, the pick of the horse in Bauchi Province, were full of guinea-corn and maize. Their coats shone and they were very fit. It was lucky no one was injured as the corned-up horses reared and lashed out with their hind legs at both us and the other horses. Eventually they were loaded, the wagon gates shut and bolted, and after some delay the train set off for Kaduna. We travelled with the fractious stallions and as the horses came down a makeshift ramp they again tried to kick out at their travelling companions.

The operation had been co-ordinated so that shortly after our arrival we met up with the men and horses travelling overland. All the Native Authority contingents gathered in a large open space near Kaduna railway station, and after inspecting them, I was relieved to find the whole exercise had gone off practically without hitch and without injury to either horses or camels. Amidst shouts of triumph and with drums beating and horns blowing, the reunited Bauchi Province contingent set off to ride and walk through Kaduna to the Durbar camp, which had been erected about five miles away on the opposite side of town to the railway station

To ride at the head of a party of 300 horses and 1,000 men, who had trekked in over a month from the remotest parts of Bauchi Province, was a great experience. Feelings of comradeship were high, encompassing tribes and religions which more often than not were in conflict with each other. The horsemen felt an elation no doubt common to conquering cavalry in the past, but extremely hard to replicate today. When we passed State House, residence of the Northern Nigerian Premier Sir Ahmadu Bello, the Sardauna of Sokoto, clenched fists were shaken in the air in a traditional mark of respect and the whole contingent let out a deep throaty roar. A few years later the Sardauna met a cruel death in this same building, when young Ibo officers gunned him and his family down in the first stages of a successful military coup.[1] After his assassination the hegemony of the North, which

---

1 On the night of 14/15th January 1966, Major Chukwuma Nzeogwu, a member of the Ibo tribe, who was serving with the Federal Army in Kaduna, led an assault on the official residence of the Sardauna of Sokoto, the Northern Premier, and shot and killed both him and his senior wife. Nzeogwu and his dissident soldiers were the Northern element in an elaborate Ibo-inspired *coup d'état* in which not only the Sardauna was killed but also Alhaji Abubakar Tafawa Balewa, the Federal Prime Minister, Chief Samuel Akintola, the Western Region Premier, and Okotie Eboh, the Federal Finance Minister. This coup brought to power the Ibo soldier Major-General John Aguiyi Ironsi (with whom

had been held together by the force of his charismatic personality, fell apart.

We reached the village of Kawo on the eastern side of Kaduna where our route took us down a minor road that led to the camp itself. As we turned off the main road, an Ibo taxi driver who was coming towards us started to hoot his horn in an attempt to force the massed horses to give way. He drove through the first rank of gesticulating horsemen, his horn blaring noisily. He had reached the fourth rank when all at once a roar went up from our men. One doughty cavalryman drew his sword and brought it down with a mighty blow on to the roof of the taxi. The blade punctured the metal of the car as though it were a sardine tin. The terrified driver leapt from his taxi and fled for his life. When other sword-bearers passed the stricken vehicle they stabbed at it in turn until a section of the roof sprung open like an opened can.

We soon reached the Durbar camp just behind Kawo village where quarters for men and lines for horses and camels had been prepared. We slept together in rooms made from straw matting and topped with sheets of corrugated iron. The horses were tied by one foreleg to a wooden stake sunk into the ground. Another rope tied the free foreleg to the adjacent hind. They all seemed settled and secure and in spite of a little bad behaviour from some of the friskier stallions, we went to bed without expecting trouble.

However, we had not reckoned on the violent storm that suddenly blew up. Great shafts of forked lightning lit the night sky as thunder rolled and crashed about us. The excitable stallions pulled at their stakes. Some freed themselves and charged about, kicking out at imagined shadows and at other horses, which in turn reared and pulled up their own stakes. Soon the relatively peaceful scene had been transformed into one of total chaos. There were, of course, over 2,000 more horses in the camp from the 12

I had served during my National Service with the Royal West African Frontier Force). In May 1966, the North retaliated, and in a bloody Northern massacre, Ibos were driven out of the North. This exodus and subsequent events led to the Eastern Region's secession from the Federal Republic of Nigeria, the founding of Biafra and the start of the bloody and ultimately futile Biafran war.

other provinces and the air was filled with the cries of panicking animals and the curses and shouts of the horse-boys who looked after them. It took some two hours to bring order to the horse lines and not until the storm had rumbled away did they settle. Again we were lucky that there were no serious injuries. As for the tethered camels, they stared at the spooked horses in amazement while they contentedly chewed their cud. The contrast in the behaviour of camels and horses under stressful circumstances could not have been more marked.

The Durbar was to take place on the racecourse near the centre of Kaduna. This covered a large grassy area and the plan was that each province would parade around the circumference of the course and past the grandstand where dignitaries were seated. To give an idea of the numbers of men and animals involved, it took more than two and a half hours for the complete Northern contingent to file past the grandstand. Strict instructions had been given not to halt in front of the Duke and Duchess or the Sardauna, otherwise the procession would take hours to conclude. Of course, clenched fists could be shaken in traditional style but on no account was the line to come to a halt. The order of the day was 'keep moving'. But some Emirs and chiefs could not resist the temptation to turn and advance towards the grandstand.

The northern-most Emirates, steeped in Islamic tradition, paraded with their Emirs and chiefs seated under large colourful umbrellas which were continually twirled over them by gaudily dressed retainers. Following behind the chief and also mounted were his traditional title holders, such as his second in command the Waziri, his war leader Sarkin Yaki, the master of the horse Sarkin Dawaki, the treasurer the Ma'aji, and the Magajin Gari, the councillor in charge of the township. These titles varied from Emirate to Emirate, but in essence each medieval court was made up of similar personages. Then would follow the court jesters, leaping about with monkey skulls on their heads, then came drummers, some on camel, others on foot or horse. Often a young boy brilliantly attired would be mounted on a magnificent horse. This would be the Emir or chief's heir or favourite son.

The horsemen from Borno who followed their Shehu (Emir) were an incredible sight. Their horses wore trousers and had quilted, multi-coloured blankets slung over their haunches like the steeds of knights in the Middle Ages. Chain mail was much in evidence and some retainers wore curious metal helmets like those of German First World War army officers. There was a contingent of hunters, dressed in black and carrying spears or bows and arrows. Other wild men led muzzled hyenas.

From the provinces where pagan tribes predominated there were spectacular troupes of dancers, barefoot and wearing loincloths with jangling bells and bangles that clanked in unison as they whirled about. The Tula trumpeters paraded with their six-foot trumpets. They were dressed, not in their traditional leather loincloths, but in long white gowns tied at the waist with a red sash that we had had specially tailored for the occasion. They also wore their traditional three-pronged headdresses made out of hide and covered with small bright red, poisonous seeds. The effect was spectacular and the low, mournful note of their horns could easily be singled out above the hectic and frenetic drumming of the rest of the contingent.

From Niger Province came a large group of nomadic Fulani followed by their young women carrying calabashes, the underside of their breasts peeking out from below their locally woven mini-singlets. In striking contrast, large juju *dodo* or spirits (in reality stilt-walkers) covered in long white cloth, pranced about in a frightening fashion, twirling hollowed-out calabashes on long strings that sounded a low eerie note.

There were also more conventional stilt-walkers from Ilorin Province; frenzied, tousled, whirling dervishes from the far north of Borno; and line after line of magnificently apparelled horses.

A contingent of Piti pagans from Plateau Province enthralled us with their horsemanship. These bareback riders wore nothing except little leather skull-caps and penis sheaths of plaited straw. They galloped excitedly up and down within their group, controlling their horses with nothing more than their legs, a bitless bridle and a single rope around the muzzle that served as a rein.

Each Emir and Chief had dressed out his retainers in brightly coloured cloth specially bought and tailored for the occasion, and there was fierce rivalry between them to present the biggest and showiest spectacle – some in quartered checks of green and red, others gold and black, others in purple and blue. The Emir's personal jester would cavort wildly among these retainers, somersaulting through their massed ranks, pausing for a moment to make a joke or stick out his tongue before careering off again on another chaotic spin.

A group of well-drilled pagan Bachama dancers from Adamawa, naked except for loincloths and massive jangling bangles around their ankles, danced by in unison, swinging beaded calabashes like castanets. In contrast, wild-eyed Bokkos pagans from Plateau Province, whose grandfathers had struck fear into the hearts of their neighbours and early European tin miners, danced by frenetically in front of their traditional enemies, their naked bodies gleaming with oil.

Tuaregs from the desert rode by on their camels, wearing traditionally dyed robes and turbans that concealed everything except for their eyes, the cloth beaten with wooden bats so that the blue-black dye shone with a silvery sheen – after a time their bodies, too, acquired the same colour as their clothing. Their womenfolk, beautifully tattooed on their arms and faces, eyes shadowed with antimony and limbs laden with silver and gold necklaces and bangles, followed behind them, eyes flashing an unmistakable message – 'Show me a man who is good enough for me!'

The dress rehearsal took too long. It ran three-quarters of an hour over time and we were told we must get our contingent to move faster. We exhorted them to speed up but on the day itself the great procession took nearly three hours to circumnavigate the racecourse as the temptation to stop and greet the Duke, Duchess and the Sardauna proved too powerful to resist. The endless line would move slowly forward and then concertina as one group after another decided to stage their own individual show. When the pagan Piti on their ponies reached the dais they couldn't resist charging up and down in front of it at a full gallop. Eventually they had to be led away, so excited had they and their horses become.

In the evening, a spectacular firework display took place on the racecourse culminating in an illuminated Northern Knot, the inter-twining symbol of a unified North, lighting up the night sky. At the end of this display all the provincial marshals were invited to a reception for the Duke and Duchess of Gloucester, who were staying with Governor Bell at Government House. We were introduced, presented one by one and given a commemorative medal to mark the occasion.

Of course, after the celebration, the men, horses and camels had to return home the way they had come and the provision and forage plans put into reverse. However, some were keener to get back to their families and villages than others and our provincial discipline broke down as scattered groups pioneered their own journey home. I returned with the horses and their grooms on the train to Jos and then rode back the 90 miles to Bauchi.

A series of interesting new Hausa words was invented at about the time of the Durbar as the language adapted to changing times. Members of parliament were called *membobi*. Parachutists were called *masu sauka da lemu*, (the men who floated down with umbrellas). And for the duration of the Durbar, provincial marshals were called *marshalloli*.

On my return to Bauchi, fresh from the excitements of the Durbar, I was told that I would have to remain in this provincial headquarters to gain further administrative experience. The prospect filled me with gloom. Tangale-Waja and the Durbar had whetted my appetite for much more. A stint as a penpusher was not at all what I wanted. Historically, young DOs were of two kinds: those who wanted to get into the headquarters secretariat and carve out a career behind a desk where they would be noticed;

and others who wanted to work in a bush district as far away as possible. I was in no doubt as to which camp I belonged.

However, for a short time I was put in charge of the Provincial Land's Office with a mandate to assess compensation for farmers whose land was being compulsorily acquired by the railway authorities for the new railway line that was to run from Jos to Maiduguri. Fortunately, the work was not too desk-bound but it involved tedious and lengthy arguments with local farmers over compensation. In some cases the line crossed valuable farmland; in others, it traversed scrubby, worthless bush, but naturally everyone was out to get as much as they could from a not ungenerous government handout. The railway line was later to transform Gombe from a delightfully sleepy traditional Emirate backwater, into a bustling and important railway town, and turn tiny Ashaka village on the River Gongola (to where I had trekked two years previously) into a polluted metropolis at one end of a huge railway bridge.

I was not involved very long in this work. After only three weeks, Leith Watt, the then Resident of Bauchi, called me to his office and told me that Nigel Cooke, Resident of Adamawa Province (who had been my Resident after Ian Gunn had left Bauchi), had requested that I be lent to him for a month. There was a need to explain to the predominantly pagan Chamba tribesmen in his area the implications of a forthcoming plebiscite. Little did anyone realise at the time that the month on loan was to extend to a period of nearly four years' absorbing work in that fascinating area and that I would be caught up in not one plebiscite but two.

'Would you be interested in such a job?' Watt asked. 'With your trekking and bush experience in Tangale-Waja you seem an obvious choice.' I couldn't wait. I knew that some of the wildest country and most primitive peoples remaining in Nigeria were located in Adamawa Province. I had heard of the wild tribes bordering Cameroon and of the legendary fastness of the Mambilla plateau where there were no roads and the approach could only be made by a climb up a 5,000-foot escarpment. This was the area more than any other that I hoped to be posted to.

And so it happened that two weeks later, Luttu and I found ourselves temporally housed in Yola, the headquarter town of Adamawa Province on the River Benue, with instructions to move to Jada in Chamba tribal country 250 miles to the south as soon we were ready to do so.

We had had an exciting interlude on the journey down when we encountered a 100-yard washout on the road near Cham. For a moment we thought that we were going to be holed up again in Tangale-Waja, but my trusty old Standard Vanguard pick-up was pushed, pulled and dragged through the swirling waters. Our supplies and loads were sodden but we reached the other side safely.

All Adamawa Province was ruled from Yola, the administrative headquarters and the home of the Lamido, the first-class Fulani Emir who governed a territory formerly misappropriated by his ancestors from pagan tribes who lived in the 1,200-mile long province that bordered the former French Cameroons. Prior to the First World War (see Preface) this area had been divided between German and British colonial rulers and was to become the battleground of two fiercely contested plebiscites.

My main job was to explain the implications of this plebiscite to the somewhat truculent Chamba – not an easy task in an area fiercely hostile to Fulani rule from Yola. The loyalties of the Chamba, who had been heavily influenced by both Protestant and Catholic missionaries and mistreated by the Fulani, were suspect. Such was their antipathy to Fulani rule that the British administration was worried that they might vote 'French', that is to say in favour of rule from the Cameroon Republic. I soon realised that I was there to be used as plebiscite propaganda – to show the Chamba that enthusiastic ADOs from Nigeria were still available to tour their area and to look after their interests so they would vote 'English'.

In Yola I met Farrant, the Senior District Officer in charge of the Southern Division (which included Jada, a Fulani-administered township and the Chamba tribal area). He armed me with files and touring diaries, and I set off on the journey to Jada.

The little town of Jada with its Fulani District Head, Wamban Jada, who had served the Lamido on Mambilla, was relatively sleepy. But in and near the surrounding hills, the Chamba were anything but sleepy, and under covert mission influence they were also strongly opposed on religious grounds to their rulers, the Muslim Fulani.

As it turned out I did not spend very long with the Chamba. After three, two-week long treks through the different clan areas – they divided into three distinct clans living east, west and south of Jada – politics determined that I be switched to the Alantika Mountains, a particularly remote mountainous redoubt where there were immediate and serious problems concerning taxation and loyalty. But before I left, my treks in Chamba country enabled me to visit the village of Kojeli where I became especially friendly with the village's Fulani chief, and where some memorable *wasani* took place.

Near the foothills of the Alantika Mountains, at a village called Mapeo, was a Catholic mission. It was here I first met Father Tim Cottar (later to become the Bishop of Maiduguri), who had lived in the area since the early 1940s. When we first met he had not seen a white man for three months, apart from his brother Father in Mapeo. I thought this tough and strange at the time, but later, on Mambilla, I experienced an even longer period of isolation from my own tribe.

When I visited him many years later in Maiduguri, Father (by now Bishop) Cottar greeted me as a long-lost friend. Sadly, there was no drink on hand to offer.

'Ah, John,' he said in his delightful Irish brogue, 'I don't think the Good Lord will mind if we unconsecrate a drop of communion wine.'

It turned out that the Good Lord did not mind one bit.

Chamba District also gave me the great advantage of meeting Jock McClymont, or Wee Mac as he was known to some. A wells inspector working under the rural water supplies section of the public works department, Mac's task was to provide well-water in villages where there was none. Whereas most of his contemporaries were content to construct wells in villages bordering motor roads, Mac made a point of trekking with his equipment into the remotest areas and living with the villagers for weeks or months on end while he sank wells and constructed wash places. Mac came from a humble Scottish crofting background and had come to Nigeria in his late 40s, but through his desire to work far off the beaten track and his wonderful ability to get on with Africans, he was not only well known and respected but eventually earned a much deserved MBE.

Although Mac was very much older than me, we struck up an immediate rapport. I would make a point of tracking him down in some remote hamlet, and he would do the same if I was on tour. After finishing our respective days' work we would enliven the evening by asking the chief to put a call out for the village drummers and dancers. We spent many happy nights together not only in the Chamba area but also, much later, further north in the Mubi area, surrounded by beating drums, swirling dust and oiled, gyrating pagan bodies. We would sometimes join in the fun ourselves and Mac's antics would cause shrieks of delight.

Because I was the DO (by this time I had been promoted from ADO) I had to be in control, no matter how wild the evening became. If things got out of hand then authority was lost. This invisible line, a very sensitive one, was crossed at peril.

The day after such a party, Mac would be up and away, trekking off to supervise his well-sinking in some remote hamlet. His legacy remains to this day and countless villagers have much to thank him for.

Mac taught me much basic bush lore. He always carried with him a tin of potassium permanganate. This had many uses – as a gargle, as a vegetable steriliser and as a purifier of filthy bath water. Woe betide, however, if one of its undissolved crystals came into contact with bare skin for it stung and burnt with vigour, so much so that the white paint on the sides of my portable tin bath were burnt completely away. I was taught to shave with the inside of a banana skin when soap was not available, to make soap out of wood ash, and to iron with a flat-sided Johnny Walker whisky bottle when there was no charcoal for the iron.

Mac invariably carried with him powdered yeast. This not only put pep into him but also pepped up a bottle of beer when perhaps a favourite old chief bemoaned that his wives were complaining about his loss of 'power'. Mac would pour yeast into a jug of beer and give it to the ageing greybeard. Immediately the brew would froth and bubble and Mac would encourage the recipient to drink it while it was 'potent'. Invariably the next day would bring forth a new and invigorated pagan – and no doubt an equally satisfied wife.

One evening, when travelling on a 200-mile journey, my old Standard pick-up had a second puncture, leaving Mac and myself stranded by the roadside. This is not an uncommon experience in Africa, and as the road was infrequently travelled we were preparing to rough it for a night with neither food nor bedding. Dusk had fallen when we saw the headlights of another pick-up travelling towards us. It turned out to be a local Native Authority vehicle which had received a message from someone who was stranded on the road near us.

'Well, we didn't send the message,' Mac said, 'but it's lucky for us that someone else did.'

The car set off to look for the mysterious caller and returned about 20 minutes later having failed to find any traveller in distress. Gratefully, we accepted the lift into Mubi. The strange thing was that in spite of many enquiries no one could identify the person who had asked for assistance. A divine providence appeared to have intervened on behalf of Mac and myself.

Sadly, Mac never came up onto the Mambilla plateau during my four years there. Nor did he accompany me to the Alantika Mountains, an area which for wildness and remoteness out-shone any other part of Nigeria, if not the whole of West Africa.

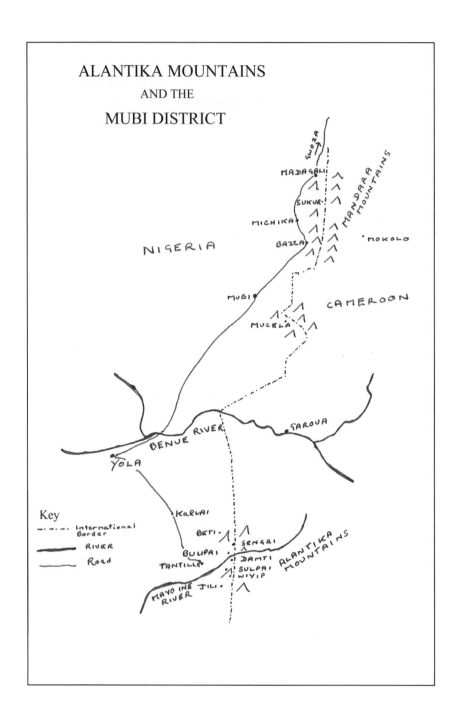

ALANTIKA MOUNTAINS
AND THE
MUBI DISTRICT

8

The Alantika Mountains

T he sheer-sided Alantika Mountains lie 40 miles due south of Yola, and run north to south for nearly 70 miles to form a natural barrier between Nigeria and the Cameroon Republic. At the highest point they reach 4,700 feet and most of the paths to the mountain villages on the top are very steep and covered with loose shingle. This makes them extremely difficult for a carrier to climb with a load of 45 pounds finely balanced on his head. The range is divided west to east in the centre by a river, which becomes the source of the large River Mayo Ine on the plains below.

The Alantika Mountains were inhabited by the Koma, by far the most unsophisticated tribe in the whole of Nigeria. The Koma comprised two distinct clans with each neatly separated from the other by the central tributary. Although they were tribal cousins, the customs, language and religious beliefs of one clan were different from the other, which pointed to their having been on either side of the divide for a very long time. Even the mat enclosures that housed their religious shrines were built differently.

At the northern extremity of the Alantika range lived the Vomni tribe, who were more advanced than the Koma. Most of them had moved down from their steep-sided mountain and built houses in the foothills and on the plains below, where they had come into contact with the more sophisticated Chamba and Fulani.

The Koma, especially those in the remotest villages, were living as they had done for centuries and were therefore, just before Nigeria's independence, something of an embarrassment to the government. The area was designated a 'closed area' on account of their warlike reputation. This meant it was unsafe and no outsider or government official was allowed to visit the Koma's mountain homeland without the written permission of the Resident in Yola. Consequently, it was on record that only 13 Europeans had ever toured the area and these had all been administrators. No mission activity was allowed to take place in the mountains. All this was a quite amazing anomaly in the year before full independence.

With the administration's mind concentrated on vastly more important matters than the plight of the Koma, they could have slipped into an independent Nigeria unnoticed and untroubled had they only continued to provide the Fulani District Head of Karlai with 12 virgins on an annual basis. Their tax rate at 12 shillings and sixpence per adult male over 16 was easily the lowest in Nigeria. But the Koma, high up in their mountain fortress, owed allegiance to no one and, with no material advantage to be gained from the payment of this tax, steadfastly withheld payment. Bunu, the wily District Head of Karlai, had, however, cleverly turned this show of defiance to his advantage. For more than 25 years he had covered up the loss of revenue, cooked the books and accepted the Koma's virgins in lieu. The Koma annually dispatched the 12 virgins to his large and lavish compound and kept their cash for more important things in life, such as salt, the one commodity that was unobtainable in the mountains. However, politics, indeed international politics of a very high order, were to put an abrupt end to this mutually advantageous situation.

After the First World War, the German Cameroons had been placed under British colonial control (see Preface). After the Second World War, and the winding up of the League of Nations, this brief had devolved to the United Nations and, although in practice the territory was run by the appointed colonial authority, when the time came for independence, the UN stepped in.

When the German Cameroons had been given to Britain to administer in 1918, the British government had incorporated the former German colony into Nigeria. The southern section, which included Bamenda (of *Bafut Beagles* fame) and the well-known landmark Cameroon Mountain, was administered as part of the Eastern Region of Nigeria. The major part of the northern section fell under the administration of the Fulani Emir, or Lamido, in Yola. It was run by the Adamawa Native Authority through Fulani District Heads and formed part of the Northern Region of Nigeria.

Historically, the people in the northern territory comprised numerous and wild pagan tribes; some had been conquered and ruled by the Muslim Fulani, and others had maintained sturdy independence in mountain strongholds. In 1918, the British placed them all under Yola – except for the extreme north, which was governed by the Muslim Kanuri Emir in Dikwa. With the advent of the missions an even greater divide took place on religious grounds, and as the Fulani and Kanuri maintained a policy of giving even the lowliest post to a Fulani or a Kanuri, a great resentment had built up among the pagan/Christians against their Muslim Fulani/Kanuri overlords. Hardly surprising, as prior to European intervention they had been consistently ravaged by Muslim slave raiders.

Just prior to Nigeria's independence from Britain and the independence of the Cameroons from France, the UN had called for a plebiscite to let the people of these territories choose whether they wanted to join an independent Nigeria or, as it was quaintly phrased, to leave it until a later date – in other words, to enjoy the status quo with their former colonial ruler. At the UN it was seen to be inconceivable that people would vote for colonial status. They saw it as a foregone conclusion that the people would opt for Nigeria, and another of Africa's intricate and untidy colonial legacies would be conveniently tidied up.

But the people, especially in the northern half of this former German territory, saw it very differently. To them it was their last chance to break free from Fulani/Kanuri domination. If they voted for Nigeria they would endorse the Fulani/Kanuri status quo; if they voted to 'leave it' they might have a chance of setting up their own independent Native Authorities under the British. A vote to postpone was, paradoxically, a vote for radical change. And so, when on 19th November 1959 they voted by an overwhelming majority of 60 per cent for maintaining the colonial structure, everyone in Whitehall and the UN was amazed.

The Sardauna of Sokoto, Prime Minister of Northern Nigeria, was furious. In an angry speech at Numan he accused the colonial administration of trying to retain the colonial status and of deliberately misleading the voters. However, the real reasons for the negative vote was fully understood by the administrators on the spot and the result came as no surprise whatsoever.

Unbeknownst to the Koma, the old international border between the former German Cameroons and Nigeria ran between their district headquarters of Karlai and their mountainous homeland. So the result of this first plebiscite cut them off completely from Yola. Their protective tax shield disappeared overnight and their comfortable existence as non-taxpayers was exposed to the administration and the world.

I was first sent to the area to try to explain to these remote people the implications of the plebiscite, which was subsequently to sever them from their former Fulani rulers. To carry this task off successfully to a people whose edge of the world ended at Yola was futile, but it had to be attempted.

The first village I visited was called Tantille. A pretty spot at the foot of the mountains, it lay on a bank of the tributary dividing the two Koma clans and boasted a natural swimming pool that had formed under a waterfall. The plain-dwelling Koma distrusted their more barbaric brothers high up in the hills, and though slightly more worldly-wise were nevertheless very shy. I had taken with me as an interpreter a likable half-caste Fulani called Hammajam who spoke a little Koma. Hammajam rapidly produced a thickset Hausa-speaking Koma wearing shorts and not the customary loincloth. This man, an ex-member of the French gendarmerie called Duwa, had been born on the 'French' side of the Alantikas, for the international boundary between Nigeria and the Cameroon Republic ran right along the top of the range.

The French colonialists were ruthless in dealing with their primitive pagans and, in accordance with their accepted methods, had forcibly removed all the Koma from the eastern side of the mountain range to the plains below many years previously. Hence the 'French' Koma were part-educated and had started to abandon their traditions, unlike their Nigerian counterparts who had been left untouched in the mountains by the British. Poor Duwa was later to pay a horrific price for this French education.

As Duwa and Hammajam started to gather together a few reluctant Koma, it soon became clear to me that they had no interest in or comprehension of the implications of the plebiscite. If this was an example of the more enlightened plains Koma, I wondered what the reaction of their wilder hill brethren would be.

I decided to see for myself, and the following day we climbed up to a hill village not far from Tantille called Jili. On arrival it soon became clear that there would be no talking to the villagers about anything whatsoever. Men, women and children lay about blind drunk – the whole village was suffering from a gigantic hangover. Two bleary-eyed drummers, who had been working flat out for some days, tried to stir the villagers to activity but eventually they too slumped to the ground.

The hill Koma were short, stocky and bandy-legged; they could climb the steep sides of their mountains like goats. They wore a loincloth made from material they wove themselves on a primitive loom. Apart from a wooden-handled knife stuck into the loincloth, they wore nothing else. They had no tribal markings on the face or body, unlike many other hill tribes who had been hunted down by slave-raiding Fulani. The women wore leaves fore and aft but had a distinguishing feature: their hair was caked with red ochre to hang in red ringlets. A small metal clip invariably pierced their lower lip. So liberal was the use of the ochre that more often than not their shoulders and breasts were also splattered bright red.

As my time was limited on this visit, I left the hung-over hill villagers of Jili and set off for Vomni country at the northern edge of the range. Stopping briefly to try to explain the wonders of voting to incredulous tribesmen in Turi and Buri, I arrived two days later at the Vomni village of Beti. By chance it was market day and some Koma men, women and children, smoking their clay-bowled, metal-stemmed pipes, had left their mountain stronghold for Vomni market. These hill villagers were amazingly self-sufficient, growing maize, guinea corn and millet on the steepest slopes and tobacco, cotton and bananas near the banks of their mountain streams. The draw of the Beti market was salt, the one commodity they lacked. I later learnt that in the remotest hill villages they even overcame this problem, and in a unique way. They kept a small black breed of cattle, which they penned in sunken stone corrals. After a beast had been contained in this way for some time it was moved into another corral. The villagers then scraped away the crystalised urine from the pit for use as salt. The Beti market product must have been a great deal tastier.

The evening of my arrival, some young Vomni girls came and danced outside the mud hut I was staying in. Dressed only in leaves and with oiled bodies and ochre-reddened hands and faces, they danced exuberantly late into the night. It was well after midnight when they gradually drifted away, their shouts and songs fading into the distance.

A month later I paid another visit to the Alantika Mountains, but this time I was accompanied by an Australian UN observer. He was a pleasant, affable man, on his first visit to Africa, and had asked to be taken to a remote part of the territory to see if the implications of the forthcoming plebiscite were well understood. So we returned to the dumb-bell shaped resthouse at Tantille, we swam in the pool and I promised to take him to the hill village of Jili. I tried to warn him of the futility of attempting to explain to such unworldly people the sophistications of a plebiscite, but he rightly insisted on going. As we set off up the steep track, I wondered whether we would find the Jili villagers once again in an alcoholic stupor.

Indeed, Jili must have been a place of non-stop celebration, for as we arrived a posse of drunken, drum-banging youths rushed out to meet us and it soon became clear that the situation was hopeless. The Australian had laboured on the steep climb and was perspiring and out of breath as we squatted in the dust while Hammajam tried to gather together enough sober Koma to make up an audience. Eventually, a few beery greybeards were assembled, clearly suspicious that the real purpose of our unwanted visit was tax-gathering. The UN official handed out pamphlets and posters and then, through Hammajam, began to enquire of his listeners whether they understood the responsibilities of voting and the reasons why the plebiscite was being held. The assessment of their political awareness by the United Nations had commenced. He had a regulation questionnaire in front of him. He waited with pen poised.

His audience belched, scratched and lay down to sleep. Koma women stared at us from the safety of their tiny mud huts. A baby ventured too close and wailed loudly as it was hastily gathered up into its mother's arms. At the other end of the village, youths woke from their drunken torpor and drums began to throb.

The Australian looked at me in despair. 'Ah, hell, you were right,' he said eventually. 'We better give up – let's watch the dancing for a bit and then go.'

The drummers and drunks cavorted in front of us. A few old hags ululated feebly from the hut where the guinea-corn beer was brewed and stored in large earthenware pots. It was tired, dispirited dancing, very much a product of the morning after the night before. Gathering up his papers and getting to his feet the Australian finally admitted defeat.

'I wouldn't have believed it,' he muttered as we followed the steep, stony track down the hill to Tantille. 'How can we expect people like this to know anything about what they are voting for?' How indeed!

I visited Tantille on polling day. Some of the plains Koma turned up to vote in the hastily constructed grass mat polling booth and watched in amazement as their hands were daubed with indelible ink to prevent them from voting twice. But none of the hill Koma ventured down. Registration officers had been authorised to tour the hill villages to explain the implications of the vote, but they had not attempted to do so because of the Koma's wild reputation. Only a few months previously a Native Authority policeman, who had been sent up into the hills to arrest a Koma, had been tied up for two days then stripped of his uniform and forced to flee back down the hills totally naked. The Koma in their mountain fastness were clearly above the law. Tantille eventually polled about 200 votes out of a registration list of approximately 3,000 voters.

One further result of the 'leave it' vote was to remove the Chamba from the jurisdiction of the Lamido and Fulani rule from Yola. Fulani rule had not affected the Koma in the same way as the Chamba who, being mainly mission-educated, had seen their sons passed over for employment with the appointment of Fulani to all levels of authority in their tribal area. Indeed, because of the covert agreement with Bunu, the District Head of Karlai, the Koma had not only been protected from paying tax but, more importantly, had been left to lead their own lives unmolested by any outside authority. With the setting up of a new Chamba Native Authority, they unwittingly came under a bright spotlight as the links with the District Head of Karlai, who remained under Yola's rule, were severed. The hastily constituted Chamba Native Authority was set up primarily to look after the interests of the Chamba tribe, the Koma's traditional enemies. The new authority needed cash and even the Koma's meagre tax was valuable. The virgin cover-up was exposed and so were the Koma.

Thus it happened that Derek Mountain, the Senior District Officer in Yola, and someone for whom I have the highest respect, was sent in January 1960 with six armed Nigeria policemen to collect the Koma's tax. When Mountain reached the important hill village of Damti, he discovered that an old and powerless

Village Head was entirely in the hands of militant pagan youths who were refusing to pay any tax whatsoever. Damti village was leading a civil disobedience campaign and had influenced all the surrounding villages to do likewise. I was delighted when I was told to return to Alantika to assist and eventually to relieve Mountain, who because of his seniority could not be spared for too long. I was to take with me a replacement unit of six Nigeria police.

Damti village lay right at the top of the middle of the Alantika range. It was a steep and arduous climb for both the police and the 15 carriers bringing supplies. When we reached the first outlying hamlets the villagers tried to frighten us away with wild shouts and angry gestures. Armed to the teeth with poison-tipped arrows they squatted on rocks and boulders along the route. Our carriers became very frightened but we shouted out encouragements and plodded on.

When we reached the central hamlet of the Damti village complex, Derek Mountain came to meet us. He told me how he had attempted to extract tax by persuasion, but the ancient Village Head had no control or authority over the wild and hostile young men who were refusing to co-operate. When the villagers had seen Derek's police packing up to leave they thought that they had scored a certain victory. Consequently, when my policemen appeared they were singularly unamused.

Derek had managed to secure a small compound consisting of four tiny smoke-blackened mud huts with juju relics hanging from the interior mud walls. They were so small that my camp bed only just fitted inside one of them. I had noticed the small black hole under my bed but still could not understand why Derek had preferred to sleep outside in a gap between two of the huts. I understood later when a cock crowed underneath me at four o'clock in the morning.

On the evening of my arrival, Mountain and I decided to pay a visit to one of the outlying hamlets and tell them that we would be back the next morning and would expect to find that all the tax had been collected – if not, it would have to be collected by force. Promises of collection were made but by the next morning the villagers had scattered. The Village Head had remained and tried to reassure us that the money was coming, but clearly it was not, and at this point Mountain signalled to our carriers to round up some goats that were grazing quietly nearby. On seeing this, the villagers, who had been hiding behind boulders, started to emerge with shouts, their bows strung with poisoned arrows. There were no women or children to be seen. They had been evacuated in advance when the men had decided on resistance.

The situation could clearly become dangerous very quickly, so Mountain ordered a policeman to lob two tear gas grenades at the villagers. They both fell many yards short of the assembled tribesmen, one into an empty compound, but the noise had the desired effect – the villagers fled into a rocky outcrop where they could watch us from a safe distance. Later we were told that the grenade in the compound had resulted in the occupant being unable live in it for a month because of the lingering gas. He and the villagers were duly impressed by this powerful 'medicine'.

Some chickens and goats were duly rounded up and sold to the policemen and carriers, the money being put towards the Damti village tax. This seemed a harsh measure but was one that the Koma understood. That night we slept fitfully as the Koma yelled and guffawed at us from a safe distance.

The following day I set off on a separate expedition to outlying Damti hamlets and returned with only a few shillings for my efforts. Meanwhile Derek had set the Village Head down in the blazing sun and stared at him eyeball to eyeball in an attempt to win him over. We had realised that Damti was the core of the trouble and the ringleader in the tax resistance campaign. If Damti gave in, the other villages in the hills would follow its lead.

Derek would have to leave the following day, and already some of our carriers, terrified by the hostile Koma, had fled; others were nervous and likely to flee at any moment. Had it not been for a cheerful Marghi tribesman who rallied them with jokes and ribald comments on the state of their manhood, we would have lost all our carriers and that would have been disaster for, not unnaturally, none of the Koma were going to carry our loads.

As a last resort, we decided to try to arrest two or three of the more truculent Koma so that Derek could take them back with him to Yola. Failing that we would remove corn from their corn bins. At first light we started to make a compound-to-compound search. Naturally the alarm was soon given but not before we had picked up three youths. Searching the compounds was a dangerous business. At any moment one could be hit by an arrow fired from the shadows, and the black, sticky poison would have been fatal. Indeed, we picked up one man just as he was stringing an arrow.

That afternoon, Derek got ready to leave with his prisoners and livestock. Just as he was setting off, two Village Heads appeared with their tax. We rewarded them generously with salt in 40 pound bags, brought up with us for just such an eventuality. It looked as though the spirit of Damti's resistance was cracking.

After Mountain had left, I set off to tour the hill villages on my own. I stayed first at Sulipai where a sizable amount of tax was collected and a bag of salt given in return. Then on to Bulipai where again there was success. The news of Damti's subjugation had spread. Bulipai even organised a dance to celebrate the payment of their tax, so we were even more liberal with the salt handouts. A lively party ensued and the villagers reeled home in a highly intoxicated state – the Koma mark of a successful party.

The Koma paid their tax in pennies, stringing together the coins, which had a central hole, into bundles of 12. These might be kept in a little bag under the taxpayer's loincloth or sometimes buried in a tin in a hole in the ground or hidden deep in a corn bin, a cylindrical mud hut about six feet high with a small entrance hole at the top just big enough to admit a man. For all these reasons, the Koma refused to handle either ten-shilling or pound notes – they were too destructible.

I had to stay two days at Bulipai because I was told by the Village Head of the existence of an unmapped village called Sengri, which lay 20 miles away in a remote valley. Maps had been made by earlier administrative officers when on tour in the

Alantikas, but Sengri had never been 'found' and consequently the villagers had never been recorded as taxpayers.

After a steep descent into a hidden gorge, to my great delight the village was 'discovered'. As I learned much later in life when venturing into the Desert of Lop in China, there is great satisfaction in finding a hitherto unknown village and putting it on the map. Of course, the vast majority of the inhabitants had never seen a white person, and when they saw us coming, most of the villagers fled into the surrounding hills, leaving the Village Head and a few stalwarts to confront us. Yes, they did know about tax. Yes, they would pay. Unfortunately we had little time to parley with them. So, when it became obvious that the villagers had no intention of paying any money at all, we rounded up some livestock and took them away with us. But the Bulipai villagers had no sympathy with their kinsmen. They cheerfully bought up the purloined livestock and called their neighbours fools and worse for not co-operating with us. It is easy to be self-righteous at the expense of your neighbour.

Our next destination was the village of Bagi. All previous visitors had recorded that when they visited Bagi the inhabitants were hostile and invariably drunk. It is difficult enough persuading truculent pagans to pay tax; if they are drunk as well it is impossible. Although they were not drunk, the Bagi villagers were not friendly either, yet the news from Damti had preceded us and we collected nearly £N200 without much difficulty.

There was another aspect to Bagi which had not been placed on record. Most villages, even remote pagan ones, usually set aside an area away from the village for use as a latrine. Not Bagi. It appeared that they were oblivious to the smell of their own droppings and they cheerfully squatted anywhere the mood took them. The resulting stench was appalling and I passed one of my most uncomfortable nights in Africa in the evil-smelling mud hut I was given.

At Bagi, one of our policemen complained of a cold and severe headache. The next day he seemed quite sick, so accompanied by another policeman I allowed him to go on ahead to the road-head at Karlai while we spent an extra night at a village overlooking Tantille. When we reached Tantille, where my horse was waiting, we found the policeman in a very bad way. His neck was stiffening and I feared that he had contracted the dreaded cerebral spinal meningitis (CSM). He was tied on to my horse and we trekked the 20 miles into Karlai where my pick-up car was waiting. I decided to get him to Yola hospital, 100 miles away over rough roads, as quickly as possible. A puncture delayed us, and by this time he was starting to become rigid, eyes protruding wildly and no longer co-ordinated. I drove to Yola with my head out of the window as I had been told that CSM was transmitted by the breath of an infected person. When we reached the hospital the policeman could no longer talk and had stiffened into rigidity. I feared that he would die that night, but I had not known of that remarkable drug sulphathiasol, which he was given on arrival. When I visited him 48 hours later he was smiling and talking. A week later he was completely cured.

Having rested at Yola for a few days and having bought further supplies to last a month, I decided to tackle the villages on the northern side of the tributary. On the first arduous day we greatly underestimated the distance between Jili and Balengi, and though we set off at 6 am we did not reach Balengi until after 3 pm. Many of the carriers did not reach Balengi that day at all. It was soon apparent that the Koma clan on this side of the tributary divide were much more amenable than their cousins – or perhaps the news of Damti's capitulation had spread. Whatever the reason, tax was much more easily collected and our supplies of salt diminished rapidly. From Balengi we trudged on to the very top of the range and the wind-swept village of Dalengi, situated squarely on the international border. It was strange to see the totally uninhabited slopes on the French side which bore witness to their policy of forced resettlement on the plains below. From Dalengi we crossed a delightful miniature grassy plateau through the village of Yebri and finally to Wiyip.

At Wiyip an earlier pattern repeated itself. The village was deserted apart from one old deaf mute who was mad. Everyone

93

else had fled. I started to walk past the outlying compounds when suddenly two armed and hostile Koma jumped up in front of me with their bows tightly drawn. I was unarmed and could do nothing more than bellow at them, which I did. Luckily they turned and fled up the steep surrounding slopes at an incredible speed.

Apart from Wiyip, this second tour was a success. I had begun to know some of the villagers by name. We had joked and danced together. Confidence was being established and I was anxious to return to the area to do something more constructive than demand tax.

The total tax collection in the whole of the Alantika area had amounted to £N488 5s 3d – not that the Koma could have got much back for it from the 20th century. Their self-sufficiency was complete and their mountain stronghold had protected them from the diseases of the plains. Smallpox and syphilis were unknown – only goitre, due to salt deficiency, was common, and to help with this problem I would line up the victims and paint their tongues with iodine as instructed by my doctor friend in Yola.

However, it is rare in government circles to have continuity. I was due for leave in three months but meanwhile was urgently requested to go to Mambilla, the remote plateau 300 miles to the south. My feelings were mixed. I wanted to stay with the Koma but Mambilla was my dream posting. If I had worked in Tangale-Waja, in Koma country and Mambilla then I would have worked in some of the remotest parts of Nigeria, if not all West Africa.

Before I left I urged the Resident in Yola not to send anyone back to the Alantika Mountains to collect tax unless he had a white skin. I knew that my skin colour had saved me at Wiyip when I was confronted by the two armed tribesmen. It had probably done the same at Damti. It would, I said, be suicidal to send an African DO or someone of lesser rank among the Koma. Anyone with a black skin, even the Sardauna himself, would be treated as a hostile foreigner.

When I returned to Yola to go on leave after my three months in Mambilla I was told to my great dismay that this advice had not been taken. Duwa, the educated Koma who had accompanied me as an interpreter on all our treks, had been sent back to Wiyip on his own to collect their outstanding taxes. He had been shot with an arrow, clubbed to death and his heart cut out and eaten. Revenge had been taken on a turncoat.

I was not only saddened but also furious; sensible advice had been ignored. The Koma and the savage murder had reached the ears of those in authority in Kaduna, and the resulting political situation had turned extremely sensitive. The territory had just been excised from Nigeria and re-named the United Nations Trust Territory although it was to be governed directly by Britain. Cannibalism, in the circumstances, was not a word that anyone wished to hear.

And at this critical point M reappeared in my life. The capital of the new Trust Territory was Mubi, 350 miles north of Yola in another area that had formerly been run by Adamawa Native Authority. M was the new territory's Resident working under a British Governor, Sir Percy Wyn-Harris, who had been brought out of retirement after successfully serving as Governor of the Gambia and with great distinction in Kenya. Our remote little colony had achieved gubernatorial status. Apparently, M had asked that I be one of the six administrative officers selected to work in the new territory. M, full of fire and enthusiasm, was misguidedly determined to teach the Koma a lesson.

I had come down from Mambilla in May 1960 to go on leave but learnt that my leave had been postponed in order for me to guide a punitive expedition to Wiyip planned to take place on 13th July. As I had spent three months in the area, longer than any other white predecessor, and as I was the only administrative officer to have visited Wiyip in recent years, the choice was inevitable. I undertook the job with a heavy heart.

During the early days of July, 50 police were drafted into Yola, maps were pored over and a great deal of nonsense was talked. The plan was for the expedition to leave Yola by Landrover, arriving at Tantille at 7 pm, just after sundown. From Tantille we were to split into three sections, climb the steep mountain slopes and encircle Wiyip. There was a long and arduous climb ahead and I calculated that we could not reach Wiyip before 3 am. The villagers were then to be surprised in their huts and rounded up, the murderers of Duwa exposed and brought back with us to Yola. The whole operation was classified as 'top secret'. It all seemed too easy.

July is the height of the rainy season and frantic efforts were made during the early days of that month to keep the dry-season road open from Yola through Karlai to Tantille. Naturally this most unusual activity did not go unnoticed, and what was supposed to be top secret soon became common knowledge. Although my sympathies lay totally with the Koma, the early days of July were lively and exhilarating. M saw to that, and I felt he had personally declared war on the poor wretched Koma.

Our time of departure was 3 pm and as we drove in a ten-Landrover convoy out of Yola, the Koma rainmakers set to work and a torrential thunderstorm broke. We knew that, in spite of the road repairs, it was going to be very difficult to reach Tantille. We had gone only 20 miles when we reached a large section of road that had been completely washed out. P, officer-in-charge of the Nigeria Police contingent and whom I had first met on my arrival in Bauchi, managed to strand a Landrover in the middle of rapidly rising waters. M bellowed instructions across the divide. P, who was an expert on horses but not on motorised vehicles, argued forcibly with him from the stranded vehicle. The son of a former Chief Constable of Nottingham who had achieved notoriety by prosecuting a party of Labour MPs for bringing undeclared contraband into Britain, P proved to be as stubborn and provocative as his father. In exasperation, M ordered P to do it his way. In the end, using a combination of tow ropes and brute force, the stranded vehicle reached the other side.

Further down the road the same thing happened again, and then again. Temporary bridges had to be rebuilt, and relations between P and M became increasingly strained. We eventually arrived at Tantille three and a half hours late, wet, dishevelled and with two senior members of the party at odds with each other. M immediately busied himself making 'Tantille toddy' as he called it (tea and brandy). Hot sausages also helped to restore a degree of harmony, but another 45 minutes were lost.

It had been decided that one group should approach Wiyip via Balengi, using the same track that I had followed on my previous visit to the area. Another party would climb to the top of the range and flank the international border to prevent the Wiyip villagers fleeing into Cameroon. In this they were to be assisted by Cameroonian gendarmerie. The third patrol was to enter Wiyip itself taking a route via Sengri. I was part of the last action group. Sengri was the newly discovered village so it was deemed essential that I accompany this patrol. I knew that in the dark the track was hazardous in the extreme, but I had not known that P suffered from vertigo and was going to have to lead his men up the steep mountain track on all fours. My sympathies were with him but this delayed us even further and did nothing for the morale of his policemen.

I had only followed the track once before. The loose shingle was treacherous and three policemen lost their footing and slid down the edge of the slope. The noise must have woken the whole of the Koma tribe. I kept expecting to see Wiyip just ahead of me – boulders turned into huts, trees into armed warriors. Our progress was painfully slow but eventually, at 6.30 am, we reached Wiyip. Of course, by this time the cocks had long since ceased to crow and the villagers had been up and about for at least half an hour. The element of surprise expounded on at great length in Yola by M had been totally lost. As we approached the village a sleepy youth, rubbing his eyes and stretching his arms, emerged from his hut. The alarm was sounded and the villagers fled. There was nothing we could do. Exhausted by our arduous trek we lay down to sleep until woken by Cameroonian gendarmerie under a French officer who shared with us their meagre rations.

In the event of such a failure M, who was 'at base' in Tantille, had ordered the village to be burnt. It was set alight and in minutes the dry grass huts were ablaze. As the black smoke and ash curled upwards into the bright blue sky it, we spotted the villagers watching the conflagration high up in the mountains.

I felt immensely saddened knowing that if common sense had prevailed this tragedy could have been averted. With patience and time, the Koma could have been eased out of their stone-age situation. But time had run out and there was none left for the administration to be patient. The British were to blame. The Koma had been untouched in their mountain stronghold while the political events in the rest of Nigeria, of which they knew absolutely nothing, had passed them by. By the time the political spotlight shone on them, the British were already scrambling to leave and to hand over political authority to Nigerian administrators. No doubt over-worked government officials had been happy to connive at the Karlai tax cover-up. As long as the tax came in, a hard-pressed administration did not have to send one of its rapidly diminishing band of officials to tour the area. There must have been other hill people in different parts of Africa who were suddenly left exposed and vulnerable as the wind of change gathered to hurricane force, sweeping the colonialists out of Africa and themselves into the 20th century.

As for the Nigerians, the attitude of one Northern Nigerian minister was made perfectly clear to me during a plane journey to Kaduna en route for leave in England. 'These people are an embarrassment to us,' he said forcibly. 'We cannot have these kind of people living in modern Nigeria. They should be bombed out of existence. That would solve the problem.'

By chance I looked out of the window. We were passing over Tangale-Waja and the vast mountain range of Dadiya. I thought of the Tula, the Cham and the hill Waja, and of all the other people who lived or used to live in mountain strongholds – and I imagined the bombs falling.

This was to be my last visit to this fascinating area. I learnt later that the murderers of Duwa were eventually captured and a school and dispensary were built at Tantille.

Years later, in the mid-1980s, I happened to see quite by chance a Nigerian newspaper – 'Military Governor discovers lost Nigerian tribe' the headline proclaimed. The story was that the

Military Governor of the newly formed Gongola State, while on a tour of a remote part of his territory, had stumbled on a tribe that had never been 'discovered'. A stone-age people, the Koma, cut off in their mountain stronghold and wholly ignorant of Nigeria, had completely escaped the attention of the outside world. The governor promised to establish a modern headquarters in Tantille and to bring the Koma rapidly into the 20th century. He would take a personal interest in their development. 'They will become,' he said, 'a showpiece of our development policy.'

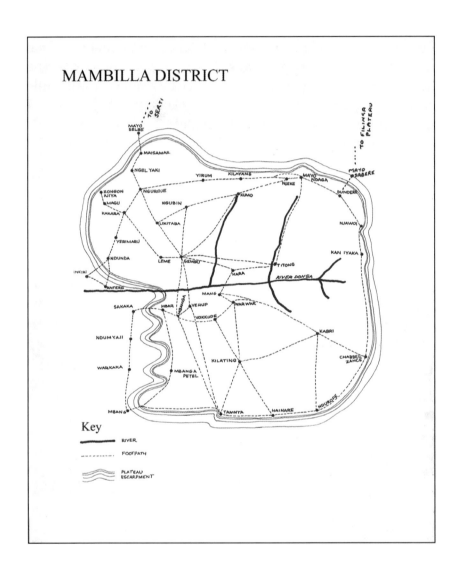

MAMBILLA DISTRICT

9

Gashaka-Mambilla Districts

'The Mambilla area is a mass of contradictions, so completely different from everywhere else in the Northern Provinces and so astonishingly remote from every administrative centre that one can only with the greatest diffidence make suggestions for its development ... between all these contradictions one must somehow compromise.' Thus wrote an administrative officer in the 1930s. Circumstances had changed, but the basic problems caused by this remoteness were exactly the same.

The result of the first plebiscite had been welcomed with rejoicing by the Mambilla and to a lesser extent by the Kaka, the small tribe who lived on the fringes of the western edge of the plateau and who sided with either the Mambilla or the Fulani when it suited their interests. The two districts of Gashaka and Mambilla had since 1918, like the Chamba District, the Alantika Mountains and Mubi District, been under the authority of the Lamido and the Adamawa Native Authority based in Yola. But the plebiscite had, by a fluke of history, given Chamba, Mubi and Gashaka/Mambilla Districts a chance to shake off this authority and free themselves from Fulani domination.

When the result of the plebiscite was known and the policy for the new administrative area – the United Nations Trust Territory – was announced, the Lamido decided to recall immediately to

Yola all the Fulani District Heads in his former territory. This was hardly surprising. The plebiscite result was a severe blow to the Lamido, whose territory had been almost halved over night. It was planned to give the local people autonomy by setting up new native authorities within which the local tribes, such as the Chamba and Mambilla, would play an active role. There would be a Chamba Native Authority, a Gashaka-Mambilla Native Authority and a Mubi Native Authority where formerly only the Adamawa Native Authority held sway.

The District Head of Mambilla, a Yola Fulani called Mukkadas, was among those recalled, in order to cause the utmost embarrassment to the British administration. Mukkadas was by no means the least competent of the Adamawa Fulani District Heads and he had been working well with Tim Healey, the Mambilla District Officer at that time. Mukkadas had even reached a degree of trust with some of the Mambilla. Government thought it wise to re-post Healey in order to convince the indigenous Mambilla that real change was about to come. In their eyes he was too closely associated with rule from Yola, hence the need to get me up on to Mambilla as quickly as possible.

It was a dramatic time. As I climbed the plateau with my 28 carriers and enough supplies for a six-month stay, I passed Mukkadas coming down. We exchanged courteous formalities but clearly he was hell-bent on beating a hasty retreat and had no time for any meaningful discussion. It was then that I realised I was climbing straight up into a power vacuum. There was no District Head on Mambilla, and Adamawa Native Authority's jurisdiction over basic services such as health, education, agriculture, veterinary, prisons and police had been abruptly removed. Nothing had been set up to take its place.

The trek to Gembu, the capital of Mambilla district where I was to live, began 5,200 feet below on the plains at a town called Serti, or Baruwa ('the place of no water'). Serti was the capital of Gashaka District and it had been decided that the district would be administered collectively with the Mambilla District under the new Gashaka-Mambilla Native Authority. But first that authority had to be established.

Sarkin Yaki, the Fulani District Head who ruled Gashaka District from Serti, was dark-skinned, fine featured and unassuming. His post had by tradition been an offshoot of the pre-colonial Fulani empire centred on Banyo, in what is now known as the Cameroon Republic. His family had long since abandoned the town of Gashaka, which lay further to the east, and owed partial allegiance to the Lamido in Yola. However, because of the former link with Banyo, he was not a direct appointee of the Lamido and had not been subject to a re-call after the plebiscite as was the case with Mukkadas and the Lamido's other district heads.

Although the districts of Gashaka and Mambilla were grouped together as one administrative unit, Mambilla had far greater wealth, with over 200,000 head of Fulani cattle and a climate suited to coffee and tea. Unfortunately, Gashaka consisted mainly of thick bush and tsetse fly. Sarkin Yaki secretly harboured dreams of ruling both districts, but not having a forceful nature he did not push his cause too hard. He was frequently diverted from such intrigue by the problems in his own headquarters as the town had attracted a good number of rootless and criminal characters. Serti was a shabby town at the end of a dusty road, housing the detribalised flotsam of the outside world: traders eager to prey on the unsophisticated Mambilla; carriers recruited from distant pagan tribes who would never return to their homelands; Fulani claiming royal connections with the former ruling Emirate of Banyo in Cameroon; and other local drifters from Gashaka District.

Because most of Gashaka District comprised virgin, tsetse-fly-ridden forest, it was unsuitable for the swelling numbers of cattle on the plateau, though it was host to some of Nigeria's last remaining large wild life, such as lion, waterbuck and buffalo. The high peaks of the Cameroons bordered this forest, peaks with Fulani names such as Chabbel Chirgu (Leopard Mountain), Chabbel Hendu (Windy Mountain) and Chabbel Wade (Mountain of Death), the last a high spot where two Fulani herdboys had died of cold and exposure.

To the north of this virgin bush lay Filinga plateau, a miniature

Mambilla, sparsely populated and only accessible by a long and arduous trek. Very few Europeans had ever been there. I have a vivid memory of trying to sleep on Filinga in a tiny Fulani grass hut, fighting off both flies and thick smoke from a fire in the centre of a space just large enough to take my camp bed. Water streamed all night from both the heavens and my smoke-filled eyes. But the Fulani headman killed a cow in our honour and the carriers slept contented.

A 17-mile stretch of track had been opened to the south from Serti to Mayo Selbe, a tiny staging post on the banks of the River Selbe and only two miles from the foothills of the Mambilla plateau. However, this was only negotiable by vehicle in the dry season; in the rains it was consistently washed out and the journey had to be undertaken on foot through a hot and humid fly-ridden bush. This could take up to six hours, so travellers spent the night at Mayo Selbe before beginning the climb up the steep-sided plateau.

The last section of the 5,200 feet climb up the escarpment was extremely steep, slippery and tortuous. It was nicknamed *biyu da sisi* (two and six) by the carriers because they were paid an additional sum of two shillings and sixpence for climbing it. As their standard daily rate of pay was three shillings, from which a shilling was deducted for 'chop' or food, this was a considerable amount of money. The *biyu da sisi* incentive encouraged them to reach the top of their six-hour climb without complaint.

During my posting I made the climb up to Mambilla 13 times and on each occasion the scene from the edge of the escarpment looking down to the plains below was different. Sometimes the plains were hazed with heat. At other times they would be seen through wisps of white cloud or, in the rainy season, obscured by black thunderclouds. In that season the escarpment was richly green and we were often soaked by the time we reached the top. In the dry season, as we poured sweat, everything would be golden brown or blackened by bush fires. Eagles and occasionally a great bustard would soar overhead. Whatever the contrasts, the scene was always majestic.

The chattering carriers saw no majesty. They were eager to cover the last four miles to the first staging post, their minds firmly fixed on food, beer and the Mai Samari prostitutes. As my leading carrier, Dan Gajere ('son of a short man'), neared the top of *biyu da sisi*, he would reach for his wooden whistle to pipe ceremoniously his comrades and me over the top and on towards the village of Mai Samari. When we finally reached the edge of the escarpment we would all rest, but not for long as the carriers were keen to be on their way. With a shout of encouragement from their headman they would help each other lift their heavy loads on to their *gammo* – the twist of grass or rag that protected the bald patch on the top of their head rubbed raw by their head-load. When the load was finally balanced to the carrier's satisfaction, he would deftly pick up his walking stick with his toes and we would move off to another blast from Dan Gajere's pipe.

Later, when I trekked to the other villages on the plateau, it was only with six or eight carriers and a headman. On these occasions, my loads consisted of a canvas bed-roll, a kitchen box containing the two empty four-gallon kerosene tins which, together with a piece of expanded metal, comprised my cook Luttu's oven, a metal cash box for the carriers' shillings, my cook's bed-roll, sundry boxes of tinned food and, most importantly, the tin bath which also served as a boat to cross swollen rivers and as a waterproof trunk for my clothes.

Having left the edge of the escarpment, we passed the first nomadic Fulani encampment of Ardo (chief) Hammadu's clan whose cattle were exclusively white. Girls churned butter by rocking milk back and forth in a long calabash or wove grass mats to cover their gourds and hid their embarrassed faces with raised hands as the carriers shouted out ribald comments.

When we reached the dense, virgin forest on the south-western edge of the escarpment, the home of the few remaining Mambilla lions, we knew that our trek was nearly over. Moments later the thatched outpost of Mai Samari came into view, the first of the three staging-posts on the trek to Gembu but the most welcome of them all.

I usually stayed in Mai Samari's one small, tin-roofed building, which had been built as a tool store for the forestry department and had the luxury of a jigger-proof concrete floor. Concrete was not only a deterrent to jiggers. When I stayed once in a round, dilapidated mud resthouse with a stoved-in thatch and a dusty, earthen floor, my silk dressing gown was carelessly thrown on the earth floor as I rolled on to my camp bed for the night. Next morning all that remained was a piece of blue silk the size of a dinner plate. White ants had feasted well that night.

On another occasion, the Mai Samari forestry store was struck by lightning when I was staying in it. A fireball shot past the deck chair I was sitting in. It was an awesome and terrifying experience which would be repeated later in my house at Gembu. Lightning victims were common on the plateau and the human ones were often brought to me for treatment. I could do little more than apply antiseptic to their terrible burns, which often turned their black skins permanently pink, cracked and blistered. Since my lightning experience in Tula, and after learning how a friend lost the sight of an eye when trying to photograph lightning, I have always treated tropical storms with the greatest respect.

After Mai Samari, the next stage on the 74-mile journey to Gembu was a 20-mile trek to Nguroje via the tiny hamlet of Ngelyaki. The plateau was undulating, so much so that in spite of an intensive survey, no piece of land could be found that was level enough to land a light aircraft. The undulations, steeper in some parts of the 550-mile square area than in others, were frequently dissected by deep rivers. These rivers were flanked by bush that included the valuable *giginya* palm, which is impervious to white ants and thus much prized for building.

Before the mass migration to the plateau of Fulani and their cattle in the mid-1920s, it had been lightly wooded. By the 1960s it was treeless apart from trees growing in river valleys (*kurame*) and eucalyptus that had been planted by the forestry department. Today, with cattle numbers far in excess of tolerable levels, the *kurame* are denuded and much of the eucalyptus has been cut down for firewood.

After my first climb up the escarpment, I would usually arrange for a horse to meet me at Mai Samari so I could cover the next part of the journey on horseback. One problem with this in the rainy season was fording the narrow, swollen rivers. Occasionally one's poor animal would be sucked down into thick mud, which meant a long and exhausting struggle before it battled through to the other side, though the Village Headmen would sometimes ease the crossing by constructing narrow, wooden bridges.

I was once trekking in a remote part of Mambilla and dismounted to lead my big, grey stallion along a rocky ledge. He was a fine horse with a wonderful silver-grey, flowing mane, but beauty is no substitute for sure-footedness and his long sloping pasterns were not designed for rocky ledges. He slipped, fell over the edge and down on to a dry, rocky riverbed. As I had hold of the reins, I went with him. We were both lucky. He fell on his side into a sandy area – just missing some sharp, granite rocks – and I landed on his soft, grey flesh. I was neither kicked nor grazed, and after recovering our wind we continued our journey along the riverbed. As the nearest hospital was at Yola, 220 miles away, I was fortunate on both this and other occasions. It would have taken six days at least to get there.

Nguroje had been built on the slope of a hill and because of the abundant rainfall – the plateau averaged 88 inches a year – the narrow pathways were so slippery that I usually had to dismount before entering the small town. But it was always a welcome sight, not least because Sarkin Hausawa (the chief of the Hausa) and Ardo'en Bairo and Bakari lived there. The Hausa had originally come to the plateau as traders, settling in the larger villages. When their numbers warranted it, they were permitted to elect a headman or chief. Their spokesman in Nguroje was particularly enlightened and interesting to talk to. He was also very hospitable. I would occasionally stay in his mud house, which was roomy, warm and, more importantly, dry. Nguroje resthouse was none of these and in addition, its dusty mud floor was full of jiggers and sand flies. Clothes, papers and people became coated in brick-red dust after a night's stay.

On one memorable occasion my bull-terrier bitch, Sally, whelped in Nguroje resthouse. She had struggled nobly up the escarpment carrying her heavy load but in the middle of a wakeful night eight pups popped out under my camp bed. Our trek was continued next day after recruitment of an extra carrier to carry Sally and her new-born pups in a box on his head.

Ardo'en Bairo and Bakari belonged to the Bawanko'en Fulani clan, who were the red cattle owners and whose territory bordered Nguroje. They were brothers, but Bakari, suffering from either delusion or something more complex, continually laid spurious complaints against his brother. Unfailingly he would slink up in the dark shortly before I went to bed to whisper about his brother's latest misdeeds, which were invariably unproven and untrue.

The Bawanko'en Fulani had retained many characteristics of the true nomadic Fulani. They no longer practised the *sharo* initiation ceremony involving a ritual chest-beating with wooden sticks of marriageable youths, but the men plaited their hair and the girls dressed in the distinctive manner of the Wodabe, the pagan Fulani on the plains. The girls were also known to be the most free and easy of all the Fulani on the plateau. Pale of face, tall and with long, dark hair, they cavorted and paired off at the local dances and festivals from the age of eight or nine upwards.

The Mambilla Fulani were nominally Muslim, and some clans were stricter in their Islamic religious observance than others. This was not the case with the Bawanko'en, and at the Muslim festivals, particularly Eid-el-Fitr which marked the end of Ramadan, they had a ready excuse to indulge in a week of dancing – and sex, at which the Bawanko'en were well known to be particularly adept. The girls seldom if ever conceived after their post-dancing coupling because they used a special herb as a contraceptive. I could have made my fortune had I discovered what it was.

In addition to the leaky, termite-infested, jigger-filled resthouse at Nguroje, there were more than 20 other mud and thatch resthouses on Mambilla plateau. Most leaked and my maintenance budget was totally inadequate – enough to repair maybe two a year. By the early 1960s the rest of Nigeria had long since abandoned the concept of non-catering resthouses, but on roadless, carless Mambilla they were still a necessity, for such was the strength of the animosity between the Mambilla farmers and the Fulani herdsmen that accepting an invitation to stay in either of their huts could have called into question my impartiality.

Resthouses were looked after by the Sarkin Bariki, the 'resthouse chief'. More often than not this venerable old rogue had only two or three customers a year and often could not be found on one's arrival. At other times he would say that he could not find wood, always a scarce commodity on the plateau but as essential for the traveller as water.

At one shilling and sixpence for a night's stay, his duties were to provide wood, water and to keep the resthouse clean. The DO's visit often gave him the opportunity to voice age-old grievances. At the end of a stay, Sarkin Bariki would produce the resthouse book which recorded both payment and visitors' comments. This stained and tattered document, sometimes stretching back 30 years, contained the sharp and amusing remarks of infrequent visitors. But as in the case of the professional carrier, Sarkin Bariki, his grievances and his resthouse book have long since disappeared.

Along with the non-catering resthouse, another of its unique feature has also vanished – the *bayan gida*. This literally translates from the Hausa as 'behind the house' and means lavatory. Usually it was made by digging a hole in the ground and placing over it two sticks horizontally lodged in the V-shaped grooves of four upright sticks – a rough and precarious perch. The grander *bayan gidaje* were thatched, but as one had, more often than not, to enter on all fours, the thatch was not always a help. The rickety structure could also be full of white ants and sometimes either my bottom or my head would bring the whole feeble structure tumbling down, covering me from head to toe in old grass, dust and disintegrating timber. I usually went out with a machete and dug my own hole.

Once, in my house in Tula, when seated on a sophisticated, smooth wooden structure neatly placed over a bucket which was emptied daily, I leaned over sideways to pick up newspaper that served as lavatory paper, when a huge pink-bellied spitting cobra reared its head. These cobras can spit venom into the eyes with uncanny accuracy and can cause temporary blindness. I dashed out of the thick, mud enclosure with my trousers around my ankles calling for Luttu. He came at a run and, grabbing one of the two spears hanging on the wall above the dining-room table, my doughty cook soon had the snake speared, decapitated and served up for his supper.

After Nguroje there remained one final trek to Gembu. I could follow a route via either Kakara or Lekitaba. Neither warranted a night stop but later I would visit them alternately to speak with the Village Headman and villagers to find out what was going on and if all was well. The journey to Kakara involved crossing a fertile plain near Kusuku, which some years after I had left became the site of a successful tea plantation.

On my initial trek to Gembu, I had succumbed en route to the temptation of opening a bundle of air-mail editions of *The Times* addressed to Tim Healey. This was a grave mistake, for in the isolation of living on the plateau with its erratic mail service, the pleasure of opening your own post was intense. Healey religiously read only one of his newspapers a day, no matter how out of date – I believe his houseboy ironed it beforehand. I had broken his ritual and paid the penalty: my welcome was frosty and tinged with hostility. He left me after the briefest of handovers, and I found myself alone with inadequate knowledge in a district without a Native Authority council or a District Head.

I soon discovered that tension on Mambilla had been heightened by the case of Ardo Adamu, the Fulani Rahaji clan chief who lived and grazed cattle near Gembu. The underlying problem on Mambilla was, and is today, the serious overstocking of Fulani cattle. Since their arrival in the 1920s, the Fulani had flocked to the Mambilla *cul-de-sac* from all parts of Nigeria – a *cul-de-sac* because it was a high plateau bordered on three sides by Cameroon. At first Fulani immigration was encouraged by the administration, if not by the Mambilla people, but as the numbers of cattle grew a ban was placed on further migration in the early 1950s. By then it was too late.

When I arrived the number of cattle was estimated at 200,000. By the time I left three and a half years later there were 220,000. Today, this figure has more than trebled in spite of an immigration ban in force for 40 years.

Under the Adamawa administration one of the biggest grievances against Yola Fulani rule was the manner in which these 'town' Fulani (*Fulanin gida*) aligned themselves with their nomadic cousins, the *M'bororo* or bush Fulani. It was alleged, with much justification, that the courts always sided with the Fulani in cases of farm damage or land disputes. This allegation was true. The Fulani with their cattle wealth had the financial muscle to bribe a corrupt court judge. A Fulani of any description was hardly ever an inmate of Gembu prison.

Just before my arrival, fighting between the Mambilla and the Fulani had broken out near Gembu. It was said that Ardo Adamu had taken some clansmen and personally speared three Mambilla who had tried to drive the Fulani cattle away from their farms. Because of its delicate nature, the case had been transferred to the court in Yola and was seen by everyone on the plateau as a test case.

Was real political change in the air or would the clever Fulani manipulate the situation for their own ends as they had always managed to do in the past? As it happened, Ardo Adamu swore on the Qur'an that he was innocent of affray. He was acquitted and just before my arrival had returned to Mambilla in triumph. Despondency was in the air. 'Nothing has changed,' the Mambilla were saying as I rode into the Gembu vacuum.

Immediate government policy was to establish the new Native Authorities, free from the ties of Adamawa administration and the Lamido, as quickly as possible. It was hoped that when a second plebiscite was held, the grateful non-Fulani tribesmen, who outnumbered the Fulani throughout the whole of the territory, would thank the administration by voting to return to independent Nigeria. A British colonial irritation would thus be neatly solved.

In furtherance of this aim, I had personally been gazetted as the Gashaka-Mambilla Native Authority. This meant that at the age of 25, I was the local council, overseeing all the council's services over an area of 550 remote and rugged square miles, a virtual dictator, with inexperienced district councillors, until a properly constituted Native Authority could be elected. Luckily for me, Malam Hammadu, the former District Council treasurer, had remained. He was a Fulani from Ngurore near Yola, but in spite of this inherent tribal advantage he was seen as unbiased. He had won the Mambilla's grudging respect and had been asked to stay on in the absence of a suitable alternative.

My first job was to try to instil some confidence into the existing District Council administration. I issued a letter to all council employees confirming them as employees of the new Gashaka-Mambilla Native Authority as of 1st April 1960 with no loss in salary. This had the temporary desired effect.

However, there was yet another potential flashpoint. The stone- and cement-built, corrugated-iron roofed council offices were situated in the centre of Gembu – at that time a thatch-roofed village of 2,000 people – and just beyond, at the end of an open space used for football and festive celebrations, the large mud compound of the District Head. Surrounded by high mud walls, this covered about five acres and was filled with living rooms and quarters for retainers, wives and concubines. On my arrival it had been vacated by Mukkadas and was completely empty. However, rumour was rife that pretenders to the throne, both Mambilla and Fulani, were about to seize the compound and claim the title for themselves. I had only one option – to move in myself.

It must be remembered that my nearest boss was more than 300 miles away in Ganye in Chamba. Ganye had been preferred to Jada as a new headquarters of the Chamba Native Authority because of the predominantly Fulani ties of Jada. My Resident was far to the north in Mubi, some 1,000 miles away. At that time there was no radio telephone link to Gembu and it was three to four days' hard trekking to the road head, longer in the rains. Therefore I had to make decisions of this magnitude on the spot without any prior consultation. Sometimes one made bad decisions, sometimes good ones. Luckily this was one of the latter.

Both tribal groups immediately noted that the DO meant business, and the situation was temporally defused as cook Luttu, houseboy Bako, brindle bull terrier Sally and I moved out of the small stone, tin-roofed croft-like District Officer's house on a hillock to the south of Gembu and into the vastness of the District Head's uninhabited mud palace. It was totally deserted. No spy, servant or concubine had been left behind.

I was enjoying a position unique in Nigeria – that of a foreigner being simultaneously District Officer, Native Authority and District Head.

My first priority was to rectify this bizarre situation and arrange for the election of a new Mambilla District Council, which in turn would elect a new District Head. This in itself was a novelty. In the past, the Mambilla District Head had been imposed directly from Yola. Now the people, through their elected councillors, were to make the choice. The Mambilla should not have had any difficulty in winning such an election as they were numerically superior to the Fulani. But the small Kaka tribe who lived in the villages on and along the western side of the plateau – Inkiri, Antere, Sakaka, Ndumyaji and Warkaka – were unreliable and fickle. Their loyalty could be bought and the Fulani knew it. The Kaka held a balance of power as both the Fulani and the Mambilla were well aware. If they put their votes in with the Fulani the Mambilla could be defeated.

We swiftly arranged for a new District Council election to be held. This resulted in overall Mambilla control of the council by six votes. However, there were five Kaka members who had gained seats on the 31-member District Council. At its inaugural meeting, the new assembly's first task was to appoint a District Head. Fortunately, on this occasion, the Kaka resisted the Fulani's blandishments and sided with the Mambilla. To my great relief a person who seemed to be an ideal candidate, 32-year-old Audu Baju, was elected the new District Head of Mambilla and given the honorary title of Ciroma. His credentials were good. He was educated, had been a schoolmaster, spoke English and was the son of the Chief of Kabri, a village which the German administration had recognised as the most significant on the Mambilla plateau. Under German rule, the Kabri Chief had been accorded premier status and given a breastplate, a helmet with the German Imperial Eagle outstretched on the top and a magnificently emblazoned red leather, gold-tooled document proclaiming that he was the Chief.

I immediately vacated the District Head's house and Audu Baju took it over. I liked him, he confided in me and we trusted each other. When I went on leave I had high hopes that he was the right person to bring the two rival tribes closer together. But of course the Fulani and their Ardo'en were nervous and apprehensive of the future. Their protective tribal shield had been removed. They were not the masters now.

On my return three months later, Audu was settled and on top of his job. Moreover he had not antagonised the Fulani cattle owners to any great degree. True, the worst of the corrupt Fulani grazing control officers had been replaced but this was only just and had been accepted by the fair-minded. The months went by. We elected a new Gashaka-Mambilla Native Authority with Ciroma Audu Baju and Sarkin Yaki from Serti alternating as its head on a three-monthly basis. Native Authority councillors were appointed and I reverted to the duties of a normal District Officer, reflecting ruefully that most of my early life seemed to have been spent working myself out of a job.

By now the United Nations had settled on the terms of the second plebiscite. This time there was to be no neutral – 'leave it' – choice, just a straightforward decision to join either an independent Nigeria or the Cameroon Republic.

The Cameroon authorities were very interested in this plebiscite. They saw it as a great opportunity to enlarge their own territory. Intrigue was rife and the loyalty of some of the plateau Fulani was highly suspect, especially those with relatives in Cameroon and historical ties to Banyo. It was an interesting time, with numerous potential troublemakers slipping over the border intent on spreading rumour and discord. Amidst all these uncertainties, I continued to try to assist the fledgling Native Authority by ensuring that the various departments under its control gained confidence and experience.

Before the poll, the UN sent Edersen, a Norwegian observer, to Mambilla. His task was to monitor fair play. Not unnaturally he was highly suspicious of the British administration's actions and motivation. Of course we wanted to see the area revert to Nigerian authority, especially as we had worked for the Northern Nigerian service and were on secondment to the new territory. But I can honestly say that when the vote took place it was as impartial as we could have possibly made it. As it happened, the Norwegian had little cause for complaint. There were an uncomfortable few days after Audu ordered the arrest of seven Fulani who had appeared on the plateau from Cameroon, ostensibly to put the Cameroon point of view. Edersen created a fearful fuss and insinuated that we were suppressing freedom of speech. It took a great deal of diplomacy to pacify him.

Without a twinge of jealousy, the agricultural officer Sven Smith and I marvelled at the comforts which Edersen's organisation provided. A separate metal house called a Uniport was constructed for his personal comfort. Then another was put up to house a guest. Specially packed emergency rations and supplies were head-loaded up to him. We spent one memorable night together playing pontoon until dawn, by which time he had lost £40. Overall he caused us little concern and his interference was minimal.

When the plebiscite was held, the northern part of the mandated territory returned to Nigeria with a 60/40 majority but the southern part went over to the Cameroon Republic with a similar percentage figure. To ensure fair play I had been excluded from Mambilla during the actual vote. I was sent down to Baissa, the headquarters of the newly formed United Hills Native Authority, a part of the mandated territory formerly administered from Benue Province. It stretched to the west from the north-western side of the plateau and was, for me, new territory.

The original plan had been to send me to Mubi in the far north but this was suddenly changed when I was ordered to replace a Baissa registration officer who had become very unpopular with the local people. To my great delight my assistants were the redoubtable Mac, and a schoolmaster from Mubi called Geoff Taylor, who subsequently became a good friend.

The Baissa UN observer was General Quo, a camera-festooned nationalist Chinese military officer. Convinced that we were determined to manipulate the result, he kept a dogged eye on all our activities. The evening before the day of the poll, General Quo announced that he was going to get up early and make a grand tour of the polling stations. Mac asked him if he would come to breakfast first. We knew of his weakness for alcohol and Mac positioned an open bottle of beer beside his breakfast sausage. This rapidly disappeared, followed by another and yet another. At 3 pm Quo finally staggered from the breakfast table. He subsequently managed to visit one polling station.

The actual voting in Baissa took place without incident, although there appeared to have been an attempt to rig the vote when wads of tightly packed voting slips were discovered in one of the boxes. But this was not serious enough to invalidate the result and eventually even the suspicious General appeared satisfied.

The next day he packed to leave in a great hurry – he had had quite enough of his brief spell in the bush. In the event, it proved to be too great a hurry, for after he had gone we discovered that he had left behind a carbon copy of his top-secret report to the UN. Naturally, it mentioned us all by name and made most interesting, if somewhat illiterate, reading. In addition, such was his rush that he had not packed up his UN kit, leaving me to do it for him. It consisted of kitchen equipment, bush lamps and general touring paraphernalia, all in mint condition. Mac and I took advantage of the situation by replacing our rather battered lamps and equipment with the UN variety before packing it away. We consoled ourselves with the thought that we had taken nothing that we had not replaced. A straight case of 'changey-changey' as Mac explained.

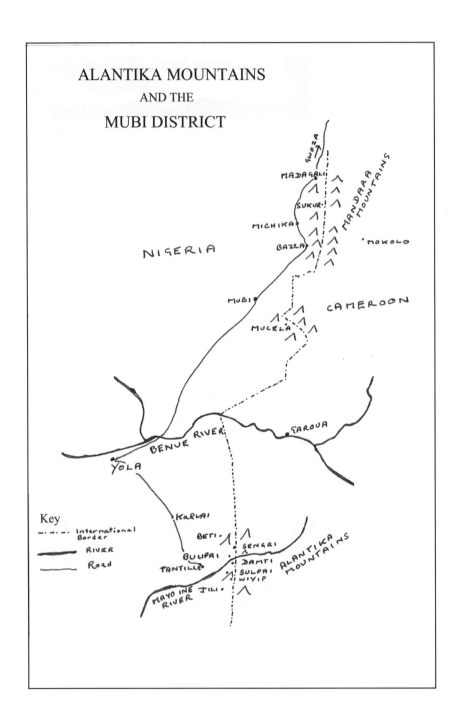

ALANTIKA MOUNTAINS
AND THE
MUBI DISTRICT

10

Mubi Native Authority

W hen the second plebiscite was over, I was told that I was to be posted to Mubi as DO to relieve Derek Mountain, who was going on leave. Mubi, almost 1,000 miles north of Mambilla, was the overall headquarters of the new Trust Territory and a new local authority, the Mubi Native Authority, had been established there. Although this posting was a form of promotion I was not best pleased because I was anxious to return to Mambilla where my real interest lay.

However, as it turned out, I had a very interesting four months in Mubi.

Although the second plebiscite had been decided in favour of Nigeria, there was still much work to be done with the fledgling Native Authorities before Sir Percy Wyn-Harris, the Governor, could hand the territory over officially to Nigeria as a functioning province.

Some of the wild tribesmen on the Cameroon side of the border were still trying to create havoc among the pagan people who lived on the great range of hills that stretched from Yola into Mubi District and then on into Borno Province, nearly 150 miles further north. This range, the Magar chain of the Mandara Mountains, runs like a spine from the northern-most lofty peak of Zaladuva (over 4,000 feet) to the southerly offshoot of Bagale hill overlooking the River Benue, and was the home of numerous pagan tribes who had taken refuge on the slopes from slave-raiding attacks in days gone by.

During our handover, Derek had introduced me to Isa Ahmadu, the District Head of Mubi, who like Audu Baju on Mambilla, was a new appointee and not a placeman of the Lamido in Yola. I took an instant liking to him; we became firm friends and developed a close working relationship.

Unfortunately, the relationship between Sir Percy, the Governor, and M, the Resident, was anything but close and friendly. M considered Sir Percy to be a bumbling incompetent – which he most certainly wasn't. Sir Percy saw M as crass, stubborn and boorish – which at times he most definitely was.

For example, shortly after my arrival I was asked to dinner at Sir Percy's modest Mubi bungalow that was serving as Government House. M had also been invited, and by the time the port was circulating he was well into a story about the antiquated plumbing in Buckingham Palace which was clearly causing embarrassment among many of the guests.

'As I sat there with my trousers around my legs,' boomed M, 'I reached up to pull the chain and …'.

We never knew what disaster befell him, for at that point Sir Percy rose to his feet, raised his glass and said with great dignity, 'Gentlemen, the Queen.'

A great deal of the four months in Mubi District was spent trekking in the mountains and I very nearly covered the whole length of them. At the far north of the range lived the Gwoza people, divided into numerous sub-clans, whose favourite sport was to raid each other's cattle and corn supplies after harvest when they were not preoccupied on their farms. Derek called these annual post-harvest hostilities 'the silly season'.

Administratively the Gwoza were not under Mubi but were run as a separate entity with their own newly established Native Authority. In the past they had proved themselves great opponents of the slave-raiding Fulani and Kanuri horsemen and had developed a lethal four-bladed throwing knife which they would launch with great accuracy to slash the tendons of their attackers' horses.

The Fali, the Higi, the Marghi and the Hithe tribes lived in the mountains south of Gwoza on both sides of the border. The French policy of forcible resettlement had resulted, as in Alantika, in the slopes on the eastern side of the range being uninhabited, but the summit and the former British western slopes were still peopled by tribesmen wearing their distinctive dress: the men in tattooed *warkuna* (leather loincloths); the women, leaves in the case of the Fali, brass prongs in the case of the Higi and Marghi, and huge metal hooks in the case of the Hithe. This extraordinary ironmongery, suspended from a strap around the waist, was a useful deterrent to uninvited suitors.

The plebiscite had unsettled the people of these tribes. My task was to try to explain what was happening politically and to reassure them that their absorption into Nigeria would not mean they would once again be subjected to Fulani misrule from Yola. Isa Ahmadu, the District Head, accompanied me into Fali country and one day we trekked to Mijilu, a remote Fali village high up in the Mandara Mountains.

On entering Mijilu, we were overwhelmed by the powerful smell of a decomposing corpse. Drums were beating and the women were singing a funereal song. In the centre of the village, a cloth structure had been erected and, through an interpreter, I learnt that the Village Head had recently died and that we were witnessing his last rites. It was explained to me that a Fali chief of his importance was placed upright in a chair and sewn into a leather shroud from head to foot. He would sit in the cloth tent for four days while mourners paid their last respects and would then be carried ceremoniously up into the mountain to be buried under the village witch doctor's watchful eye.

There appeared to be no objection to my paying my own respects, so I plucked up courage, for the stench was overpowering, and entered the tent. No part of the actual body of the corpse could be seen. It was completely sewn up in cowhide and placed upright in a cloth-covered chair, hands resting on knees. The buzzing from a thousand flies nearly drowned out the distant drumming and I soon left feeling somewhat sick. About an hour later the corpse was carried up into the mountains on the shoulders of Sarkin Tsafi, the witch doctor, followed by a long line of ululating women and villagers. I learnt that the corpse would be buried vertically in a rocky shaft and after decomposition the skull would be severed from the rest of the body and kept safely with the skulls of the Chief's ancestors.

That night I had to sleep in one of the village mud huts, there being nowhere else and the nearest village some miles away. The sickly stench of death clung to my clothing for days.

One notorious Fali from the Cameroon side was suspected of supplying guns to dissident Nigerians. He slipped into Mubi from time to time and we were determined to catch him. Having received information that he was on his way into town, we planted some uninhibited Mubi girls near the quarter in Mubi he was known to visit. Their instructions were to give him the warmest of welcomes and to extract relevant information over the pillow. For this work they would be paid, both by their client and handsomely by us.

We struck gold when one of the girls who had slept with him informed us the next day that he had arrived with guns. She brought a US gun catalogue of weaponry and pointed out the type of gun he was smuggling – an American automatic rifle. We had received information as to the whereabouts of a hut that he used in the mountains when crossing from Cameroon into Nigeria. So after receiving further information that he would leave Mubi and spend a night in the hut before returning to Cameroon, we mounted a dawn operation to seize him. We entered his hut just after sunrise to find him stark naked on a bed with a woman. He was amazingly cheerful at having been caught with his trousers down and surrendered without resistance.

Policeman P was in Mubi at this time and his house was very near mine. P was a precise, upright and very punctual man who used to return home at two o'clock every afternoon, have lunch and then retire to his bed for an hour's snooze at three. One day I persuaded, with a monetary inducement and for a bit of fun, the clever girl who had caught the Fali gunman to slip into his bed before he had returned home. On the stroke of two P returned and crouching behind a large bush at the bottom of his garden I watched the unfolding drama. His lunch had been prepared and was on the table. He washed his hands, put on a record of Gilbert and Sullivan of which he was inordinately fond, sat down and ate lunch. At precisely three o'clock he got up and the bedroom door closed behind him. There followed an eruption. First bellows then screams and moments later a terrified, semi-naked girl ran out of the house followed by an overheated P waving a loaded pistol. The clever spy had certainly earned her money.

The Fali were a cheerful people not normally given to smuggling weaponry, and it was a pleasure to trek among them. Mac was sinking wells on the plains at the foot of the hills at the time and occasionally we would meet up at a village where he was staying called Muchela. This would be an occasion for a *wasa* in the evening and the lively, laughing Fali girls provided versatile entertainment. The girls' bodies were heavily scarified in elaborate patterns all over their backs and sometimes on arms, breasts and bellies as well. There was a Catholic Father who ran a tiny mission in Muchela at the foot of the hills. I went there for Christmas communion and witnessed the bizarre sight of scarred, leaf-clad, but otherwise totally naked pagan women listening to a mass in Latin and muttering the appropriate responses.

In contrast to the affable Fali, the Higi and the Marghi were hostile and difficult. They were heavily missionised, the Augustinian Fathers having established missions at Bazza,

Michika and Madagali. Fights were frequent and violent. Murders were common, drink or a dispute over a woman usually being the root cause. A particularly violent murder took place in a village I was staying in and I had the unpleasant task of photographing the result and disposing of the body. Most of my carriers on Mambilla, a thousand miles to the south, were tough and truculent Marghi/Higi pagans and they also made formidable soldiers, but luckily they committed no murders during my time with them on the plateau.

Shortly after my arrival in Mubi, the Matakam tribe, with clandestine backing from the Cameroon authorities, raided the Hithe, who were kinsmen of the Marghi. This tribe lived in the hills behind Madagali which are characterised by awesome rock structures – the rocks at Kapsiki just over the border in Cameroon are an outstanding and much photographed example.

The Matakam had plundered the mud corn stores of the Hithe, smashing them open and stealing the grain, and three people had been killed in the attack. As soon as the news reached Mubi, M ordered me to go immediately up into the area – some 90 miles from Mubi – with police officer David Angus and eight policemen. It was dark when we reached the track at the foot of the mountains leading to Tur, the village where the worst of the raiding had taken place. There was no moon. We slithered, slipped and groped our way up the steep slope, totally reliant on our local guide. As dawn broke we reached the village, and after resting assessed the damage. It soon became clear that the trust of the Hithe tribesmen in the ability of the British to protect them was negligible. Something had to be done to restore their confidence, and quickly. I sent a note back to M via one of the policemen to that effect, suggesting that a rapid supply of grain to replace what had been stolen from the shattered corn stores would help to restore morale.

Although M could be inept at analysing a situation, once he identified with a cause, he could act with great rapidity and enormous energy. He received my note at dusk. That night he personally went into Mubi market and roused the corn merchants from their beds. A lesser man would have been deterred by their protests and calls to wait until the morrow, but not M. By six o'clock the next morning, not only were lorries setting off on the road from Mubi laden with sacks of corn, but other lorries were following full of blankets and salt. A note reached me later that day that these relief supplies were at the foot of the hills and could I organise carriers to head-load them to Tur. That evening, 24 hours after our arrival, the corn and blankets arrived in Tur. The next day we were handing them out to the tribesmen. They were impressed. Someone did have their interests at heart after all.

After this fracas I was asked to visit the *Chef de Sub Division*, my counterpart across the international border in Mokolo, to make sure that such a raid would not be repeated. It was felt in Mubi that the remnants of the French colonial administration were intent on stirring up inter-border strife. I took some whisky as a peace offering and headed for the remote border crossing. On arrival I discovered to my horror that I had forgotten my passport, although I did have my medical certificate. I showed this document to the official at the border. He held it upside down, stared at it for a long time and waved me into Cameroon. My French counterpart was charming and hospitable. He denied any involvement with the Matakam and said that he would ensure there would be no further trouble. There wasn't.

The most remarkable Marghi village was Sukur, situated on a remote plateau on the Sukur massif in the Mandara Mountains, which towered above the plains of Madagali. The Chief of Sukur, the Llidi, was respected by all the Marghi people, and even by the neighbouring tribes, as a divine priest with formidable powers. These extended into every facet of a tribesman's life, for the Llidi was much more than a witch doctor or a hereditary chief – he was God on earth.

The village contained impressively built stone houses, far superior to ordinary pagan huts. It also boasted a unique paved causeway, which led from the north-western gate of the village to a valley nearly 2,000 feet below. Five to ten feet wide and nearly two miles in length, the causeway had furnished this impregnable fortress with an all-weather road for horses and soldiery setting out to raid their neighbours. In addition to this remarkable construction, the Llidi's compound occupied half an acre and was surrounded by an eight-foot wall of unmortared stones. Outside this enclosure were two enormous sacred stones known as Fula and Dula, one about 12 feet high, the other eight. Legend had it that they were brought to the Llidi's compound by two early villagers who boasted that one was stronger than the other.

Blacksmiths held great authority in Sukur because, in the past, the village and its surrounding area had had a monopoly on iron, and iron bars made in Sukur had once been used as legal tender. This must have greatly contributed to the authority of the Llidi, although even he recognised a higher authority and paid a tribute, in iron bars, to the village of Gudur in the Cameroon Republic, which had a special spiritual authority over many of the tribes in the area.

However, the head smith, the Llagama, had another function, that of tribal castrator, and his services were required to protect the virginity of girls in the Llidi's compound. His talents were also in demand from other quarters, as this extract from *The Nigerian Field*, Volume *XXV* shows:

> In the Northern Cameroons the most skilled operator was the Llagama of Sukur. His work reached a peak during the reign of Hamman Yaji of Madagali, though there has always been a pair of eunuchs, the Birma, on guard at the compound of the Llidi to look after his children. Under Hamman Yaji [the activities of Hamman Yaji, a Fulani District Head of Madagali who terrorised the Marghi, will be described in more detail shortly], the male prisoners, mostly from Matakam and Moda, were sent up to Sukur for gelding before they entered his compound as custodians of his harem. Behind the Llidi's house is a small rock on which

the operation was performed. An eye-witness described how the wretched man was placed sitting on the edge of this stone, his hands bound to a stake in front of him and his legs forced apart by four slaves, with another four grasping his body in a manner reminiscent of the way in which a boy is handled in the typical circumcision operations of the Adamawa tribes.

The practice was to cut out the testicles with a small iron blade and then to pour hot oil on the wound. If it healed at all, the eunuch would be on duty within two weeks. More often the victim died, with as little ado as his fellow-sufferers in the northern deserts who were buried waist-deep in sand to allow the wound to heal, or those in the Orient who were hopefully planted in a dunghill for nature to do her best. Mbuka and Dali [the blacksmiths] were acknowledged experts, but the casualty rate was enormous. They expected to lose 90 per cent of their cases.

The people of Sukur looked on the Llidi as the source of their prosperity, of pleasure or hardship, of rain or drought, of good or indifferent harvest. To fulfil these massive responsibilities, the Llidi supplemented his inherited powers with those of divination using a land crab. In his book entitled *Tribal Studies in Northern Nigeria,* published in 1931, C K Meek gives an account of this practice:

Three pieces of nut shell are placed near the crab's hole, together with a number of stalks of grass, each stalk representing some question or individual. Thus if a man had died his friends might ask a diviner to ascertain how he had died, and the diviner would assign certain causes of death (e.g. witchcraft, poison, natural causes) to each stalk of grass. If it had already been determined that witchcraft had been the cause of death the diviner would be asked to name the witch. Names of suspected individuals would be assigned to the stalks of grass. The answer is obtained by watching to see if the crab deposits a piece of shell on one of the stalks of grass. In order to obtain a clear decision the crab is expected to deposit the shell on the same stalk of grass three times running.

One District Officer related how, in the 1950s, he made an

unscheduled visit to Sukur, climbing the great paved causeway in a thick *harmattan* mist that shielded him from view. On arrival at the Llidi's compound, he discovered him seated with his crab in its calabash of damp sand. 'My crab told me that you were coming half an hour ago,' the Llidi exclaimed, to the astonishment of the visitor.

Even when I visited Sukur in the early 1960s, the Llidi still retained remarkable power and prestige, and in spite of the ever-growing activities of the missionaries, a unique bull-killing ceremony at the end of the harvest continued to be observed. This involved the fattening of a young bull in an underground cellar near the entrance hut of an individual's compound. Two holes, one for feeding and the other for the extraction of dung and bedding, were the only points of access. The bull was incarcerated and fattened for two years, after which it was so huge it could hardly move. On the day of the festival it was released from its cavern and paraded in Sukur. After the parade it was killed in a very cruel and painful manner by roping it to a specially constructed crossbar and stabbing it in the throat with a knife. The wound was then pressed tight to prevent loss of blood – valued as a nutrient – and the creature eventually died from internal haemorrhage.

The ceremony was followed by dancing, organised by the blacksmiths. The bull was dismembered and the meat given to the relatives of the owner, while the bones, marrow, offal and blood were ground into a paste and stored in pots for use until the next ritual slaughter two years on. Like a Mercedes owner in modern Africa, a householder who kept a bull confirmed his social standing within the tribe; sometimes two or three households would club together to buy a bull in order to impress their neighbours.

In the 1960s the Llidi was still wearing his sacred hairlock into which had been plaited the hair of his ancestors. This could, in no circumstances, be seen by anyone and was protected by a special cap that the Llidi wore day and night. When his head was shaved by the barber, he would twist the cap around the hairlock to shield it from his hairdresser's view.

Sukur was situated in Madagali District, and Malam Risku, the District Head of Madagali, the headquarter town of the district, was a Christian who, as a young boy, had been carried over the mountains to escape the depredations of the notorious Fulani slave-raider Hamman Yaji. This ruthless man had been appointed District Head of Madagali in 1902 by the German administration and terrorised his subjects until 1927. He recorded his activities in a diary kept in Arabic script. It is nothing if not to the point:

> 1912, December 27: The pagans of Sukur brought me two cows as a peace offering.

> 1913, May 12: I sent my soldiers to Sukur and they destroyed the house of the Arnardo [the pagan chieftain] and took a horse and seven slave girls and burned the house.

> July 20: I sent my people to Sukur and we killed 15 and wounded very many and captured 18 slaves.

> 1916, Oct 19: I sent my soldiers to Sukur and they captured 18 slaves.

> 1917, August 16: I sent Fad-el-Allah with his men to raid Sukur. They captures 80 slaves of whom I gave away 40. We killed 27 men and women and 17 children.

> 1920, October 23: While I was at Nyibango I heard that the pagan named Diskin had raided Wappara, so I made arrangements and sent Fad-el-Allah with his men to raid Sukur. They captured from them 39 slaves and 24 goats and killed five men.

An eye witness account relates that, 'On one raid Hamman Yaji's soldiers cut off the heads of the dead pagans in front of the Chief of Sukur's house, threw them into a hole in the ground, set them alight and cooked their food over the flames. Another time they forced the wives of the dead Sukur men to come forward and collect their husbands' heads in a calabash; and on yet another occasion, to take all the heads down to Madagali for the Fulani to see.' Another witness relates how he had seen children have a coil of wire hammered through their ears and jaws by the soldiers, while another described how, when Hamman Yaji learned of the great significance of the burial rites in the village of Sukur, he ordered his soldiers to cut up the bodies of the dead so that they could not be given a tribal burial.

It seems the Sukur did retaliate. There is a story that on one occasion, the Sukur pagans ambushed a party of 15 Fulani retainers sent by Hamman Yaji to capture some raiders from Borno. The pagans succeeded in killing all these men. Hamman Yaji's retribution naturally followed on a full military scale, and against arms of precision even pagan courage was hopeless.

Though the British assumed responsibility for the Northern Cameroons in 1921–23, the activities of Hamman Yaji were not revealed until 1927 when he was deposed. Before the reign of Hamman Yaji, the Sukur people had been impregnable in their mountain fortress. But Hamman Yaji's superiority was paramount after he acquired rifles from the Germans. Amazingly, he was able to continue his activities long after the establishment of British colonial administration. His descendants – and with a ready supply of captive virgins there were many of them – still live in the area. In the highly political early 1960s it was thought prudent not to dwell too much on their infamous relative, and details of his diary were suppressed.

It was while touring among the neighbouring Higi people that we learned of a major outbreak of smallpox. It had always been endemic in the area but this time it seemed to have taken a strong hold. I was instructed to return to the area and to supervise the building of matting isolation camps some distance from the affected villages. I was no stranger to smallpox. Once, during my short stay in Yola, an exuberant Yugoslav doctor called Crkvenac called for me to come and see him in Yola hospital. 'There is something here that you will never see in your lifetime again,' he said. 'It is quite fantastic. Doctors in England would give their eye-teeth to see it.' Intrigued, I hurried to the hospital and was ushered into an isolated ward where I was confronted with an elderly woman whose head and face were completely covered in a suppurating, yellow crust. I could not identify any facial features. It was horrific and I felt quite sick. 'Look at that!' said this extraordinary doctor. 'The finest case of smallpox that you will ever see.'

I rushed out and away. Once home I examined with mounting concern my vaccination certificate. It was three months out of date. I dashed back to the Yugoslav. 'Vaccinate me! Vaccinate me!' I pleaded, rolling up my shirtsleeve. He smiled and did so.

In contrast to the enthusiastic Slav, there was in Mubi at the time of the Higi smallpox outbreak, a young doctor, a new arrival from England. He had a wife and a tiny, three-month-old baby. When the isolation camps were finished, he was asked to accompany me to the worst affected area to initiate a campaign of intensive vaccination. Strangely, he insisted on bringing his wife and child. The baby was in a carrycot covered with a mosquito net, and I could not help noticing that it seemed to have a bluish tinge. It was very still and to my lay eye, did not seem at all well. 'Are you sure your child is all right?' I queried. 'Oh, he's fine,' replied the doctor.

We spent a long day in the bush and drove back to Mubi at dusk. That night, we had all been invited to M's for dinner and the doctor and his wife duly came. Halfway through the meal the telephone rang. Their houseboy was on the line to tell them that their baby child was dead. Death had been caused by cerebral malaria. They buried their child in Mubi and left the country, never to return to Africa.

While I was still in Mubi, Independence Day, 1st October 1961, dawned for the Cameroons with Derek Mountain still on leave. Not only was Sir Ahmadu Bello, the Northern Premier, coming for the handover but so also was Alhaji Sir Abubakar Tafawa

Balewa, the Nigerian Prime Minister. The ceremony was due to take place on the laterite Mubi airstrip. The band was lined up and the dignitaries, chiefs and local officials seated in a matting enclosure. I had by now acquired my starched white uniform and Wilkinson dress sword. At exactly ten o'clock four small planes landed and the Nigerian Prime Minister and Northern Premier alighted. The Nigeria police band played the national anthems of the two countries as the Nigeria flag was run up on one flagpole and the Union flag was lowered on another.

The Northern Cameroons were free, and part of an independent Nigeria. Five new Native Authorities had been established in 18 months in areas formerly under the rule of Adamawa and Borno.

The two leaders inspected the massed police lines and were then introduced to the chiefs and local dignitaries. The short but solemn and historic ceremony went without a hitch. The lands of the former German colony had been put firmly on the Nigerian map and a few fortunate administrative officers had helped to put them there.

After this ceremony and the subsequent official junketing, little changed in our lives except for the departure of the Governor, the redoubtable Sir Percy Wyn-Harris. He had had a difficult time with the irascible M, but he had earned the respect of all his other staff.

Sir Ahmadu Bello stayed on for two days after the Prime Minister had left and the chiefs and dignitaries from the former Trust Territory were summoned to meet him. They naturally included Audu Baju from Mambilla. The meeting was held in the Mubi Native Authority council chamber and during it the Sardauna (the honorary title of the Northern Premier) asked if anyone had an idea for a name for the new Nigerian province. M immediately put forward *Taka Lafiya* which means 'step forward peaceably'. This rather contrived suggestion received little support.

'What about Sardauna Province?' chipped in Mambilla's Audu. No one could object to this. The sycophantic group of chiefs applauded, and so the new province was named.

Before Sir Percy finally left, Mac persuaded him to join us deep in the bush for a *wasa*. He suggested that Sir Percy stay in a village hamlet, which he knew well, and spend the night on a camp bed in a mud hut. To his great credit Sir Percy accepted. He was flown into this remote area, his plane landing on a grassy strip; he brought no radio or means of outside communication, just his personal pilot. The Governor just 'disappeared': it must have been one of the very few occasions when a remote hamlet had the territory's Governor to themselves for a whole night. The frenzied, cheerful dancing and drumming went on until well after midnight and Sir Percy was persuaded to join in the dancing himself. It was a night, he said, that had taken him back many, many years to his early days in Kenya.

Sir P Wyn was a short, powerful Welshman, full of energy and keen intelligence. In 1933 and 1935 he had got nearer to the peak of Everest than anyone since Mallory and Irving, returning with Mallory's ice-axe.

Later, at the time of the independence of the Gambia he sailed his own boat from Woodbridge in Suffolk to Bathurst, now Banjul, to celebrate independence with his former subjects.

11

Gashaka-Mambilla 2

Much as I had enjoyed my exciting four months in Mubi, I was anxious to return to the remoteness of the Mambilla plateau and to find out how the intrigues and tribal rivalries had developed in my absence.

Derek Mountain had returned from leave, and with John Harvey-Kelly, who had been standing in for me at Gembu, about to go on leave, there was nothing further to keep me in Mubi.

The troubles stirred up by the Matakam tribesmen in the Mubi area had been repeated as far south as Mambilla. The Cameroon authorities seemed bent on stirring up trouble right along the length of the 1,000-mile border with Nigeria. To counteract their incursions, M had come up with a grandiose scheme to police the length of the border with mounted patrols, and my old friend P, a keen and competent horseman, had been ordered to assist with this. Consequently it had been decided that I take back with me to Gembu a squad of 15 armed Nigeria policemen who would be quartered in the two abandoned United Nations' Uniport houses. I would purchase horses for them and turn them into mounted police. There had never been armed policemen previously on Mambilla, the policing having been done by the unarmed and less sophisticated Native Authority policemen.

It was August, one of the wettest months of the year, when I set off from Mubi in my ancient and battered kit-car with six months' supply of foodstuffs. It could well be six months before I returned to civilisation and I had bought a considerable quantity of basic supplies.

As we left Mubi it started to rain and when we reached the village of Song 50 miles to the south it was pouring. I knew that the one-track laterite road ran through a low-lying swamp shortly after Song. This could flood and prove impassable for days. I felt that we had to press on. The police were following behind me in a 15-ton lorry. My carriers and headman were in a similar vehicle. I worried that it would be these vehicles that would get stuck rather than mine.

When we reached the swamp we passed a road labourers' camp which had been completely washed away. 'We'll be lucky if we get through this,' muttered Luttu. As Luttu had once put his head straight through my car windscreen on an earlier brush with a culvert, he not unnaturally regarded my rainy season driving with some suspicion. Luckily, he had been asleep at the time and so relaxed that he had suffered no ill effects.

As we rounded a sharp corner with water flowing beside the raised level of the road, Hammadu, my Fulani boy, suddenly shouted out that the police lorry had gone off the road. No sooner had we digested this piece of news when we had our own problems to contend with. In front of us a drift – a concrete base built over a riverbed – had filled with fast-flowing water and was impossible for us to cross.

We stopped the car and watched disconsolately as trees and debris came sweeping over the drift. I walked back to where the police lorry was stuck fast in the mud, the water swirling past it, and told the policemen to sit tight. As I started back I saw to my alarm the small wooden bridge between the police lorry and my own car being swept away on the flood. The situation had suddenly become more serious, added to which it would soon be dark. Fortunately we had brought along some planks for just such an emergency, and throwing these across the gap left by the bridge we managed to cross on foot, but they wouldn't be strong enough to take the weight of the vehicles. My car was stuck on a narrow piece of road about 40 yards long, cut off by swirling water before and behind it.

Suddenly I heard shouting. A woman laden with a huge head-load was stuck in the river in front of us clinging to a tree. She had been trying to cross but had not reckoned on the force of the water. By edging my way along an overhanging branch I first managed to retrieve her loads and then pull her up onto the branch and to safety. It was a risky exercise – had she fallen into the swirling water she would almost certainly have drowned.

By this time the rain had ceased but the water had not stopped rising and was now lapping round the car's axles. We bedded down for an uncomfortable night. The mosquitoes from the surrounding marshland immediately went on the offensive. Huge and vicious, they filled the kit car, entering from goodness knows where, and in no time we were covered in bites. Then it started to rain again.

I immediately thought of the food we had stacked on top of the car to make more room for myself, Luttu and Hammadu. We hauled the precious, and by now sodden, bags of flour and sugar, tea and coffee into the back of the vehicle, and thoroughly soaked ourselves as we tried to squeeze into the remaining space for some sleep. But soon the water was flowing under the door of the car and through the interior. The vehicle started to shake. The road was so narrow that had a tree hit us and pushed us over the side we would certainly have been trapped and drowned. Hammadu started calling to Allah for salvation. I listened to his moaning and gritted my teeth.

Either Allah or some other god heard us, because after a sleepless night we were still on the strip of laterite when dawn broke. The rain had stopped. The sun was trying to break through and the waters were slowly subsiding.

As luck would have it, a Landrover with a winch and cable suddenly materialised on the other side of the drift. It was driven by an acquaintance of mine from Yola. Once the water level had dropped to a point where we could wade across, my friend taped up the vulnerable parts of my car's engine, then with water flowing over its bonnet and the engine running, the Landrover managed to pull my car across the drift.

He then drove his Landrover across the drift, constructed a makeshift bridge with his own planks and eventually reached the lorry. An hour later after much shouting and steamy, muddy confusion the lorry was man-handled back onto the road and in no time we were all safely on the southern side of the drift. But my supplies were ruined and had to be entirely replenished when we reached Yola.

On the trek up the escarpment and on to Gembu we tramped and rode through more torrential rain. When I eventually reached Gembu my sugar, salt and flour were ruined again.

My food supplies on the plateau were always a problem. Although I grew my own vegetables, which thrived on my horses' manure, I was often badly in need of the basics and there was no way of obtaining these on the plateau.

My Cameroonian opposite number lived in Mayo Darle, at the foot of the escarpment on the Cameroon side. It was a tradition that correspondence with each other was carried out in one's native language, whether or not the recipient understood it. Once when I was very short of basics, I wrote a letter to the French *Chef de Division* at Mayo Darle in carefully constructed English saying that I was sending down three carriers with £N40 in cash. Could he kindly buy me flour, tea, biscuits, sugar etc? In addition a little wine would also be very welcome. The carriers disappeared. They could of course have disappeared with the £N40 – a lot of money for them, but I had selected them with care and hoped for the best. A week later they returned, staggering under heavy loads. We took the heavy boxes into the house and unpacked them. Inside were 48 bottles of red wine and 48 bottles of white, but no foodstuff of any description whatsoever.

On reaching Gembu I duly took over from John Harvey-Kelly. He had lived there with his wife Julia and she had brought a feminine touch to the bachelor croft that was the DO's house. There were other improvements as well. A new Native Authority council chamber had been built and work had started on a motor road from Gembu to Mayo Selbe using village communal labour. There was obviously a need for a road up the plateau and at least two expensive surveys had been completed.

In addition, M had launched an amazing scheme for building a ski resort-type chairlift. I viewed these projects to bring the internal combustion engine to Mambilla with mixed feelings in the knowledge that a road would not only bring vehicles but also rogues and vagabonds who would exploit the unsophisticated Mambilla inhabitants. But I also knew that a road was inevitable – I just didn't want it to be completed while I was living there.

There were other more immediate problems. Harvey-Kelly had told me that the uncertainties and intrigues of the plebiscite campaign had encouraged some of the Fulani to conspire against Audu Baju, the Mambilla District Head. I soon realised that this was having a considerable effect on the poor man. He would frequently invite me to talk to him in the privacy of his house. He had heard, for example, that he was on a terrorist blacklist. Did I think that an attempt would be made to poison him? His mental stability started to deteriorate and he turned increasingly to drink. Worried about his personal safety, he cut all the rope bridges leading to Cameroon. This was a very different man from the cheerful, optimistic Audu Baju I had left four months earlier.

Immediately after the result of the second plebiscite two more elections had to be held to return members from Gashaka-Mambilla to the Federal and Regional Legislatures in Lagos and Kaduna. On 30th November 1961 the regional election to the Northern House of Assembly in Kaduna was held.

On roadless Mambilla, all the ballot boxes had to be nailed to wooden planks and head-loaded out to the remote polling stations. They would then be sealed by the polling officer and head-loaded back again. During this period of frequent elections this tedious and lengthy procedure was continually in the course of preparation. And, of course, the time-consuming method of transport meant that electoral results were considerably delayed; it sometimes took up to six days to bring in the boxes from the farthest polling station. As the area's designated electoral officer I acquired a great deal of electoral expertise.

In this particular election, counting started at three o'clock in the afternoon of 5th December, but at 4.15 pm the count was temporarily disrupted – and much enlivened. I was seated with my back to a crude and badly fitting pair of wooden doors that closed the entrance to the District Council hall. I was facing the vote counters who were piling the candidates' votes on trestle tables and watching for any irregularities. Suddenly, the counters in front of me jumped up, oblivious to the scattering of papers, and retreated to the other side of the room urging me to join them. I was angry. What did they think they were doing? The ballot papers would be muddled.

'What do … !'

My angry outburst was cut short as, looking over my shoulder, I saw that a large spitting cobra had slid under the ill-fitting door and was silently working its way towards my chair. I rapidly joined the electoral staff on the other side of the room while the snake was swiftly dispatched.

In 1961, the ruling political party in Northern Nigeria was the Northern People's Congress (NPC). Naturally, with the return of the Northern Cameroons to Nigeria, the Sardauna (or 'the Sardine' as he was dubbed) was well pleased with his administrative officers who had worked in the area during the second plebiscite. The NPC candidate in the Gashaka-Mambilla election was Hammagabdo, the son of Sarkin Yaki, the District Head of Gashaka District. Although a Fulani, he was not a Yola Fulani and he had been accepted as a moderate by most of the Mambilla and by Audu Baju. But not all the Mambilla were happy with this choice and Zubeiru Kabri, the brother of the Village Head of Kabri, had declared himself to be an independent candidate against Hammagabdo. He had earlier opposed Audu for the District Headship of Mambilla and consequently Audu was frightened and suspicious of his motives. Audu had tried hard to persuade Zubeiru not to stand and when he had refused, Audu conducted a hostile campaign against Zubeiru during the run-up to the election.

It was soon obvious that Hammagabdo was going to win. The piles of paper alongside his name on the trestle tables grew larger and larger by the minute. For a time during the count, Audu disappeared and then returned smelling strongly of alcohol. I had tried to persuade him not to drink on public occasions, telling him that it reduced any standing he might have with the mainly Muslim Fulani. But he had ignored this advice and he started publicly to insult Zubeiru for having the audacity to stand against Hammagabdo. In the face of this abuse and before the landslide result in favour of Hammagabdo was announced, Zubeiru stalked out of the chamber. At six o'clock I left an elated, inebriated Audu and returned to my house.

Next morning, shortly after I had reached my little thatched office at the foot of the hill, Yaji Mbar, Audu's head servant banged on the door.

'Come quickly, *ranka ya dade*. Please come quickly,' he called out in great agitation. 'There is something wrong with the Chief. We are calling him but he does not answer us.'

I quickly ran over to the District Head's house and entered the compound that I knew so well. When I reached his bedroom the dispensary attendant, Musa Song, was already by Audu's side, trying to give him artificial respiration. But he was long past the stage when this could have been of any assistance; his stiffness showed that he must have been dead for at least three hours. The empty bottles of brandy and beer by his bed gave clues to his sudden demise.

The district was stunned. Rumours spread that he had been poisoned or was the victim of a violent juju, engineered by the powerful Zubeiru. I believed that he had just drunk himself to death, but it could not have happened at a worse time. Just when we had managed to introduce some stability into Mambilla politics, the delicate balance had abruptly reverted to one of uncertainty and instability. The Fulani had been given an unforeseen opportunity to politic for a Fulani ruler, and they were determined not to let it slip away.

On the very night of Audu's demise the intriguing began.

The Kaka were under psychological attack from the Fulani, who wanted their precious votes. It was imperative that an election be held soon. Until the matter of the vacant District Headship was settled, there would be no stability on the plateau. The morale of the Mambilla, which had been sky-high after the election of Audu Baju, was sinking daily.

The newly elected Mambilla District Council was to choose and confirm the appointment of the new District Head of Mambilla. Such was the uncertainty that even the quiet and diffident District Head of Gashaka, Sarkin Yaki, was being encouraged to stand for the chieftainship of a combined Gashaka and Mambilla area. I quickly dissuaded him by saying that if he won, the government would not ratify his candidature. There was no mandate to govern both districts.

Three candidates were put forward by the Mambilla but two, Wazirin Mvua and Malam Musa Kakara, were disqualified, much to their supporters' annoyance, on evidence of their having accepted bribes in the past. The third candidate, a man of good reputation and long service as a court scribe, Malam Tafi Warwar, was eventually formally adopted. More conservative and less flamboyant than Audu, he seemed nevertheless to be a candidate who would command the respect of moderate Fulani.

On the Fulani side an interesting outsider appeared. Before the advent of the colonial powers, the territory of Gashaka had not been administered by the Lamido from Yola but by a Fulani kinsman who ruled from a town called Banyo. In those days, the plateau was virtually uninhabited and evidence shows that the Mambilla only came up onto the plateau in the mid-19th century. The Banyo empire had been powerful and widespread, but the colonial carve-up placed the larger part of it under the French and the tail-end Gashaka portion under the Germans. As we have seen, this territory devolved to the British and was subsequently placed by them under Yola Fulani rule. However, there was no doubt that in former times the Banyo Fulani had had authority over Gashaka District, though whether this authority extended to the plateau was arguable.

Malam Salori, the Fulani candidate, staked his claim as a great grandson of Mohammadu Gabdo (Dandi) who had founded an empire in about 1835 comprising the sub-Emirates of Kwancha, Banyo (in present day Cameroon) and Gashaka (formerly in British Cameroon and now in Nigeria) (see Appendix 5). His credentials in this respect were sound, as he had been born in Nigeria. But his father, Munsuru, had attempted to force his way into the District Headship in 1939 by creating a disturbance in Mayo Ndaga. In spite of this, it appeared that the Fulani had cleverly found a candidate who was not too tainted with Yola but who nevertheless had pure and royal Fulani blood in his veins. He had been practising photography in Bamenda, and when I first met him he brought his camera and talked at length about his photographic prowess with total self-assurance. As we eyed each other, we both knew instinctively that we were not going to get on.

About this time a new and revolutionary development had taken place on the plateau – the installation of a radio telephone link with Ganye and Mubi. The significance of this is difficult to appreciate in this age of mobile and satellite phones, but it meant that I could talk to my immediate superior, John Matthew, the District Officer in Ganye, and that on a lucky day I could even contact M or Derek Mountain in Mubi. However, we soon discovered that we could be overheard on the radio sets which some of the inhabitants of Gembu town possessed. They must have had great fun tuning in to our conversations and listening to our outspoken comments on individuals and their politics. To try to maintain some form of secrecy we developed an elaborate code for communicating and, for example, the South American term 'estancia men' was used to describe the Fulani.

The election for the new District Head of Mambilla was due to take place on 18th February 1962. As I wandered round my house on the night of the 17th I could see and hear that the town was alive with intrigue and suspense. Lamps were moving from one compound to another. There was the excited buzz of conversation. The Fulani were putting both the Mambilla and

Kaka elected members under great pressure. I felt certain that the Mambilla would stick together – not even large sums of money could dent tribal loyalties on this crucial issue – but as for the Kaka, I was not at all sure.

I had hoped that they would be able to reach an amicable conclusion without having to resort to a vote. It was a naive hope. As the debate next day in the District Council meeting room developed into an acrimonious shouting match, I urged restraint and brought out the ballot box – the redoubtable democratic tool that outsiders have wished on to Africa.

A polling booth was hastily erected behind a piece of cloth, and one by one the council members came forward to cast their vote. Tension was high. This fateful day could determine the whole future of the area for years to come, for unlike other less remote parts of Nigeria, the District Head of Mambilla still exerted great authority. I had calculated that even if all the Kaka supported the Fulani candidate Malam Salori, the Mambilla candidate Malam Tafi Warwar should, on tribal voting lines, still win with a very small majority and I had advised my superiors accordingly. But I had not taken into consideration the old adage that there is nothing that money cannot buy. Four Mambilla councillors sided with the Fulani as did all the Kaka. Malam Salori won by one vote.

Immediately there was uproar. Hundreds of Fulani, Mambilla and Kaka tribesmen had gathered on the football pitch just outside the chamber, and in no time, two angry groups stood facing each other. Not only could the two main tribes start fighting but the Kaka turncoats might also be sought out and killed. The Nigeria police with their firearms had been recalled to the foot of the plateau; the Native Authority police had nothing more than wooden truncheons. I could only rely on my white skin.

I decided to walk between the two hostile ranks and order them to disperse, to go to their homes and to accept a fair result.

Miraculously this tactic worked. The crowd started to drift away, no fighting broke out, no one was hurt. A potentially explosive situation had been defused by sheer bluff. But the

Mambilla were shattered, in stark contrast to the wild Fulani jubilation. The new District Head was proclaimed Damburam by his supporters and he ruled Mambilla for many, many years

All I could do was to get on the radio telephone and explain that my earlier prediction of a win for the Mambilla candidate was wrong. The *'estancia* men' had won through the power of the purse.

The Mambilla were so depressed that I realised something had to be done quickly to boost their morale. I proposed that a *wakili* or second-in-command be appointed to represent the Mambilla interests in the district. This suggestion was enthusiastically received, and after yet another election, Zubeiru Kabri, the man defeated in the Northern Region election against Hammagabdo, was elected as Damburam's *wakili*.

To begin with all was well and the Damburam appeared anxious to placate the Mambilla. But a worrying tendency soon began to develop. He started to surround himself with drummers and praise-singers who gave him the nickname, *al'Qur'anin Dutse* (the Qur'an of the Plateau). These professional flatterers are common throughout Northern Nigeria and elsewhere and they always dance attendance on chiefs and dignitaries. But Damburam encouraged them to such an extent that I had to ban his pre-Friday mosque drumming, which tended to begin at 9 am.

He also toured the plateau with an army of flatterers, followers and wives. The tiny Mambilla villagers could not support such a phalanx of people, nor were they supposed to. Mediaeval court customs had been considerably curtailed in other parts of the North. I spoke to Damburam about this and for a time he took my advice.

During my time in Mubi, I had been dealing with contracts as chair of the Mubi Native Authority contracts committee, always a source of potential scandal. An Ibo contractor who ran a bar in Bama, to the north of Mubi, had attempted to bribe the committee with a massive sum of money. The evidence was clear and in writing, and as a result of my investigation he was remanded for three days in Mubi jail. I thought little more of it. After all, such cases were common, especially in the dealings of the Ibo with the so-called unsophisticated northerner.

Some months later I was startled to learn that I was being sued for a million pounds by this self-same contractor. Apparently, when the case against him had come to court the vital piece of written evidence was missing. I was later to go through the appropriate police file and the numbered pages read 65, 66, 69, 70. Pages 67 and 68 were nowhere to be found and it was suspected that an Ibo policeman had been bribed to remove them. The case collapsed and he sued me. The plaintiff justified the huge sum of money by claiming loss of goodwill in the contractor's bar, loss of profits and general character assassination. In such circumstances a government servant had a civil case to answer and it was clear that my Resident M was taking the matter seriously. I was assigned a Queen's Counsel and a preliminary hearing was heard in the court in Mubi, which resulted in the case being transferred to the High Court. I must confess I took it all very lightly even though others didn't, and I have the magnificently worded document to this day.

I returned to Mambilla and in my preoccupation with Mambilla politics and affairs totally forgot about the disgruntled Ibo contractor. Then one day a letter arrived. The delivery of mail in head-loaded canvas mail-bags sent up by foot from Serti was always an operational hazard, especially during the rains. Sometimes the bags would be sodden, having been left for days at the foot of the plateau in torrential rain. With Mambilla's 80-inch annual rainfall and the consequent state of the roads and the difficulties of travel, letters from Mubi invariably took three weeks and letters from England up to five. One frustrated visitor to the plateau, anxious for news from his fiancée, slit open a mail-bag while climbing the escarpment and retrieved his post. The Post Office sued him for tampering with Her Majesty's mail – a heinous offence!

So when the letter arrived on 23rd May summoning me to answer a case of wrongful and malicious prosecution in the High

Court in Jos on 15th May there was little I could do except laugh and shrug my shoulders. In the event, the plaintiff did not appear and the case was dismissed. Several years later, the Ibo contractor met an end that I would not have wished on him. During the riots in 1966 when the Hausa/Fulani and Kanuri turned on the Ibos in the North, he was chased through desert land in Borno by Kanuri who were eager to settle old scores. His car broke down and he was thrown down a well. I was told that his fingers were stamped on as he clung to the side, screaming for mercy.

There were, however, other urgent matters to attend to. I had felt for some time that the only way to solve the perennial disputes between the Mambilla and the cattle Fulani was to demarcate the plateau into specific grazing and farming areas. This would eventually involve mapping the whole of the plateau, constructing concrete beacons as boundary markers and producing properly surveyed maps. A set of these maps would be lodged in Kaduna as well as in Mubi and Mambilla. I managed to get the full support of Kaduna, Mubi and the Mambilla council for this scheme and immediately began to set it in motion.

Many weeks were spent trekking to the most hotly disputed areas on the plateau, as I was convinced that I should supervise the scheme personally, especially in the initial stages. Much time was spent arguing with both Mambilla and Fulani before decisions were finally reached. The concrete beacons had to be built, not an easy task on rainy Mambilla, where cement had to be head-loaded in and would be ruined if it got wet. Finally, draft sketches were drawn showing the numbered beacons in the demarcated area. Gradually the scheme caught on. The courts began to make rulings based on the agreements reached.

There was a clamour for me to visit numerous disputed areas, but I could do only so much. The whole process could take years, and I also knew that when I finally left the plateau for good my decisions would be deliberately misrepresented. Hence the urgent need for accurate mapping. I managed to persuade the authorities of the validity of this argument, and an African surveyor was sent up to assist us.

This crucial problem of farmer/grazier disputes was exacerbated by a tragic failure of the maize harvest, the staple Mambilla crop. It was too high an altitude for guinea corn, and millet only grew in certain areas. Famine threatened, and with the District Council's promise of monetary support we sent out urgent messages for assistance. Soon sacks of maize were being head-loaded up the steep sides of the plateau. But it was often a case of too little, too late. Even when the grain reached Gembu, it had to be divided up and sent on to remote and distant hamlets. Corrupt officials could easily help themselves or sell the corn at inflated prices, and they often did. A pound of corn soon cost one shilling and eight pence on the plateau, as against six pence in the rest of Sardauna Province, and distribution was very difficult to supervise effectively.

A policeman was caught stealing potatoes and an old man collapsed and died of hunger in Gembu. Shortly after these two incidents, the tragic case of Buba the Leper occurred. Buba the Leper lived with an old man on an isolated hillside near the village of Leme ten miles from Gembu. He was an outcast from society, greatly feared and shunned by the local people on account of his violent temper, a frequent side effect of the leprosy drug Dapsone. One evening, a young Fulani boy stole some sweet potatoes from Buba's farm, which surrounded his hut. The leper chased him, caught him, stabbed him to death and was subsequently arrested. At the Preliminary Inquiry into the case held in Gembu, I recommended that he be sent to the High Court on a charge of first-degree murder. He was then remanded in Gembu prison pending instructions from the High Court and was still on remand when I was returning on foot to Gembu from a trek via Leme.

As we entered Leme, the Village Head rushed up to our party and begged us to stop. Something was obviously very wrong, for we could see groups of Fulani pointing to an isolated hut on a hillside two or three miles away. This was Buba's hut. It transpired that he had returned home after escaping from prison by squeezing himself through a latrine drainage hole at the bottom of the 20-foot mud wall surrounding the prison. He was, according to the villagers, alone.

The Fulani had been incensed by this particularly brutal murder and unless action was taken they might easily have taken the law into their own hands. I asked my headman, Abba, to select three of his most reliable carriers. We then walked up the hillside towards the hut.

Motioning to the carriers to surround the hut, I went up to the entrance and called, 'Buba, come out. We know you are inside and we have come to take you back to prison.'

There was no reply.

'Buba, *ina da bindiga.*'

This was pure bluff as I never carried a gun on Mambilla or anywhere else. There was total silence from within. I moved towards the doorway, apprehensive lest Buba should come rushing out with a bow and arrow or a spear.

'This is your last chance,' I called out. 'Come out or I am coming in with a gun.'

From inside there came a muffled, '*To, shi ke nan,*' and shortly afterwards out came Buba, a broad grin on his face.

We escorted him to Leme, tied him to a horse and sent him back to Gembu prison to join the old man, who had been imprisoned for aiding and abetting but who had decided not to escape. Buba later stood trial in Jos, but the court was lenient and took the effects of the drug into consideration. After a few months in Jos prison, he and the old man were released. Buba returned to the plateau and jokingly informed me that his imprisonment had been worth it.

Gradually we came through the worst effects of the crop failure. But it had been a tough time and had done no good for Mambilla/Fulani relationships.

Bauchi

A Zar woman from Bauchi

Gombe

The Fulani initiation ceremony of sharo

Fulani District Head

Gombe

A mud house in Gombe, beautifully decorated using hands and fingers in wet mud

Fulani women come to the Gombe market to sell milk and butter

Tangale-Waja

Duck-seller

The self-government Durbar

Mounted Kanuri

The self-government Durbar

Bachama dancers

Wrestling with a hyena

Two jesters

Tula trumpeters

Mubi

Matakam warrior from the French Cameroons

Results of the Matakam raid on the Hithe corn stores

Giving out salt to the Hithe people after the raid by the Matakam

Marghi woman and baby

Fali woman's 'beauty' incisions

A Hithe woman

*The Fali had a great sense
of humour*

A Koma woman come to the market on the plains to buy salt

Vomni girls dancing

My carriers who brought my loads up on to the Mambilla Plateau

Biyu da sisi – *the part of the climb on to Mambilla for which the carriers were paid an extra two shillings and sixpence*

Mambilla terrain. No aircraft could land on the plateau

The view from the edge of the Mambilla Plateau

Mambilla

The Mambilla chief of Kabri

Mambilla corn store

Mambilla

Fulani girl with baby

Mambilla girls. They did not carry burdens on their heads

Fulani dancing on Mambilla

Fulani girls at Mai Samari, *Mambilla*

Mambilla

Hausa trader in the Gembu market

*View from my house in Gembu overlooking the River Donga
filled with low cloud*

Mambilla

Pro-Nigeria posters for the 2nd plebiscite on Mambilla.
The French were exploding nuclear devices in the Sahara at the time.
The Hausa reads, 'Vote to join Nigeria because she feels sorry for you' and
'Vote to join Nigeria because she gives education to everyone'

Sarkin Tsafi – *a witch doctor*

It was about this time that Mambilla suffered a cruel blow and I lost a good friend. Ardo Musa of Kakara, the clan leader of the Butanko'en, was one of the most sensible of the Fulani chiefs. He was able to see beyond the sectional struggles of his fellow Fulani and worked for the good of the whole of Mambilla; he also worked well with the able Jauro Musa, the Mambilla Chief of Kakara.

Ardo Musa's face was lean and hard; he had honest eyes, a shrewd yet gentle nature and a long, black, goatee beard flecked with white. I suppose that at that time he must have been about 45 years old. He always wore a white turban, drank hot milk out of a mug half full of sugar, and lived near Kakara in the southern half of the plateau. His counsel was accepted by the distrustful Mambilla, for he kept his clan's cattle in check and farm damage in his area seldom occurred. He was also enlightened and fair – not common characteristics among the Fulani.

We were holding a district council meeting at Gembu. Not a meeting of great import, but the five shilling a day sitting fee encouraged the council members to leave business unfinished, thereby ensuring an extra day's debate and a double payment. It was late afternoon when the meeting broke up and an angry, black line of clouds and distant rumbling to the west told of a mighty storm to come. The meeting had generated no inter-tribal animosity, and the members broke up chatting amiably and slowly scattered to their Gembu lodgings. All except Ardo Musa.

'I can't stay, I have to go home,' he explained.

'But why?' I queried in amazement. 'Look over there. You will never reach Tamnya before that storm breaks. Why don't you spend the night in Gembu like everyone else?'

'No. I have to go,' he said adamantly.

'But the sitting-fee?'

'I have to go,' his eyes were firm and resolute.

Nothing, not even an order from his DO, would have persuaded him to stay. He had to go and so he went, followed by his wives and retainers, riding or walking with him.

By the time they reached the village of Leme, ten miles from

Gembu, the storm had already broken. Just beyond Leme, Ardo Musa's stirrup was struck by lightning and he died instantly. No one else in his party was hurt and as soon as the news reached Gembu they ran to tell me.

'But why? Why did he try to go home? Why didn't he spend the night in Gembu?' I asked,

They looked at me with pity.

'He had to go,' they answered. 'It was written.'

12

Elections and Filinga

I was shortly immersed in preparations for yet another election, this time to the Federal House of Assembly in Lagos.

Abel Gelchi Warwar, a Mambilla schoolmaster, stood for the ruling NPC. The opposition Action Group (AG), the party run by the powerful Yoruba politician, Chief Awolowo, the Premier of the Western Region, did not process its candidate's application in time and Abel stood against a solitary independent and won easily.

The Action Group complained bitterly, but they had totally underestimated the distances on Mambilla and the time required to trek to Gembu to lodge their application. By a simple miscalculation of time and distance the application arrived late. I was criticised for being a Sardauna placeman, but to no avail. The electoral rules had been followed to the letter.

Abel was a hothead and had a fiery temper but I managed to get on with him. Unfortunately, even on Mambilla and before he became a Federal MP, he liked his drink, and his electoral success, an MP's expenses and the bright lights and temptations of Lagos contributed to his rapid decline. Sadly, he followed Audu Baju, the other Mambilla leader with unfulfilled potential, and died an alcoholic in his mid-30s. At a time when they most needed leadership, the Mambilla lost two potential leaders in rapid succession. Fate had played into the hands of the Fulani.

However, before this election and its subsequent tragedy for the Mambilla, the Northern Region Minister for Information, Ibrahim Biu, and the Under-Secretary for Lands, Yusufu Tanko, visited the plateau. Very few politicians were prepared to climb up the steep escarpment and there had only been one previous political visitor.

On the first evening of their two-day stay in Gembu, they held an election rally for the NPC. Naturally, I distanced myself, for although I was now working for the Northern Nigerian government it was important for me to be seen to be politically impartial. At this rally, Yusufu Tanko made a speech which deliberately undermined my authority. He told the people that the day of the white man was over, that Nigeria was independent and that Africans were in charge now. They should not be misled because they still had a white District Officer.

My messenger came up the hill to my house at great speed to tell me what had been said. I was working in Mambilla at the express request of the Premier of the North, the Sardauna, and it was common knowledge that very few Nigerian DOs relished the chance to work in such a remote place. But there was little I could do and I felt despondent. If this was the political line, what was the point of my staying?

However, to his great credit, Ibrahim Biu came to my house that evening and completely repudiated what Yusufu Tanko had said. He apologised and said he would personally speak to the Sardauna about it, adding that the government had absolute confidence in my work and in me. Yusufu Tanko, who was junior to him, had no right to speak out as he had. A few weeks later I received a letter of abject apology from Yusufu Tanko and I knew that the Sardauna was, for the moment, still on my side.

I was due for home leave, but although I had been on my own for many months, I was so caught up in Mambilla affairs that I had to be persuaded to go. I can well remember the startled faces of the Mubi Club members when I came in to say good-bye as I kept breaking into Hausa to explain myself. I could talk about nothing else except Gashaka/Mambilla politics. It was definitely time for me to have break, even though I did not realise it myself.

An African District Officer who was prepared to work in such a remote situation had come to the plateau to stand in for me while I was away: Joseph Gomwalk from Plateau State, who would in a few years become the State's Governor – only later to be executed for corruption. His coming was a foretaste for the Mambilla and the Fulani of what Yusufu Tanko had been alluding to. Times were changing fast and Mambilla was moving with them.

Just before I left, a British Army engineer officer suddenly appeared at my front door. I was staggered. My intelligence system did not usually let me down, and I thought I always knew well in advance when a visitor was on his way to Gembu. But David Charlesworth was no ordinary officer. Full of energy, he had doubled up on the normal trekking stages and had completed one trek of more than 30 miles in a single day. He had been sent to survey the road. When the survey was complete, British Army sappers were to begin to tackle the projected road from the foot of the escarpment. Preoccupied as I had been with my grazing problems and the mapping of the plateau, I had given little time to the road. But it was now the government's top priority and consequently Gomwalk gave it a great deal of his attention.

Before boarding the plane to London in Kano, I stayed with M. He had left Mubi two months earlier and was deeply enmeshed in an inquiry into the misdeeds of Sanusi, Emir of Kano. It was a one-man inquiry, the Sardauna had appointed him personally, and M was thoroughly relishing his new role of grand inquisitor, a position which provided him with a welcome atmosphere of excitement and drama. He drove me at breakneck speed through the streets of Kano, 'to avoid the marksmen who are after me'. Policemen in gym shoes patrolled his house, 'so that the blighters cannot hear my bodyguards moving about'. The city was tense. M had created tension and thrived on it.

However, by appointing M as the sole commissioner, the Sardauna had not only devised a method of deposing an Emir who had been challenging his authority but also a way to ease out M himself. For although M had performed loyally, the Sardauna no doubt felt that the continued presence of this larger-than-life character in his post-independence administration could prove embarrassing. As it turned out, the Sardauna accepted a part of M's report – the part that incriminated the Emir – but the sections that implicated other prominent members of Kano Native Authority were suppressed. M resigned in a fit of pique and the Sardauna's dual purpose was successfully achieved. M realised too late that he had also been a victim of a Machiavellian plot.

I must have looked most odd on my journey back to England to take up my leave, there being no opportunity to buy clothing while working on Mambilla. When my shirts and trousers eventually fell to pieces I had them replaced with local cloth tailored in the Gembu market. Consequently they were makeshift and ill-fitting. I must have looked like one of the refugees who were at that time flooding out of the Congo during the tribulations involving Katanga, Tshombe and Lumumba (which made for riveting listening on my radio).

Added to which there were the skins. A Native Authority bounty of five pounds a lion skin meant that from time to time magnificent skins were handed over. This saddened me as there were too few lions on the plateau and those that were left were helping the government in its stated aim of controlling cattle numbers. Therefore when a veterinary officer in Yola sent me a canister of cyanide to bait meat to kill lion, I discreetly buried it. At one point a company of Nigeria army soldiers was sent to the plateau to reduce the lion population, but they made so much noise that the lions slipped away from the area until the soldiers dispersed and not one was killed.

However, Jauro Bello, the Fulani Ardo of Chabbel Zance, had given me a leopard skin and I myself had acquired a lion skin, but the year-round damp atmosphere on the plateau made them difficult to cure, and in spite of my primitive efforts with salt, they both smelt strongly of putrefying flesh.

So the combination of my clothing and the malodorous skins stuffed into an old parachute bag made me a somewhat eccentric traveller. It was not surprising that the customs officer at Heathrow waved me hastily through. (Today the skins would have been impounded.) I headed straight for the renowned London taxidermist, Rowland Ward, and deposited the skins in their immaculate showroom. They batted not an eyelid. For them it was an everyday occurrence.

I then went on to London outfitter Austin Reed and purchased trousers, jacket and shirts, giving the startled assistant my African clothes to dispose of as he wished. Finally I arrived home where I was congratulated on my smart appearance.

On my return from leave, I stopped for a break on the journey to Mambilla to visit J, who was District Officer, Jalingo. The small town of Jalingo, the headquarters of Muri Emirate, lies just off the main road half way between Beli and Yola. In the early 1960s it was under the jurisdiction of the Lamido in Yola but was administered as a subordinate Emirate by the Fulani Emir of Muri, who ruled over the Muri Fulani and the volatile Mumuye pagans who inhabited the surrounding hills. It had never been part of the former German Cameroons.

J, born far too many years after his time, was wild, hard drinking and totally unpredictable. He had a brilliant brain and was greatly loved as a character by both the Fulani and the Mumuye. At the same time he was a considerable trial to his superiors. He often acted out fantasies, going through phases of being Mister Midshipman Hornblower or, more sinisterly, a member of the German Third Reich. It was impossible to know if what he was saying was true or false. He once defused a potentially explosive NEPU opposition political rally by goose-stepping with them through Jalingo town and teaching them to chant '*Sieg Heil*'.

He was also a notable mountaineer, and just after Nigerian independence he climbed a high peak in the Himalayas, placing the new Nigerian flag on top of it. This earned him a sepia-coloured photograph of his exploit in *The Illustrated London News* magazine. J also climbed Wase Rock in Bauchi. An earlier observer described it as: '… a remarkable pillar of rock visible for many miles around. Sheer up from the farm land at its foot it rose for 600 feet or more, its flat top whitened like a tablecloth with the droppings of countless birds, the vultures, pelicans, white-breasted crows and others being its only visitants. The smooth grey sides gave no sign of hand or foothold other than the smallest cracks and excrescences of weather action, and on them nothing grew.'

Before J climbed Wase it was thought to be unclimbable, and there was an old legend that the Emir of Bauchi, anxious to find out if it could be climbed, agreed to reprieve two murderers if they could scale it. They volunteered to try and were taken to the foot of the rock. One of them climbed half way up, then dropped to lie dead and broken at the bottom. The other actually succeeded in getting to the top, but once there, unable to face the awful descent, went mad from thirst or fright or both and left his bones on the summit.

Having many powerful African friends in important positions in Kaduna, J acted by his own rules and usually got away with it. In 1960, a group of British parliamentarians visited Jalingo on a fact-finding mission just before independence. J had been designated to give them lunch and to show them what progress was being made in preparing the Emirate for independent rule. He served drinks, then just before lunch he began to scurry backwards and forwards to the kitchen hastily bringing on plates of food.

'I do apologise,' he muttered, 'the cook has misbehaved himself and I had to tie him up outside. I'm afraid this a do-it-yourself lunch.'

Political eyebrows were raised. 'What on earth do you mean, J?'

'The man was unbelievably rude to me. There's no other way to teach them,' replied J with a straight face. 'Come outside and I'll show you what I mean.'

The Members of Parliament scuttled out into the garden behind the house, where to their horror they saw the wretched cook, spread-eagled on the grass, his wrists and ankles tied securely to stakes.

'Absolutely intolerable! Quite outrageous!' muttered Tories and Socialists in unison. 'You'll be hearing about this. Your days in this country are severely numbered.'

The party left without their lunch, whereupon J untied his beaming cook and gave him the promised five pounds. An official recommendation for immediate dismissal was lodged with the Kaduna government but J had got his message in first; his African superiors fully appreciated the joke and nothing was said.

One day when I visited this highly unpredictable character, a burly Public Works official was seated on the sofa, his left arm around a beautiful Fulani girl. His intentions were obvious and the girl appeared complaisant. We drank beer with an affable J who suddenly turned to the other man and said, 'Of course you ought to know, Peter, she's a contagious leper.' And she was.

That was the way of J. An impressive conjurer, he enthralled the Africans with his magic and they credited him with supernatural powers. Eventually he married a girl who nursed him in a London hospital on one of his leaves to Britain. But the drink and his fantasies caught up with him, and I last saw him years later in a sad state in Kano.

On arriving back in Gembu, and after a brief hand-over from Gomwalk, I quickly settled back into Mambilla affairs. The road up the escarpment had made great advances and enthusiasm for it was high. I gave it top priority. But the demarcation of the plateau was still uppermost in my mind. Road or no road, it was vital that the long-standing farmer/grazier antagonism be resolved. The opening of the road and the subsequent influx of aliens would only make the situation worse. In fact this is exactly what happened: politicians flooded up when access was made easy; land was acquired; and cattle numbers increased dramatically. Fortunately for me, this all happened after I had finally left.

One crucial element of the scheme was to encourage cattle to move off the plateau, especially during the dry season when grazing was at a premium. I was determined to try to encourage permanent emigration and had identified what seemed to be a natural area for overflow cattle on the plateau of Filinga to the north of Mambilla in Gashaka District, a third of the size of Mambilla and virtually unoccupied. But its complete isolation from markets and villages was a natural discouragement.

Shortly after my first arrival on Mambilla, Maclennan, a veterinary officer, had made a brief visit to Filinga, but a proper survey of the area had never been attempted. I determined to go to Filinga and assess the situation for myself. It was June, a very wet month in Gashaka-Mambilla, but I had to seize this opportunity to make the trip. There might not be another chance.

I decided to approach the plateau from Serti. I would make my way through the old Banyo Emirate headquarter town of Gashaka and from there on to Filinga via the tiny village of Yakuba. Sarkin Yaki, the District Head of Gashaka and father of the politician Tafida Hammagabdo, lent me a horse and a guide and gave me encouragement. I had come with my faithful headman Malam Abba and my wild Higi and Marghi carriers who were by now welded into a tough, competent and loyal team.

Gashaka belied its former greatness as an outpost of the Fulani Banyo empire. Virtually deserted, only the remains of the mud wall that used to surround the town indicated its former size and importance. The population was elderly and lived in poverty; they were not eager to sustain for too long the burden of our visit.

From Gashaka, the 18-mile trek to Yakuba crossed dense primeval rain forest where vast trees sent roots looping in all directions into the damp earth. There was a constant drip from the foliage overhead and often the sunlight barely filtered through. I had never experienced anything like it on any trek in the North. Sometimes the track was obliterated and the carriers, under instructions from Sarkin Yaki's portly guide, would have to stop and hack their way through the twisted stems of vine and creeper that climbed up the massive trees to the canopy above. We were all tired, drenched with sweat and exhausted when eventually we reached the tiny hamlet of Yakuba, where the friendly inhabitants looked after us well. At four o'clock the next morning we set out for the Filinga plateau.

Plateau is a misnomer, for Filinga consists of three separate plateaux linked by stiff climbs. Filinga plateau is the lowest at about 5,000 feet. A further 1,000 feet leads to Chabbel Chirgu ('leopard plateau'), and another 500 to Chabbel Hendu ('the windy plateau').

As we started the ascent, the first streaks of dawn across the sky revealed the looming outline of Gangirwol. The highest peak in Nigeria (7,936 ft), the slopes of Gangirwol straddle the international border. At that time only one European had reached the tiny plateau on the top of this steep-sided massif. Gangirwol translates from Fulani as 'something else', a wonderfully descriptive name. I would dearly have loved to attempt the climb, but there was no time. The foothills were trackless with virtually impassable undergrowth which would have taken days to hack through. Another Fulani name for Gangirwol is Chabbel Wade ('hill of death'), which commemorates the death from exposure of two Fulani herdboys who had managed to climb to the top.

While climbing Filinga we thought we heard the booming of gorilla sounding on the slopes of Gangirwol. At that time, it must have been one of the last places in Nigeria where gorillas could be found.

As we climbed higher, the escarpment of Mambilla was visible to the south, separated from Filinga by a huge stretch of uninhabited, dense and seemingly impenetrable bush through which we were planning to return. When I saw for the first time just how far it stretched, I wondered if we were wise. Half way up the escarpment a storm broke. We had seen the huge black clouds approaching but were unprepared for the freezing hail and ferocious wind. Lightning flashed and thunder crashed all around us. We took shelter as best we could but when we restarted our ascent our clothing and loads were thoroughly soaked.

Filinga is the name not only of the plateau but also of the only village on the top. Before we reached it we were caught in another terrific storm. When eventually we arrived, the Fulani villagers made us very welcome. They let us stay in some of their sturdiest mud huts and brought chicken and rice for both the carriers and myself. I was able to repay them with good news. On account of their extreme isolation we had persuaded the Native Authority to reduce their tax by two thirds, saving each adult male 30 shillings. We had also reduced the cattle tax to two shillings per animal. Both these tax reductions were designed to encourage Fulani immigration. But it had little effect. The lack of villages and markets and the dense tsetse-fly-riddled bush surrounding the plateaux were too great a deterrent.

After two days with the Filinga villagers, listening to their grievances and attempting to explain to them the stupendous changes which were going on in the outside world, I determined to climb up to Chabbel Chirgu. There was a Fulani encampment on the top, kinsmen to Ardo Jibo of Mayo Ndaga and white cattle owners.

The climb involved crossing a small intermediary plateau and scrambling up a steep track bordering a beautiful waterfall that tumbled down from Chabbel Chirgu overhead. The morning was bright and sunny and a myriad of wild flowers, some of which I had never seen before, made the trek particularly delightful. In the distance on a grassy abutment we spotted a herd of buffalo, the only time I have ever seen them outside a game park in Nigeria.

When we finally reached the tiny Fulani grass hut encampment on the top we were treated to another warm welcome and this time a cow was killed in our honour. The carriers gorged themselves and sun-dried the surplus meat for use on the remainder of the journey.

I had been given a Fulani grass *bukka* (hut) to sleep in. As accommodation was tight – our party almost outnumbering the permanent residents – Luttu and Hammadu shared this shelter with me. It was much too small for a camp bed, so we bedded down on grass mats, with a smoky fire smouldering all night beside us. As the hut also had to serve as a kitchen for all of us, the combination of flies, smoke and sweat was a novel one.

In the evening my messenger and I borrowed horses from the Fulani and rode up to the highest plateau, Chabbel Hendu. The track was not too steep and the horses were easily able to cope. We found ourselves in a marvellously lush grazing area, as good as any that I had ever seen on Mambilla. It was virgin territory and seemingly very fertile. But it was very remote and I doubted if any Mambilla Fulani, rendered soft by the abandonment of their nomadic way of life, would come here – even with the incentive of reduced taxation.

The next day we made a very early start as we had decided to descend to the plains and attempt to reach Yakuba. The long journey down was made through yet another crashing thunderstorm, and we eventually arrived in Yakuba thoroughly saturated at about 3 pm. But I was exhilarated by my journey to the three plateaux. Very few, if any, Europeans had seen what we had seen and I did not know if any had ever reached Chabbel Hendu before me.

The next trek was going to be very tough and we all knew it. We were to travel through 20 miles of thick, practically uninhabited, bush and climb a quarter of the way up the Mambilla escarpment where a small hamlet would provide a base for our overnight stay.

The going was indeed tough. Our guide lost his way and the path we were attempting to follow was frequently non-existent.

We were cut by sharp elephant grass and soaked by sudden storms. The distance to the escarpment seemed unending – as we advanced it appeared to retreat. About noon we broke from the dense undergrowth on to a grassy plain, where a solitary hunter had constructed a primitive and temporary shelter. He was tanning the hide of a buffalo and told us cheerfully in Fulani that he had secured enough meat for the next six months.

We pressed on through inhospitable, tangled bush, reaching the foothills of the Mambilla escarpment at 4 pm to begin our climb, already thoroughly exhausted after trekking continuously for 12 hours.

Two hours later, as the sun was about to sink below the horizon, we reached our destination, the tiny outlying hamlet of Mayo Sabere. But on arrival, disaster. The Village Head had not had news of our intended arrival, had no food available for the carriers and had prepared no shelter for any of us. More rain was approaching, and there was no possibility of either trekking on or sleeping outside. Luckily Sarkin Yaki's messenger was still with us (we were still in Gashaka District) and he managed to goad the recalcitrant old Village Head into some sort of action. I was concerned for my carriers; they had performed a miracle of trekking and the last thing they needed was an inhospitable welcome. Fortunately they still had their dried Filinga meat, and their bellies were filled with maize flour and gravy provided by the village.[1]

---

1   The route we followed to the Filinga plateaux now runs through a game reserve. The Gashaka-Gumti National Park was gazetted in 1991 and is Nigeria's largest national park. The total area covers about 6,402 km^2. According to the park's guide book:

> There are few other places in the world that contain such spectacular scenery and such diverse wildlife. The hidden corner of West Africa that is Gashaka-Gumti National Park is surely one of the continent's best kept secrets.
>
> It is the sheer variety of different habitats within Gashaka-Gumti National Park that makes the area so uniquely rich in wildlife. In fact the park is actually an intricate mosaic of montane grasslands, savannah woodlands, swamps, lakes, mighty rivers, dark lowland rainforests, and luxuriant, montane rainforests strewn with ferns and orchids. Each habitat supports

The next day Sarkin Yaki's rotund and jovial messenger left us and we set off on the hard climb to the outlying Mambilla village of Dundere. Dundere sat on a tiny plateau abutting onto the side of the Mambilla escarpment, and Ardo Jibo, the Fulani chief of the Karawanko'en clan who held grazing rights surrounding Mayo Ndaga, used it as a dry season grazing area. So at least one enlightened Ardo had accepted the principle that you cannot keep your stock on the same patch of grazing all the year round. The following day we were soon on the rolling downland of Mambilla plateau itself, amidst wild pig and scampering duiker. After a further nine miles along an undulating footpath we entered Mayo Ndaga.

Mayo Ndaga, the large Hausa/Fulani trading settlement on the north-eastern edge of the plateau, was administered by Madawaki, Sarkin Hausawa, a man in his 50s and the proud possessor of a complete set of false teeth. He had once lost all his teeth, but a thoughtful predecessor had had a set of ivories made in England and they appeared to be a superb fit. A small, energetic and fiery little man, who did not suffer fools, he had become a good friend, as also had the Kara. Fortunately for Ardo Jibo, there were not many Mambilla settlements in his area and consequently farmer/grazier disputes were not common.

I spent many hours chatting with both Sarkin Hausawa and Ardo Jibo whenever I visited Mayo Ndaga. On this occasion I

---

its own distinctive community of plants and animals.

Rainforests provide a haven for animals such as the giant forest hog, leopard, yellow-backed duiker, golden cat, and many different primate species including chimpanzees. Woodland savannahs are home to buffalo, lion, elephant, and wild dog, as well as various antelopes such as waterbuck, Roan antelope, kob, hartebeest and the world's largest antelope, the giant eland. The mountains of the park harbour populations of the rare Adamawa mountain reedbuck, in addition to black-and-white colobus monkey, baboon, warthog, oribi, and klipspringer. Whilst its largest unspoilt rivers contain hippos, crocodiles, otters and a wide variety of fishes.

The park is officially labelled as one of Africa's 'Important Bird Areas' – and with more than 500 species found here, this is certainly no exaggeration. Visiting bird watchers constantly add new species to the list. An additional abundance of creatures such as butterflies, flowers and trees, makes this park a naturalists' paradise, unrivalled anywhere for diversity.

learnt for the first time that Damburam, the new District Head of Mambilla, was trying to discredit the Madawaki and have him dismissed. In 1939, Damburam's father, Munsuru, had tried to seize the District Headship of Mambilla by force. Madawaki Sarkin Hausawa had been the Village Head at that time and helped to thwart his claim. Damburam was bent on revenge, but I felt that this energetic little man was, for the moment, capable of looking after himself.

In front of the steeply pitched grass-roofed, mud resthouse was a large open area, ideally suited either for racing horses or for dancing. That night, as a celebration for our safe return from Filinga, Sarkin Hausawa and Ardo Jibo organised a *wasa*. By nine o'clock a tremendous party was underway. The Fulani girls of Mayo Ndaga were particularly beautiful with straight black hair and very light skinned. Some could have passed as coming from the Levant. One particularly graceful girl caught my eye and we danced opposite each other for a long time doing the slow shuffling dance of the nomadic Fulani.

After the dancing had finished Hammadu left to ask whether she would come to my resthouse. He returned some time later to tell me that she was Ardo Jibo's youngest wife, but that nevertheless she would come. I waited and waited and in the very early hours abandoned all hope. The next morning I commented on the fact that she had never appeared. 'She did,' Hammadu replied, 'but you were asleep and we did not want to disturb you.'

The next day we double-trekked the 22 miles back to Gembu.

13

The River Donga and the Southern Divide

The River Donga bisects the Mambilla plateau in almost two equal parts, rising in the mountainous area that straddles the international border to the east. For a few miles it forms part of this international border between Nigeria and the Cameroon Republic, and then flows north-west, eventually to merge with the mighty River Benue. To reach the southern half of Mambilla, where the southern Mambilla and Kaka tribes live in roughly equal proportion, the River Donga has to be crossed.

From the front windows of my house perched on a hill at 5,200 feet, I could look down on the Donga, some 3,000 feet below. On a typical morning in the rainy season the valley would be filled with fluffy, thick white cloud resembling snow. Slowly the cloud would lift until by 11 o'clock in the morning the river was visible again. But the mood of the weather could change rapidly, and I once watched as forked lightning from a heavy jet-black thundercloud chased two vivid rainbows up the riverbed.

The river flowed brown and muddy even in the years of drought, but at the height of the rains, from May to September, the water would often be fast and dangerously deep. To ford the river during this period, horses would have to be swum across to the other side. The helmsman of the canoe that carried us had to gauge carefully the strength of the current and the potential drag of up to three horses swimming beside his craft. Horses can swim quite naturally when out of their depth, and for the crossing they were held only by a rope attached to their head collars. In spite of having to make these hazardous crossings many times in a year, neither my loads, my carriers nor myself were ever tipped into the Donga.

The Kaka villages of Ndumyaji, Warkaka and Sakaka are situated on the south-western slopes of Mambilla and face the plateau of Bamenda in the Cameroon Republic. Most of the Kaka tribe live on Bamenda, having been divided, like so many other tribal groups in Africa, when the international border was delineated arbitrarily in 1923.[1] As Bamenda was more accessible, a high level of mission activity there had given the Kaka on that plateau the opportunity to learn building skills, such as carpentry and stone masonry. As a result, most of the contractors and building artisans employed by the Gashaka-Mambilla Native Authority were Kaka. The village of Ndumyaji had also produced one of the Native Authority's ablest councillors, Musa Ndumyaji, whose portfolio included courts, police and prisons. In 1972 Musa became the first person from the plateau to visit England, and he stayed at my home in Hampshire.

It was easy to understand why the Kaka had taken so readily to construction work, for their own houses were very well built – round yet large and constructed with a tightly woven frame of supple but strong sticks and vines infilled with mud and straw. A circular thatch, again tightly woven, was made separately on the

1   Nigeria Cameroon International Boundary.
There has been consistent trouble over the past two decades [1990–2011] between Nigeria and the Cameroon Republic over their international border – in Nigeria in the north near Lake Chad and in Cameroon in an oil-rich area known as the Bakassi Peninsula. Fortunately the line south of Lake Chad to Mambilla, which I helped to demarcate before the territory became independent, has not been under dispute.
On 22nd November 2011 the Secretary-General of the United Nations congratulated both countries on reaching agreement in these two hotly disputed areas. The judgment agreed had been made at the International Court of Justice at The Hague, so this has been no trivial dispute. I was fortunate my amateur attempts at settling disputes on the border in the 1960s had not been called into question.

ground and once completed was lifted on to the rim of the house.

Kaka villages were spread out on steep yet lush slopes in beautiful countryside some 2,000 feet below the edge of the escarpment, and as a result marauding Fulani cattle did not trouble the inhabitants. This was the main reason for their easier relationship with the Fulani compared to that of the Mambilla with the Fulani. At the height of the rains these grassy slopes would be covered with exotic wild flowers, which included species of lilies, fritillaries and gladioli. I wondered whether some of these had yet to be classified by botanists.

The Kaka villagers' only real problems concerned medicine and baboons. Baboons and monkeys were always raiding their farms and I was always being begged to shoot them. Not having a gun, I never did. The medical problems were acute and of greater concern to me, there being no dispensary in any of the three villages and the climb to Gembu a stiff one for an ailing patient. Measles was a great scourge of young children and seemed to be particularly prevalent in this south-west corner. Sadly when an epidemic occurred there was little that either myself or the Native Authority could do.

Getting hold of a regular supply of medicines on the plateau was a perennial headache. They had to come from Jos nearly 600 miles away and the problems of head-loading supplies in all weathers and the difficulty in obtaining them in the first place often made for acute shortages of even the most basic drugs. During my stay of nearly four years we had a visit from only one doctor. This was Dr Crkvenac, the resolute Yugoslav who, though known to be a very competent bush doctor, was also thought to be more attracted to our remote outpost by the possibility of shooting Mambilla's dwindling wildlife.

It was eventually agreed to build a hospital to serve the area, but much to our dismay it was sited at Ganye, 100 miles to the north of the Mambilla plateau, hardly an improvement on the existing situation. I always carried with me a box of medicine as I had been given some basic training in administering injections and simple medicines by a doctor in Mubi. After the day's work was over I would often sit and try to treat the most terrible ulcers, wounds and suppurating sores. Although I could usually provide only aspirin for a raging fever or worse, this could work wonders. The fact that the little white pill had come from my medicine box was often enough to initiate a psychological cure – and there was always the medicinal yeast for the chief or greybeard who needed a boost to promote matrimonial satisfaction.

Partly to ensure I had slept in every Mambilla and Fulani settlement on the plateau, I determined to visit the two outlying Kaka villages of Inkiri and Antere. They were situated on the banks of the River Donga in lush rain forest and were reached by trekking south from Leme and climbing 5,000 feet down the steep-sided escarpment. Once at the foot of it there was a 12-mile trek to Antere through thick rain forest.

The route was criss-crossed by streams over which the Kaka had built a series of suspension bridges. These suspension bridges, a building speciality of the Kaka, were cleverly constructed from twisted vines and suspended from overhanging trees. Just below the village of Antere one had been suspended across the Donga stretching for at least 150 yards – it was an engineering masterpiece. I crossed over it and into Cameroon, the muddy water of the Donga threshing through boulders and rocks beneath me.

The two villages were very remote and had not been visited by anyone for many years. Consequently there were many young adults who had never seen a white skin and they clustered around me trying to touch my skin and stroke the hair on my arms and legs. The Village Head of Antere, a man of great character, was a cured leper. His face was deeply lined, his teeth neatly filed (in former days a sign of cannibalism) and he had a wide grin and ready laugh. Though trusted and respected by his people, he was also greatly feared for it was commonly believed that he could change into a leopard at will.

Transmogrification, or *rikida* as it is called in Hausa, is a commonly held belief throughout Nigeria. I was told the story of a European tin miner who lived among the Bokkos, a pagan tribe on the Jos plateau who had a great reputation for *rikida*. The area around the miner's camp was plagued by hyenas and by one in particular, which boldly used to howl outside his house. In desperation he set a trap for the animal and one night an intense and continual howling assured him that he had successfully caught his tormentor. The next morning he was amazed to find a sturdy Bokkos pagan firmly caught by the leg in his trap.

A C C Hastings recounted a similar extraordinary tale in his book *Nigerian Days*:

> A friend and I had set a spring-gun trap and a dead village dog as bait to get a particularly troublesome hyena who had been stealing goats at night. In the middle of dinner we heard the gun go off and seizing our revolvers and a lamp apiece, dashed out to have a look. The bait still lay there, with teeth marks in the head, but close to him was a pool of blood and a piece of jaw lying near. From the tall guinea-corn farm in front we heard a moaning sound which told us a hyena was wounded in there, and following the noise we dived into the stalks to get him. This was our mistake, for, as I learned afterwards and I believe is quite true, hyenas are in a sense ventriloquial and can make their howl come from another point than where they actually are. We searched a long time, hearing the mournful howl coming from this quarter and that until it died away, and we lost him altogether.
>
> The sequel to this was rather weird. Next day I heard a certain villager, well known to be a wizard, had been seen returning in the dawn, his jaw bound up in a bloodstained rag and looking very sick. He died before the sun went down, and all the village rejoiced because that dreaded hyena man would trouble them no more, saying how fortunate it was that he had been attracted by the dog bait before he went on to catch a human being.

Although I asked the Chief of Antere to show me how he accomplished the unusual feat of transmogrifying into a leopard, he politely declined. He did however, in common with the Chief of Inkiri, have a problem with his tax collection, and my presence in both these villages helped to bring in some outstanding cash. At the time I met the Chief of Antere he boasted nine wives, and as I stayed in one of the huts in his compound, his extended family, plus innumerable goats, chickens and ducks provided me with a lively time.

In contrast, the Village Head of Inkiri was dour and unsmiling. His main source of pride and prestige was that a relative was the Gashaka-Mambilla schools' manager. It was difficult to make much headway with any conversation, so after the business of the day was done, I asked him to call up the Inkiri drummers and dancers. The evening was spent jigging with the Kaka, watched in amazement by my solemn host. Neither the Fulani nor the food shortages affected these two Kaka villages, and the villagers' lives were contented and trouble-free.

The southern divide of the River Donga also contains a number of Mambilla villages in addition to those of the Kaka. Here, historically, their tough women wore absolutely nothing at all except a colourful string of beads, which was remarkable in their cold, damp climate. In addition, the temperament of these southern villagers was fiery and more virile than that of the more docile Mambilla who lived on the northern divide. This can be partially explained by the fact that the Mambilla have no common title for themselves and were divided into numerous groups or clans. Each village group called itself by the name of its locality or by that of the village founder or of some especially distinguished chief. There was, and is, no tribal organisation, and a next-door neighbouring villager was frequently a principal enemy in spite of intermarriage. Paradoxically, intermarriage commonly created hostility. A Mambilla, if asked who his traditional enemies were, would answer: 'The member of such-and-such a village for we marry their daughters and they marry ours.'

The Mambilla, on the southern divide, had become skilful farmers with a staple diet of maize supplemented by sweet potatoes, pumpkins and groundnuts. The introduction of coffee by the agricultural department as a cash crop was a major boost to their income. The Mambilla also grew a legume which they called *yom*. This was harvested when six feet tall and the stem used for firewood, invaluable on the treeless plateau.

The Mambilla excelled at basketwork. They were not head-load carriers, hence my need to import carriers from far afield. But they wove a strong and utilitarian basket that was supported with a strap around the forehead. Their corn bins were also made from basketwork rather than mud. These cylindrical baskets were woven over a framework of poles and bark and could be anything up to six feet high, topped with a neatly woven lid. Baskets were so tightly woven that they could also be used to hold fermenting beer. There was an even more elaborate form of corn bin, the lower section containing tools and cooking utensils, the upper section being a tightly woven corn store with a hinged roof.

One of the nearest Mambilla villages to the south-west of the River Donga was called Mbamga, where a young and truculent mission-educated chief called Peter embodied all the fiery spirit of these southern villages. He challenged me on every political development no matter how trivial and sent an endless stream of letters of complaint to my office in Gembu.

From Mbamga village there were alternative routes to the villages of Tamnya and Bang. Tamnya had a dilapidated and leaky, jigger-ridden resthouse perched on a hill some way from the village. The view from this hillock to the plains of the Cameroon Republic was quite awe-inspiring, the plains often acquiring a blue tinge as if reflecting the sky. Ardo Adamu, the best of the Fulani Rahaji Ardo'en or Chiefs, had control of the grazing in the surrounding area and plied me with welcome hot milk when the resthouse roof was letting in basinfuls of water.

From Tamnya I followed the escarpment edge to Hainari and the Hausa settlement of Dorofi. The track would then cut north-east towards Chabbel Zance, the Ardo'ate of the largest cattle owner on the plateau, Jauro Bello, who despite his vast herd of over 2,000 head lived in great simplicity. His house was of primitive construction, his apparel quite unostentatious. It was a popular call for my carriers as a bullock was usually slaughtered in honour of our visit.

Jauro Bello eschewed politics being completely apolitical, and as there were few Mambilla settlements in his area he avoided the common complaints raised against most of his fellow Ardo'en. But his cousin, Daudu Wawu, who lived close by, was very different. He had engineered a mass migration of the clan's 77 herds – some 8,000 cattle – from neighbouring Cameroon in 1941 to avoid a levy of forced mining labour by the French authorities. This was before the ban on bringing new herds up onto Mambilla came into force. The Emir of Banyo was incensed and wrote to his brother Emir across the border in Yola asking to have Daudu Wawu extradited. As a sweetener the Emir of Banyo offered the Emir of Yola 1,000 head of cattle. But the Lamido of Adamawa in Yola, happy with the prospect of extra revenue from cattle tax, took no action and the Emir of Banyo had to be content with the imprisonment of Daudu Wawu's kinsman, Jauro Dewa, who had remained behind but whom he felt was implicated in the plot.

But of all the southern Mambilla villages the one that remains fixed in my mind to this day is Mbar, along with its highly volatile Village Head and his notorious son, Yaji. Yaji Mbar had been the trusted adviser and confidant of Audu Baju, the late District Head. It was Yaji who had knocked on my door the morning after Audu's untimely death. Not unnaturally his star had been in steep decline after the Fulani Damburam was appointed Mambilla's District Head. Yaji's services as a retainer were rapidly dispensed with, he turned to petty crime and was jailed for theft. On his release from prison he produced a piece of paper purporting to show that he had been an official Native Authority employee. It confirmed that during the time of Audu's tenure as District Head, Yaji had filled the position of Native Authority Messenger, and he therefore appealed in court that his dismissal after Damburam attained office was illegal. He entered a petition of wrongful dismissal and a claim for arrears of salary and compensation for dismissal without notice. To the amazement of many he won his case. My review of the proceedings could find no fault with the judgment.

At exactly this time the position of District Council representative for Mbar fell vacant. A by-election was to be held and the eligibility for candidature stipulated that one had to be born in the Mbar village area and to have been a tax-payer to the Village Head for the previous two years or to have been a Native Authority employee. The court had ruled in Yaji's favour on the latter count, and as he had been born in the area and paid his taxes he was able to put forward his candidature.

Damburam was horrified, for Yaji was an implacable opponent. By gaining a seat on the District Council he could in theory get himself elected to the Native Authority council itself. If he achieved that status, he could become a powerful and hostile troublemaker. The Damburam camp was scandalised. But legally Yaji Mbar was in the right and his name went forward as a candidate.

The matter was complicated further by the character of the Village Head of Mbar and the fact that his son was the opposing candidate. The Chief of Mbar was tyrannical, hot-headed and unpredictable. As Yaji owed no allegiance to the Village Head and had had his own reputation vindicated, his opposition became a catalyst for discontented villagers. At the first attempt at voting, the Village Head concealed a small boy in the matting roof of the polling station from where he could see into which box ballot papers were put. As the voters entered the boy forcefully reminded them of the fate awaiting them if they voted in opposition to the chief. Meanwhile, Yaji had persuaded non-registered people to cast votes for him. The whole proceedings became so chaotic that the election was declared null and void. Tension in the area was by now so high that I realised I would have to supervise the election proceedings in person, so I headed across the River Donga for Mbar.

The village comprised a scattered group of compounds rather than a coherent unit. There was no resthouse and I reluctantly had to stay in the entrance hut, *zaure*, to the Village Head's house.

Polling day dawned wet and foggy. Yaji insisted on a rigorous inspection of the polling booth and I poked at the matted enclosure with a sharp stick to make sure no spy from the opposition camp was concealed there. When everyone was convinced that the dilapidated structure was spy-free, voting began punctually at

173

eight o'clock. As it did the heavens opened and within no time ballot papers and voters were sodden. Ink smudged, tempers rose, both sides tried to introduce bogus voters. These were painstakingly weeded out and the wet and bedraggled queue of sullen voters filed slowly into the polling booth.

Initially, the Village Head's supporters outnumbered Yaji's and by mid-morning his son was clearly in the lead. But as the day wore on and more and more legitimate Yaji supporters turned up, the Chief of Mbar's temper started to rise. After I had turned away a voter who was attempting to vote twice for Yaji's opponent, the explosion occurred. With a great roar, the Village Head leapt up from his chair at the entrance to the polling booth and ran towards his house, followed by a soaked and motley group of supporters. The voting continued. The rain fell. An hour later the Village Head returned, smelling strongly of drink and without a word to me resumed his seat. Then at 4.30 pm, as the last voter in the line cast his vote, he suggested that we should start the count. 'No one will come now,' he said. 'We are just wasting our time sitting out here in the pouring rain.' Had I agreed to this suggestion the election could once again have been declared null and void because the official time to close the poll was 5.30 pm. We sat in silence in the mist and rain – no further voter appeared. At 5.30 the mist lifted and, for the first time that day, the sun shone.

By now, a large and excitable crowd of Mbar villagers had gathered outside the polling station to watch the count take place. Many had been well primed themselves with powerful locally brewed corn beer. The political temperature was rising rapidly. Our polling booth had been constructed on a small hill away from the scattered compounds and about half a mile away from the market place. I realised that to start the count under the eyes of this potentially explosive mob was to invite disaster, so I told them that the count would not begin until they had all moved away to the market. They realised that I meant exactly what I said and started to drift away with muttered threats. When they were finally gathered in the market place the count began, watched by the candidates and two each of their supporters.

The Village Head's candidate's box was the first to be opened. His final tally was 151 and although this was respectable everyone knew that Yaji Mbar had won. The Village Head said nothing but as we began to count Yaji's dank and sodden ballot papers the tension grew. When Yaji's total passed 151, the Village Head jumped up in an uncontrollable rage, grabbed the Nigerian flag and ran with it into his house. The flag was always carried on tour and erected on a makeshift pole outside the place where I was staying, a colonial practice that had been continued by the Nigerian government after independence when it had replaced the Union Jack. We stolidly counted on until the final slip confirmed the total of votes cast for Yaji as 222. But before we reached that figure a deep-throated roar of approval rose up from the market place. As far as the villagers were concerned, their man had won, and it emerged that many who had voted for Yaji's opponent had done so through fear of the Chief of Mbar.

After the appropriate forms had been filled in and the result officially declared, I retired to the Chief's compound. Neither the Chief nor my flag was to be seen, and a cow that had been tethered outside my hut for slaughter in celebration of a win for the Chief's son was quietly led away to enjoy an unexpected lease of life. The next morning my flag was returned, and the volatile despot of Mbar appeared and chatted to me as if nothing untoward had happened. Yaji's extraordinary career was rejuvenated and Damburam was confronted once more with a formidable opponent. Yaji Mbar's appeal in court and subsequent election generated a great deal of comment on the plateau, but the facts were clear – Yaji had legally and rightfully been elected. However, my relationship with Damburam was not improved.

Shortly after these electoral high jinks I became preoccupied with a much more serious problem which occurred in the southern divide. The Mambilla had formerly practised trial by ordeal. This involved giving both complainant and accused a mixture containing the bark of the sasswood tree. If drunk, this highly toxic substance rapidly caused death unless it was vomited out of the system. Captain Izard, a British administrator in the 1920s, had persuaded the Mambilla to abandon the practice and instead administer the concoction to cockerels, the death of a cockerel proclaiming the owner's guilt. But with the attainment of independence, the tribal elders believed that their former custom could legally be revived. This is what independence meant to them – a reversion to the habits and customs that the British administration had banned.

The revival of trial by ordeal must have been going on secretly for about 18 months before it finally came to light. In part its reappearance was due to a Native Authority councillor having, for an appropriate fee, given permission for the custom to be revived. But a relative of someone who had died from the poison came to me and complained. The whole practice then came out into the open.

There were two gruesome cases, both of which had been presided over by an old man called Luludinku. In the first, seven people had died, four of them dropping dead by the side of the track as they made their way home. In the second, three people had complained against another that the accused had put a spell on a child who had recently died. The three complainants drank the poison and within minutes were dead. The accused vomited up the sasswood and lived.

After the cases came to light I held a preliminary inquiry to see if a charge of murder had to be answered. If this appeared to be the case then the accused would be sent for trial to the High Court at Jos. Luludinku appeared to be the culprit. Pathetically he pleaded the cause of Nigerian independence and the fact that the unscrupulous councillor had given him permission to resurrect the former tribal custom. The case was referred to Jos and Luludinku was hanged. The councillor was given a short term of imprisonment. Justice was not done. The two sentences should have been reversed.

During the preliminary inquiry, Luludinku had to be sworn on oath. The Mambilla method of swearing in a witness was achieved by striking an iron gong, shaped like testicles and the size of a hand-bell which was used for oath taking before evidence was given. The Mambilla were much in awe of this simple instrument and it was also used during ceremonies held for the installation of their chiefs.

Before finishing this account of the fiery and war-like Mambilla who lived with the Kaka on the southern divide, it is worth recording their traditional drinking and eating habits. Their three main festivals were held at the time of crop sowing, harvesting and the opening of the first corn store when, in common with many other pagan tribes, great quantities of beer would be drunk. Formerly, in the case of the Mambilla, it would have washed down a great deal of human flesh. In 1931 the anthropologist C K Meek wrote:

> All the Mambilla groups were cannibal until recently, and most of them would be cannibal still were it not for fear of the Administration. They ate the flesh of their enemies killed in war, and among their enemies might be members of a neighbouring village with whom they had intermarried when at peace. Thus it might happen that a man would kill and eat one of his own relatives. Instances have been reported of a man killing and eating his wife's brother during an affray between two villages. But it was stated that if a man killed and ate his father-in-law, he would fall ill and die. There is evidence, too, that these groups sometimes sold their own dead for food.
>
> Religious ideas were not prominent in the cannibal ideas of the Mambilla. Tribesmen who were unwilling to answer questions stated clearly that they ate human flesh purely as meat. When they killed an enemy, they cut pieces off his body and ate them raw, in situ, without any formalities. Pieces were taken home and given to the old men, who ate them from sheer lust of flesh. In such cases the flesh might be eaten raw or cooked. Even the intestines were eaten, being ripped up, cleaned and boiled.
>
> On the other hand, it was stated that young men were compelled to eat in order to become brave, the conception being, apparently, that by eating the flesh of a slain warrior they absorbed his courage. The skulls of enemies were preserved, and when the young men first went to war they were made to drink beer and a certain medicine from one of the skulls, with a view to making them fearless. Women, however, were not permitted to

eat human flesh, and it was not permissible for married men to eat the flesh of women who had been killed during an attack on a village. But wifeless old men might eat the flesh of women with impunity.

The Mambilla had, when I lived among them, transferred this liking for human flesh to the flesh of dogs. On being asked why so many dogs were kept in a compound, the Mambilla owner replied that they bred so much better than goats. At least dogs, unlike shoats (sheep and goats), did not contribute to Mambilla's huge problem of soil erosion.

14

Journey's End

Frightful rotters, the British, absolutely satanic. Don't know what we
should do without them. Who are we going to blame after they leave?
Balachandra Rajan, *The Dark Dancer*

Although my life on Mambilla was utterly absorbing and
followed no set hours, there were long periods when I was
entirely on my own. At one stage I did not see a white face for
over six months. Not everyone, whether in their 20s or older, can
cope with isolation from their own tribe for such a long time. I
was keenly interested in the people on Mambilla, their problems
and their conflicts, but I was fully aware that undue familiarity
would lead to more than contempt. It would destroy authority,
especially if through untoward familiarity it was thought I
favoured one tribe over another. For these and other obvious
reasons I had to find non-addictive diversions, which would
keep my sanity intact without impinging on my authority. It was
a delicate balance and a very thin line was trod. Loneliness had to
be confronted and overcome – without 'going native'.

There were a few people with whom I could relax and discuss
the parish-pump politics of the plateau. One in particular was
Malam Dodo Mallumfashi, the resident veterinary officer, who
was a Hausa from Katsina Province. Malam Dodo was greatly
respected by Fulani and Mambilla alike. Quiet and unassuming,

he studiously avoided involvement in the inflammable Mambilla politics.

A relaxed chat in my house with either Fulani, Mambilla or Kaka friends would have excited the unscrupulous to hint at intrigue. So for the most part, a visitor of this kind had to be an outsider. One such was Malam Ibrahim, a mechanic who after repairing my wireless came back on numerous occasions to chat. We talked at length about the habits of the Fulani, and he told me the following story, which he had personally experienced. When passing through Gombe he had invited a beautiful young Fulani girl to visit him at night. The girl, who was married, arrived and they lay down together. Suddenly, in Malam Ibrahim's words, 'There was a flurry of feathers and a loud squawking. The "girl" ran out of the hut in the guise of a chicken.' The husband, so he believed, had detected her whereabouts and manipulated the change. Malam Ibrahim told me that he had never been so shaken in his life. I could believe him.

Then there was Malam Sidi, who was an itinerant Arab from the Niger Republic. The remote Mambilla *cul-de-sac* attracted many such travellers from other parts of Nigeria and beyond, some of whom came to exploit the unsophisticated, others to escape justice. Whether Malam Sidi was on the run I never learnt, but he was soon attempting to exploit the unsophisticated Fulani herdsmen. He would frequently arrive at my house on a Sunday morning for a chat. I did not discourage him, as he was totally apolitical as far as the cut-throat politics and tribal intriguing of the plateau were concerned. Our conversations ranged widely and included instruction on the intricacies of Islam; he even taught me how to perform the ritual ablutions correctly. He had the unfortunate habit of clearing his throat with a hawking rasp, lifting up the corner of my carpet, and depositing his spittle beneath it. Protestations were in vain. He apologised, forgot himself, and did it again.

His exploitation of the gullible Fulani herdsman took the form of *buga kasa*, best described as divination in the dust. I believe it involves drawing circles with one's forefinger in the sand, throwing in twigs, and reading the signs, rather like reading tea leaves. The Fulani would pay to be told when they should undertake a journey, what day was auspicious for making approaches to a girlfriend or her parents and whether or not the outcome of their advances would prove successful. However, there were rumblings that not only was Sidi overcharging, but that his forecasts were proving worthless. I thought of a scheme to try to dissuade him from continuing.

On one of his Sunday visits I asked him to show me the upturned palm of his right hand. Studying it intently, I remarked that he must be aware that the lines were etched by Allah himself. He was.

'But are you aware that some people have the gift to read these lines of Allah and to foretell what future lies in store?' He was not aware of this.

'Sidi,' I continued seriously, 'I have that gift.'

'I believe you told me that you have just married a beautiful, young Fulani wife.' He nodded. 'Unfortunately, Sidi, in a little while she is going to run away.' He looked at me in alarm. 'But she will return.' A sigh of relief. 'Then, less than a month later, she will run away again.' Utter consternation. 'She will never return.'

'And then?' he enquired anxiously.

'No, nothing.' I do not know to this day what made me say this.

'Is there nothing that I can do to prevent this happening?'

I looked up and released his palm. 'Give up practising *buga kasa*,' I replied.

'I will, I will,' he responded fervently.

But he didn't, and the strange thing is that everything happened just as I had foretold. First the young girl ran away and then returned. Then, two weeks later, she ran away a second time and he never saw her again. On this second occasion I was trekking towards Lekitaba when Messenger Abba saw a horseman pursing us at full gallop, his gown billowing behind him in the wind. It was Sidi, turban askew.

'Bring her back, please, bring her back,' he pleaded.

'Stop the *buga kasa*,' I replied and this time he did – but she didn't return.

Apart from casual visitors there were other distractions. A predecessor had started the Mambilla Turf Club, which he had unsuccessfully attempted to have registered with the Jockey Club in Britain. This club organised races for the Fulani horsemen at which there was a tote. Race day was held near the Senior Primary School three times a year and was often combined with children's sports, Mambilla wrestling, mock fighting with shields and spears and of course, dancing. It was the dancing that really kept me sane.

I had been apprenticed under Mac's tutelage and was now a past master at gauging the political temperature of the dancers. But on Mambilla, with the great animosity between the Mambilla and the Fulani, one had to be particularly sensitive. If the Fulani were called to the house more frequently than the Mambilla, prejudice was assumed. I tried hard to ring the changes.

The nomadic Fulani's dance was a slow shuffle, the men and women rotating round each other sedately and in separate lines. The music was provided by hour-glass-shaped drums with either two or three drummers, one of whom was a 'caller' who would sing to the rhythm of the drum. Nowhere on the plateau were there drummers to touch my three good friends from Hainari and Dorofi on the edge of the southern escarpment: Peuri ('the one who was born on a cold night'), Hari ('the one who was born on a windy night') and Sambo. These three virtuosos were magnificent and whenever I travelled to Hainari or Dorofi the evening was always enlivened with whirlwind drumming and dancing. Ardo Musa, the dour Rahaji Muslim, whose cattle roamed the area, did not really approve of the festivities, but in contrast the Village Head of Hainari was a great supporter.

The 'town' Fulani, together with the resident Hausa, would come to perform the dances of Adamawa; the Mambilla alternated with the Fulani, jigging and jogging to the throbbing beat of their large drums. But nothing could rival the mastery of my three friends from the south of the plateau.

One evening, bored and lonely, I put on a Hausa robe and turban, rubbed my face with brick-coloured earth, and with Hammadu walking in front and carrying a dimly lit bush-lamp, wandered down the hill towards Gembu market. Hausa dancing was taking place and I sat in the shadow of a *zaure* watching the dancing and listening to the conversation round about me.

'Who is that?' I heard one man ask his companion.

'A stranger,' came the reply. 'I have never seen him before.'

This moment of tension passed and I returned to my house some two hours later with my disguise intact.

Roy James David, a young Kaka who ran the Gembu postal agency, was another colourful character. His actual name was Gutuk Ndumyaji, but since acquiring the elevated station of postal agent he thought that this tribal name was inappropriate so he bestowed on himself three new names. Before his appointment Gutuk had been sent on a clerical course. He had failed the course but his eyes had been opened to the wonders of the outside world. The course had been held in Kaduna, where streets were named and houses numbered. On his return he set about rectifying Gembu's backward situation by naming its streets and numbering the houses, 'to improve postal facilities'. He named his modest mud hut 'Charity Gardens' and sited it in 'Essenbury 5, Gembu, NW1'.

He had also noted in Kaduna that by writing to organisations and individuals around the world most unexpected benefits could result. He consequently became heavily involved in correspondence with Israelis, American cosmetic manufacturers, Buddhists and publishers. One old and well-respected publishing house in England unwittingly became engaged in a lengthy correspondence with Roy James A David, the Prior of Morrigan, Gembu, who was, at the time of writing, 'looking forward very keenly to be seeing your efforts for my prior [sic] convenience'.

He discovered *Whitaker's Almanack*. The Grand Order of the Knights of St John most sincerely regretted that they did not have a vacancy in their ranks for the illustrious Prior. The Very Reverend Pastor James A David was unable to find the sponsors he needed to propose him for membership of the Marylebone Cricket Club. Unfortunately Herr Krupp did not reply to the offer to form a joint venture partnership in bicycle spare parts on Mambilla.

For some reason Roy James David became obsessed with Mussolini and all that he had stood for. This unhealthy influence led to his demise, for shortly afterwards he helped himself to the petty cash and sadly spent a brief spell in Gembu prison. But although he lost his position with the Native Authority he retained his sense of humour and his interest in writing to the world at large, much to my continual amusement.

Although James did not write the following, he could well have done so as his style of writing was exactly the same. This letter was in fact received by a fellow District Officer:

To the District Officer, King, Sir,

On opening this epistle you will behold the work of a dejobbed person and a very much childenised gentleman. Who was violently dejobbed in a twinkling by your goodself. For heaven's sake, Sir, consider this catastrophe as falling on your own head, and remind yourself as walking home at the moon's end of five savage wives and sixteen voracious children with your pocket filled with non-existent cash. Not a solitudery sixpence, pity my horrible state. When being dejobbed and proceeding with a heart and intestines filled with misery to this den of doom myself did greedily contemplate culpable homicide, but Him who protected Daniel (poet) safely through the lion's den will protect his servant in the home of evil. As to reason given by yourself esquire for my dejobbment the incrimination was laziness.

NO SIR. It were impossible that myself who has pitched sixteen infant children into this valley of tears can have a lazy atom in his mortal frame, and the sudden departure of eleven pounds monthly has left me on the verge of the abyss of destitution and despair. I hope this vision of horror will enrich your dreams this night, and good Angel will meet and pulverise your heart of nether Milestone so that you will awaken and with as much alacrity as may be compatible with your personal safety, and you will hasten to rejobulate your servant. So mote it be, Amen.

Yours despairfully,

Subusu

Note by District Officer:

Gentle Reader, do not sob:
Subusu, has been rejob.

One Armistice Day we organised a Remembrance Service. A motley crew of Native Authority policemen in their fezzes and shorts were lined up on the football pitch outside Damburam's house. At 11 o'clock sharp the large piece of metal suspended outside the prison was struck 11 times. Resplendent in my official white uniform, I called the 15 members of the guard to attention, Wilkinson sword at the ready. My horse stood perfectly still. Two minutes later I intoned '*Za mu tuna su*' ('We will remember them') in a sonorous voice. '*Za mu tuna su,*' came the deep-throated and well-rehearsed response. In such ways, I suppose, I retained my sanity.

I shaved every day, convinced that if I let that discipline go I was on a slippery path. I was lucky with my health although I broke my wrist in Tula when my horse put its foot in a hole. This meant a drive to Jos to have it re-set, then after that two-day journey it had to be re-broken by the doctor. Some months later, I had to return to Jos hospital for two weeks to recover from jaundice, which had resulted from a dirty needle after an injection for polio. On Mambilla I was perfectly healthy except for one bad attack of malaria which was entirely my own fault. These were the only medical problems in nearly eight years – I was lucky.

One personal absorption was the building of the new Gembu court house. The old mud-built building was very dilapidated and as a goodwill gesture the British government had made a grant of £4,000 to build a new one. It was clear that a reasonably substantial and permanent building could be erected for half that sum and the balance put towards much-needed dispensaries. The answer from on high was unequivocal. The court house must be built for the sum which had been officially designated.

On hearing this, I decided to turn myself into an architect. If they wanted a splendid folly, then they would have one. But I quickly discovered that while I was able to draw a ground plan incorporating two courts, rooms for Muslim women plaintiffs, a wide protective veranda, a huge central arch and a spiral staircase to nowhere in particular, I could not readily gauge the height. So, as the hand-knapped stone walls rose on their substantial foundations I would visit the site daily to try to estimate the eventual height of the central arch. My eye was the judge; the Kaka contractor, long-suffering. The supporting walls rose higher and higher until at last the visual aspect seemed just right. 'Put it there,' I commanded, and there it was put. Turrets and gargoyles were constructed to siphon water from a concealed roof. The building was magnificent and the Native Authority was mightily pleased. At least they were until the rains came in earnest.

Unfortunately, the gargoyles could not cope with the volume of water that collected on top of the concealed roof and quickly found its way down the newly painted inside walls The court officials officiated in pools of water and the splendid new building was soon leaking like a classic sieve. The 'architect' was called in. Reluctantly the gargoyles knocked down and the roof re-built with a much steeper pitch. The turreted wall to the rear of the building was also demolished so that the water could run freely off the roof. But this alteration was concealed by the turreted wall above the magnificent frontal arch, and I hope the Gembu court house still stands proudly to this day.

My house was never locked, and a thief would have found no difficulty in entering. One evening when I was in bed, Sally, my bull-terrier bitch, who was with me in the bedroom, gave an unusually sharp bark. I thought no more of it until the next morning when I found that my locked metal cash tank in the sitting room, which contained my petty cash and the carriers' wages, was missing. It had been stolen. The uproar and outrage were extreme. Never in the history of Mambilla had such a thing happened. The police cast about and Malam Sidi cast spells but the culprit was never discovered, although the battered cash tank was later found near the foot of the escarpment.

The demarcation of the grazing areas gradually progressed as did the road, under the enthusiastic leadership of army officer Charlesworth. Willing village communal labour had nearly completed a through track from Gembu to Mai Samari and Charlesworth was using his impressive engineering skills to tackle the escarpment itself. My feelings remained mixed. I knew that the road was both wanted and needed, yet my romantic nature rebelled against the violation of the isolated splendour of Mambilla.

In 1963, the Nigerian census took place. This highly emotive exercise was of crucial importance to the government. Seats in the Federal House of Parliament in Lagos were allocated on a regional basis and the size of the population determined the number of constituencies. The exercise was much more complicated than the numerous elections in which I had been involved, for we were counting not only men, women and children but Muslim women as well, which involved taking into account delicate religious susceptibilities. The census form also provided for the count of all livestock from cattle to chickens. I undertook this difficult operation as best I could. We checked and rechecked the data as it came in. With no roads in the 550 square miles of scattered hamlets and nomadic Fulani compounds, it was a long and time-consuming process. Remote areas such as Filinga had to be tramped over by some reluctant volunteer.

At last, after many weeks, the result was reached and the information was passed to Kaduna. One of the statistics produced was that there were 88,532 males of voting age. Some weeks later a letter of thanks was received from the Sardauna's office for a job well done. In it I was informed that my total had been increased to 143,000 males. I then knew that it was time to leave. Although the Sardauna asked me to reconsider, as he would like me to remain on Mambilla, I knew I could not stay.

And so, in November 1963 I sadly and reluctantly left Mambilla for the very last time. More than 50 horsemen accompanied me on the journey to Mai Samari, including the District Head Damburam, who I am certain was not sorry to see me leave. We dismounted and I shook hands with them all in an emotional send-off on the edge of the escarpment. As I turned away from Damburam, his horse kicked out hard and caught me on the shin. Was it conveying its master's feelings?

I reached Kaduna to learn that President Kennedy had been assassinated some five days earlier. I must have been one of the last people in the world to learn the news.

Appendix I

Why I Went to Nigeria

In 1957, green and still wet behind the ears, I found myself striding out full of energy and idealism as a colonial administrator into the vast expanse of Africa – as if I had been recruited in the early part of the British Empire's heyday.

Why had I enlisted in a service entering its death throes? As I was setting out my superiors in the service were taking early retirement, streaming home and collecting at the exit door a generous government severance package known colloquially as 'Lumpers'. The country to which I was posted would gain its independence in three years.

Certainly, my father was none too enamoured of my career choice, which had a distinct lack of long-term prospects. Yet deep down, he must have understood – it was in the genes.

As a 12-year-old, having read and re-read the gripping details of Colonel Fawcett's search for a lost city in the Matto Grosso in Brazil as described in his son's book *Exploration Fawcett*, I informed my bemused mother that I wanted to be an explorer. Eight years later, older and wiser, I realised that if I wanted to explore, I would have to find the appropriate organisation to send me to a country where it was still possible to undertake exploration.

As for genetics, the case is cut and dried. I had side-stepped the overriding and militant 'holy' gene of the Hare family – several of whom went into the church – to be imbued, fortunately, with the conflicting gene of high adventure. My father's great-grandfather had led an abortive charge to take Bhurtpore in India in 1826 and his brother, a naval captain, took part in actions against pirates in the Straits of Malacca in 1832. My father's grandfather, Henry Press Wright, had been the first archdeacon of British Columbia and his own mother spent her early years being carted around north-east Canada in a saddlebag.

Some years earlier, before being appointed archdeacon, Press Wright, as senior chaplain to the British forces during the Crimean war, had petitioned Lord Raglan to send Florence Nightingale to the Crimea. My father's grandmother, who had gone out with Press Wright to Scutari to welcome Nightingale, travelled home on a small ship ahead of her husband – the only woman on board with the exception of her young daughter, my grandmother.

Halfway through the voyage it was clear that the captain was permanently drunk and incapable. The crew begged the only adult female passenger to order the captain to delegate his duties to the first mate, otherwise they would mutiny. She accepted, persuaded the captain to agree and the first mate brought the ship safely home with my great-grandmother by his side.

Another relative by marriage, Colonel Arthur Hogge, had accompanied Francis Younghusband as his aide-de-camp on the ignominious 1903 expedition that resulted in a small diplomatic mission turning into a full-scale invasion of the last unexplored country on earth, Tibet.

My uncle was a senior chaplain in the Indian Army. My father's own early years had been spent in tea in Ceylon, before the Great War had put paid to all that. But in the war he had displayed great bravery at Ypres, where he was awarded the Military Cross, and at the first day of the Somme where he lost a leg.

So it was hardly surprising that I would want to follow in the spirit of a great-grandfather, who as a boy had 'longed earnestly for adventure and travel wherever it may be found'. Thus it was that at the age of just 22, I found myself styled Assistant District Officer, the administrative baby of a rapidly dwindling service.

I had already spent 15 months in Northern Nigeria. Commissioned in the Oxfordshire and Buckinghamshire Light

Infantry during my compulsory military National Service, the thought of spending more than a year in West Germany with the regiment doing nothing but pointless military exercises appalled me. Questing for adventure, my chum Jon Stallworthy and I scanned the noticeboards and saw that newly commissioned officers were being offered choices to satisfy the most romantic soul. Volunteers were required for the Somaliland Scouts, the King's African Rifles and the Royal West African Frontier Force. Flouting the convention of the military axiom, 'never volunteer', I, together with Jon (who joined up with me at Cowley Barracks, Oxford on the same day) put in for the mounted camel brigade of the Somaliland Scouts. Seven days later we both received a summons informing us we were to be sent to serve, not with the camel corps but with the 5th Battalion, the Nigeria Regiment as part of the Royal West African Frontier Force. We shared a house, a horse and a sense of fun. Jon later achieved much fame as a poet, a biographer of Wilfred Owen, and as a leading expert on the poets of the Great War, and as Professor of English Literature at Oxford University.

Fifteen months later, having greatly enjoyed my National Service in Nigeria and been thoroughly seduced by Africa and the excitements of the African bush, I was determined to return. But my father, remembering his happy years in Ceylon (Sri Lanka) in the years before the First World War, had arranged for me to go there as a 'creeper' – a learner tea planter – on my godfather's tea estate.

Nuwara Eliya tea is some of the finest in the world and the estate is, I believe, one of the highest on the island. I was intrigued to learn it had originally been carved out of the jungle by Sir Samuel Baker, the renowned Victorian African explorer. Baker is remembered not only for clearing the bush at Nuwara Eliya but also for discovering Lake Albert, one of the sources of the Nile. He is also remembered for buying his 15-year-old Hungarian wife Florence in a slave market after she had escaped from revolution in Hungary, been caught and educated in a Turkish harem.

The memory that is impressed on my mind during my

short time in Ceylon has nothing to do with tea planting at all. 'Cinders' Sanders for whom I 'crept' took me to the Hill Station in Nuwara Eliya for an evening meal shortly after my arrival. The Hill Station was a tall, dark, cavernous old colonial building and there was only one other person in the dining room. During our conversation my name was mentioned and towards the end of the meal a solitary, distinguished-looking gentleman came over to our table.

'Did I hear the name, Hare?' he enquired.

'Yes,' I replied, 'my name is John Hare.'

'Did you have a father who lost a leg in the First War?'

'Yes, I did, his name was Lancelot Hare.'

'I was the surgeon who cut it off,' said the man solemnly.

I didn't ask if he had still got it.

Africa had entered my bloodstream and I found tea management and life on a well-manicured estate much too tame. I was instructed to count and write down the names of the female Tamil tea pickers at six o'clock in the morning. When their baskets were full I weighed the tea and recorded the total. It was a task that soon palled. Moreover, my short time there coincided with a violent national election and inflammatory anti-white statements by Mrs Bandaranaike. It soon became clear to me that the days of the European tea planter were numbered. The one vivid memory I have of Tamil tea pluckers was their penchant for digging 'cat's eyes' out of the middle of a newly tarred tarmac road and using the luminous round dials as nose ornaments. When driving around the tea estate at night the girls glittered like fireflies.

With the explorer gene still well in the ascendency, I decided after six months of 'creeping' to return to England at my own expense, which I did, much to my father's incredulity and annoyance – although Cinders Sanders thought it was a wise move.

Appendix II

A C C Hastings, a District Officer based in Gombe, described in his book Nigerian Days an early encounter with the Tula in about 1906 as follows:

I awoke to the sharp challenge of a sentry, and the rush of quick pattering feet. The false dawn was in the sky, the cold stars twinkling down upon the stirring camp. I heard a brief murmur of conversation, and shortly after Loba came to my tent door to tell me that the Tulas were coming to the ridge and massing at its foot, in readiness to attack at daylight. They were moving with great silence, he said, but lying in the thick grass, he had heard the elders talking, and saying with gibes how they would come indeed to the white man's camp and eat him up. Quickly we made our preparations. Carriers and servants were ordered to lie down behind the thorn fence for shelter, while the four sections of the company filed outside the *zariba* [fence] and lay down, each taking a side of the square, for it was uncertain whether all sides would be attacked. The horses were taken to the rear fence and securely tethered, the Maxim [machine gun] placed at the left front corner of the camp, with the gun section under Austin's charge; and all being ready, Utterson and I took charge of the two front sections facing the ridge.

The true dawn gleamed and spread upon the horizon behind us, and one by one, just as on a photographic plate, the rocks and trees upon the valley sides and ridge developed and sharpened before our eyes. Again the full day came and showed us the valley full of naked forms, slinking, creeping, running, and making to approach on three sides of the square. Among them walked the chiefs, with white plumes of ox-tails fastened to fantastic head-dresses, and carrying enormous shields of hide. The Tulas came on in silence to within a few hundred yards, evidently expecting an easy job, with an apparently half-empty camp to tackle. Again I walked out a few yards towards them, shouting a warning to be wise and disperse. Yells of anger, or, it may be, derision, greeted my remarks. I can well believe they contained advice to me to 'cut the cackle' and get on with the work, so giving it up as a bad job I walked slowly back and signed to Utterson to carry on and let them have it.

The pagans now came on quickly, letting fly scores of poisoned arrows, and plucking at their quivers as they ran. The Maxim opened fire at this moment, but only for a dozen rounds; the belt jammed and despite Austin's frantic efforts to clear it, refused to work again. Checked only for a moment by the noise but not the bullets, which had done no damage, the Tulas came with a rush once more, the arrows came flying into the camp, and a few throwing spears struck the ground just short of us. This time they got it hot and strong from the rifles. A white plume went down kicking and thrashing in the grass, and 30 or 40 black forms lay scattered on our front. Still they came on to within 50 yards of us, but there their courage failed them, and they broke and ran for cover, and shortly after we saw the whole attack dissolving into a general retreat to the ridge. Our casualties were seven carriers and soldiers hit with arrows, but the wounds were not serious as the poison on the tips was old and dry, and none proved fatal, as would have been the case had the heads been freshly dipped.

Appendix III

A selection of reports written by Mr W F C Holme in 1907 and Mr T F Carlyle in 1912/1913 to the Resident, Central Province in Naraguta when each was the Assistant Resident Gombe and when Tangale-Waja was directly administered from old Gombe on the River Gongola. The move to the Gombe township of today was not made until the early 1920s when the town was laid out by the government.

The reports graphically illustrate the state of administration in Tangale-Waja at that time. They also show that my experiences with the Koma in the Alantika Mountains were remarkably similar to those of Mr Carlyle nearly 60 years earlier, and that in many respects the problems of Tangale-Waja – tax collection, witchcraft and murder – had not changed at all in the intervening years.

21/8/07 W F C Holme to the Resident, Central Province, Naraguta:

The Sarkin Ture [Chief of Ture] came here [Gombe] yesterday and brought a complaint to me that the Awok people are reviving an old established warfare against his people. While eight men were working on a farm some Awok people came and killed them. Three men were killed after they were returning from Ture to Panda after buying corn. [Note: both Holme and Carlyle refer to Panda. Carlyle calls it Tula Panda. I can only think that it is the old name for Tula Baule, which was known to me when I was in

Tula and which was one of the three main sub-divisions of the Tula tribe. The other two were Tula Wange and Tula Yiri.]

Awok town is of considerable size and half of it is inhabited by the Kolamanies who on both the above occasions have been the aggressors. Sarkin Ture assures me (through his interpreter Buba Difa) that he has not given cause for this outburst and that since the white men forbade him to fight and kill and eat men, he has not done so nor has he retaliated on Awok.

I gained the following information from him: Sarkin Ture is the Chief of the district and four towns follow him. Awok is independent and controlled by no one. Waja is ruled over by Sarkin Gelengu who is at variance with Panda and Ture. Panda follows Galadima Ako and is on friendly terms with Ture.

I informed the Sarkin Ture that he did quite right to obey Government orders and come to complain to me and that the towns that went to war and disobeyed orders and refused to pay their taxes would be punished. This is the first occasion on which a pagan Sarki from that country has appeared to bring a complaint and I am glad he has done so though it puts us face to face with the difficulty of controlling the Waja Tangalto pagans. [Note: the Tangalto are a sub-division of the Tangale tribe.]

All the pagans in that country have refused to pay *jangali* (cattle tax), the Fulani there have paid and Sarkin Ture informs me that his town and the towns that follow him possess no cattle and have removed or killed their cattle and I have no doubt that no tribute will be forthcoming, nor does it appear to me quite fair to expect the Sarkin Ture and Panda to pay tribute unless one can give them protection. The pagans do not yet realise the power behind us. It is quite clear that unless steps are taken Ture and Panda will ultimately follow the example of their neighbours, besides the prestige that the Government will lose, in the eyes of the Fulani if the control of these pagans is allowed to lapse.

I of course said nothing definite to the Sarkin Ture as I thought it probable that you would prefer to postpone undertaking an expedition against them until the tribute fails to come in.

I have told the Sarkin Ture to return to me with the Sarkin

Panda in about three weeks and bring me the details of population in their districts. I can then inform him of the steps the Govt will take when I hear from you.

I would further suggest that it is probable that an expedition such as took place last year will only have a temporary effect, unless some steps are taken to have the country properly administered.

W F C Holme

Resident, Central Province, Naraguta to W F C Holme:

Your No.15/07 of 21st August.

1. A similar murder was committed when Assistant Resident Phillips was in the district and he made Awok pay compensation. They should be fined this time.
2. Waja is divided into several units previously independent. The sub-District Heads officially recognised are the Sarkin Gelengu, Sarkin Dela Waja and Sarkin Reme.
3. The Waja and Tangale pagans should not pay *jangali* this year at any rate, even if they have cattle. They have suffered severe losses of stock last year at the hands of expeditions.
4. It is not intended that the control of the pagans shall be allowed to lapse. Nor have I any intention of 'undertaking an expedition' against them. After the two expeditions which have already been through their country there is no likelihood of an organised resistance being offered. I propose that you should re-occupy the Ture station about the end of this month and remain in charge of the Tula-Tangale district. Detailed instructions will be sent to you later. If you see the Sarkin Ture again you may assure him that it is not the intention of Government to abandon him.
5. Re Buba Difa. I wish to caution you against placing reliance on this man. He is plausible, but quite untrustworthy, and previously caused a great deal of trouble on the Gongola, being

finally sentenced to three years' imprisonment for extortion.

        W F Gowers, Resident Central Province, Naraguta

Mr Holme was then asked by the Resident Central Province to hand over the division to Mr Carlyle and to proceed to Ture and re-occupy Ture station. In the Resident's letter of 3/9/07 to Mr Holme he said:

4. I propose to arrange for an officer and 25 R & F [soldiers] to accompany you to the Tangale District in order to enable you to arrest the persons responsible for the recent murder reported from Awok, and any others who may be found to have been guilty of lawlessness since the late Mr Phillips' death. [*It will be recalled that Captain Phillips died climbing Tangale Peak, Chapter 5.*]

Mr Holme proceeded to Ture and undertook the patrol to Awok together with Lieut Gubbins in charge of the R & F.

26/10/07 W F C Holme to the Resident, Central Province, Naraguta

Sir,

1. I have the honour to send you herewith my report on the tour at Awok and our dealings with it on the 25th instant. I shall be glad of your instructions.

2. Please send me as soon as possible £20. I came from Gombe with £10 which will not last me long.

3. I wrote to Mr T F Carlyle when I heard that I was to proceed here and asked him to send me some more money – but I have not heard from him. Cloth will be of more use than money if you have any to dispose of, as I have to change it into the former or into salt at Deba Habe.

I have the honour to report as follows:

1. Arriving at Ture on the 24th inst. I proceeded to further investigate the charges against the Awok tribe.

2. There has been a feud for years between that tribe and Ture and the latter has not (at all events of late) been able to hold its own.

3. The famine spoken of by the late A R Phillips was apparently local to Ture and was caused by raids by the Awok people which prevented the proper working of the Ture farms.

4. This year Ture are again short of corn in consequence of their farm, which lies between Ture and Awok, having been raided three times, which has so frightened the Ture people that they are afraid to approach it.

5. I was unable to obtain any messenger whom I could send to Awok, as no one would go near the town, though in addition to the Ture people I had with me men from Pindiga, Tangale and Deba Habe.

6. It was consequently necessary to approach the town and trust on getting near to find some man whom I could send with a message to the Sarki.

7. At daylight on the 25th inst. accompanied by Lt Gubbins and 25 R & F [soldiers] I started from Ture and reached the Awok hill after proceeding about 5 and a half miles.

8. There are two roads [Note: when Holme and Carlyle speak of 'road' they refer to footpaths, not a motor road] up this hill and we chose the one on the S.E. side which was the better of the two. This road was very steep and difficult to climb and it was not until we were near the top that some Awok men appeared armed with spears, shields of elephant hide, bows and poisoned arrows and dressed in their war paint consisting of feathered and beaded head gear.

9. I at once spoke to them through an interpreter telling them that there was no need to fear and that I wished to speak to their Sarki. I told them to send a man to call him and I further told them to wait there for their Sarki.

10. They replied in a threatening manner that their Sarki would not come but that his brother was coming out to see me.

11. I told him that I would wait there and see the Sarki's brother.

12. All this time their numbers had been increasing until about 50 and 60 fighting men had collected. These men were gradually approaching nearer and near until they were within about 30 yds of us.

13. I told them that until their headman's brother came I wished them to stop at a point which I indicated about 100 yds away – but they refused to move and told us to go away.

14. I then ordered them to disperse and they replied by shouting, laughing and brandishing their weapons.

15. I again ordered them to go back but with a like result.

16. It was appearing to me that it was a matter of imminent danger to have them so close in continually increasing numbers. I told the officer in charge of the escort that if he considered their presence a danger as I did I wished him in self-defence to take what steps he thought necessary to drive them back.

17. Lt Gubbins thereupon ordered them to retire three times and told them he would fire if they refused.

18. This having no effect he opened fire upon them with half a dozen men.

19. The savages then retreated but formed up again about 100 yds away and he again fired driving them from the spot.

20. We then remained where we were for about half an hour in the hope that the Sarki would come, but then seeing the savages forming up in two or three places in the valley between two points on the hill – individual firing was commenced and we proceeded to clear them from the villages through which we went.

21. The Sarki and some old men were then seen approaching and on asking why they refused to come and see me they said they intended to come, but that the young men would not agree.

22. I then informed the Sarki that as he had come there would be no more fighting if he did everything I told him and he said that he would do so.

23. Our position on the hill being far from secure, I ordered the Sarki to lead us down to the valley where a stream ran, to bring us wood and food and to collect and bring me all the arms. This

he said he would do.

24. We then guided by the Sarki descended to the valley where we awaited the fulfilment of the Sarki's promise.

25. In the course of time about 20 men led by the Sarki came down with some small goats and a little guinea-corn. I sent them back and said all the arms were to be collected and brought down at once. Presently six men came down with small quantities of corn but still without any arms. These men I again sent back with a message to say that if the arms and some food was not brought down directly I should have to come up the hill again and do as I had done before. They assured me that they should be brought and said that they had had enough fighting. There was however no fulfilment of my orders except that the Sarki had sent them to say that he refused to come down again. I again sent a message to say that if they brought all their arms into Ture the next morning no further action would be taken.

The remainder of this document is missing but the Resident, Central Province, Naraguta's reply to this report is as follows:

[*date illegible*]   W F C Holme from Resident, Central Province, Naraguta:

Your 1/07 forwarding report of patrol to Awok.

Your Paragraph 3. I am glad that the scarcity reported is not general.

Paragraph 5. I cannot understand the present attitude of Awok and the unwillingness of messengers to go there. They paid a fair proportion of their last year's tribute to Mr Hastings Assistant Resident without the use of force and they subsequently do not appear to have offered any resistance to Mr Phillips who visited them.

Paragraph 16. You appear to have exercised as much forbearance as was possible under the circumstances; apparently they would have attacked you if you had not fired. Were any arrows actually fired or spears thrown?

Paragraph 23. You could hardly expect a tribe living in the midst of other armed natives some of them on unfriendly terms, to give up all their arms. Such an order was certain not to be complied with.

Paragraph 31. In view of the fact that you are to go on leave shortly and there will again be no officer available to administer the district, I greatly regret that I cannot take further steps to subjugate Awok. Such measures unless followed by continuous occupation do little permanent good, and had I anticipated the change in the leave regulations and the consequent necessity for your early departure I would have postponed the present patrol. I hope however that the lesson they have already had (Lieut Gubbins reports that they lost 46 men) will have a satisfactory effect and that with patience you will get in touch with them.

W J Gowers Resident, Central Province, Naraguta

Subsequent events were as follows:

8/11/07 Lieut. Gubbins to the Resident, Central Province, Naraguta.

Sir.

8. [*paras 1–7 of marginal interest*] On the 27th ulto I received a message at Ture sent through Kanu from the Sarkin Awok to say that he refused to come to see me or to bring in any arms. Later the same day a message from Awok was brought by two Panda men who gave me a small bundle of sticks and said that the number of men killed was 27 and that they were going to kill a corresponding number of Ture men at the first opportunity. I told the men to go back and inform the Sarkin Awok that I should hold no communication with him until my orders had been

obeyed and that he had better avoid any further provocation to the Government.

9. On the morning of the 28th inst. I left Ture with the intention of staying at Tula Wange. When nearing the top of the steep hill leading into their country we found stones ands cross sticks placed on the road which means the road is not to be followed. It was however not possible to turn back without a considerable longer journey – but in order to avoid fighting, we decided not to stop near the towns but to proceed further and camp at Tula Panda.

10. This we did and though we met with no active opposition – men were hidden in various positions watching our movements. I twice told natives of Tula Wange who were near enough that their Sarki was to come and meet us at Tula Panda, but he neither came nor sent a message.

11. I afterwards received a complaint from the headmen of Tula Panda that two of their men who had followed me through Tula Wange had been caught and detained – probably because some Tula Panda men were guiding us. There was no man in Tula Panda who would carry a message to the Sarki: re the men they had caught and to avoid bringing another fight I could take no steps towards their release.

12. I found the Tula Panda people very friendly. As soon as they knew we were coming they prepared us a good camp and I had no trouble in procuring food. The Sarki and all the old men of the town came to complain about the two men who were caught by Wange. They told me that though Tula Wange and Tula Yiri normally followed Sarkin Tula Panda, he had no control over them at all, that they are robbers and cannibals, that he dare not even send a messenger into their town. I said that I would bear in mind what they had told me and said that I would also enquire into an alleged murder of 5 of their men by Balanga. As previously stated, however, I made no attempt to punish Tula Wange as I was sure from the attitude of the men of that town whom I saw that any attempt to procure the Sarki by sending soldiers would mean bloodshed and I did not feel justified in taking such strong

measures without further orders. I think that both Tula Wange and Tula Yiri require breaking and disarming.

I consider my force quite sufficient to clear this town of its fighting men and destroy it. But I have not sufficient men to compel them to bring in their arms or otherwise obey your orders.

Mr Holme's comments in the same letter were as follows:

I feel that the following steps should be taken before any political officer is sent to take charge of the Tula/Tangale district with a small escort:

1. The Sarkis of Tal and Tangale should be forced to come in and pay a levy.
2. Awok should be totally disarmed and should pay a large fine in food stuff to be given to the Ture people as compensation for the murders and the impoverished conditions into which they have been thrown.
3. Kamu should be made to come in and partially disarm for sheltering the Awok tribe when they were in insurrection against the Government.
4. Tula Wange and Tula Yiri should also be forced to come in and pay a proportion of their arms.

Such a course will show the friendly towns that they have been wise in accepting the inevitable and obeying the orders of the government and it will also weaken the powers of the towns who have been disloyal and leave their neighbours less at their mercy.

Signed Lt Gubbins and W F C Holme

In 1912/1913 T F Carlyle, whose name became a household word in the area, was in charge of Gombe Division which included Tangale-Waja. He first took control of the division in 1907. In 1912 he asked permission

to undertake a tour of the Tangale-Waja area in Gombe Division in the following letter The subsequent correspondence reveals the outcome of that tour.

16/11/12 From T F Carlyle to the Resident, Central Province, Naraguta

Sir,

Subject to your directions it is my intention to spend the 1st quarter of next year among the Wajawa and the independent tribes to the south of this division. If you are unable to accord me assistance during that period the Emirate [of Gombe] will be able to look after itself. Thereafter I do not consider that any assistance will be necessary. During my visit to the south I hope to be able to collect sufficient material to complete the Resident assessment reports of this division.

2. As regards escort I should like if possible to be accompanied by a section of 30 R & F.

3. I ask for this patrol to minimise the possibility of armed resistance, which cannot be regarded as altogether remote. The tribes of Cham and Dadiya and Pero have not been counted and as this task will necessitate a compound to compound visit I think it well I should have a strong force in the vicinity when I subject the pagans to such close contact. Cham I understand has not been visited during my absence.

4. Mr Lonsdale was accompanied by the Dadiya section when he visited Pero in May this year. The people of that tribe were actually armed in order to resist payment of tribute which they refused to bring into Dadiya. But the advance of the troops to the foot of the town and Mr Lonsdale's persuasion brought the pagans to submission. I do not think that the tax which they then paid was adequate but it was a first payment.

5. The troops are actually necessary in Tula-Tangale but their presence will greatly facilitate the collection of the increased tax due from those tribes.

6. If the troops left Nafada on January 15th and joined me in

Waja they could be back in Nafada before the end of March.

7. I believe that this patrol and possibly a similar patrol next year will result in the final pacification of the pagans of this division.

T F Carlyle

29/11/12 From the Resident, Central Province, Naraguta to T F Carlyle

Your minute No. 655/1912 of the 16th instant

1. I have asked for the <u>escort</u>.
2. Please do not use the word 'patrol' unless you mean something like a punitive expedition.

Resident, Central Province

22/2/13 F Carlyle to the Resident, Central Province, Naraguta

Sir,

I have the honour to present the following interim report on my tour among the pagan tribes of Gombe Division. A regrettable incident, which occurred at Gwandon (Pero section of the Tangale group), is the immediate cause of this report.

2. I left Nafada on January 21st 1913 with Lieut. J R Geoghegan and 30 R & F 'C' Coy, 2nd NNR). We arrived at Awok (Tula group) on the 27th January, moving thence to Ture on 31st Jan., Kaltungo (Ture group) on 3rd Feb. and Tal (Tangale group) on 6th Feb.

3. I found all these people in an amenable condition and the tax which is increased this year (1912–1913) from 3d to 6d per householder was collected without friction. Some considerable preparation had been made and as I had brought with me a large

following of traders the pagans had no difficulty in raising the whole of their tax in cash and at fair prices.

4. In the group several complaints were settled. A fight which had occurred in Larika in October last and in which two *maza* [men] had been killed was dealt with by a fine of 75 shields and 300 spears on the *angwas* [hamlets] concerned. The head *angwa* of Kalwa were fined 30 shields and 100 spears for an assault on Kutal, a *mai angwa* [hamlet headman] of Banganji. These fines were paid immediately.

5. Shippo, a man of Banganji charged with being concerned in the death of a Wurkum who disappeared in November but was arrested by Sarkin Banganji.

This matter is under investigation.

6. On 11th February at 11 a.m. we arrived at Filiya (Pero). The Pero faction had refused to come to do their usual clearing nor did any of them come out to meet us.

7. On our arrival at the usual camping ground I sent a courier [Note: in Carlyle's day government messengers were called 'couriers'] to call the Sarkins Filiya and Gwandon. The former came at once and submitted, the latter refused to come in and repeated calls during the day with the intimation that I should visit Gwandon the following morning in force failed to have effect. On the contrary, the people of Gwandon replied that they had not married children of the white man and they did not intend to clear roads, pay tax or have anything to do with him. I regarded his remarks as 'bluff'.

8. On the 12th February at 7 a.m. I set out for Gwandon with Lieut. J R Geoghegan and 23 R & F. Gwandon is situated on the sides of a precipitous hill, its compounds resting on built up terraces and being massed close together. The total population (with sub-villages) I have since found to be 2323; 829 of which are male adults.

9. We climbed Gwandon Hill until we came close up the compounds where we were met by 2 unarmed natives who made the usual demand that we should go down the hill again and parley at the bottom. I replied that I had no desire to fight but that

we would parley with the Sarki and elders of Gwandon where we stood. The reply was that the Sarki was not there but he had gone away. This I had reason to believe was false. I therefore replied that we should occupy the town but that we would not fire if the armed men I saw among the compounds would put down their arms. The 2 natives thereupon retired daring us to advance. I therefore asked Lieut. Geoghegan to occupy the town.

10. We advanced through the compounds making straight for the highest point. The advance was soon impeded by a large number of armed and painted natives whose threatening attitude and vicinity to us was such that Lieut. Geoghegan was obliged to open fire. Some natives were shot, the remainder then retired and firing at once ceased. We thereupon occupied the chief height in the town but meanwhile an attack was made by the pagans on our rear where they had massed in force. Firing began again whereupon the pagans drew off.

11. We remained in the town about 2 hours and then as the natives refused to come in but remained among the rocks around we returned to the camp by a circuitous route which left us no part of the town unvisited.

12. The same evening Sarkin Gwandon (Weenan) came in with his elders and made submission. They reported that 16 natives of Gwandon had been killed and 4 wounded. These figures I believe to be correct. Sarkin Gwandon explained that the reason which had prevented him from coming in in the first place was that the young men had all prepared for fight and he had lost control over them. That preparation for war was made out from the following facts:

> All the women and children had been removed before our arrival.
> The warriors to the number of at least 500 were ready to meet us in their war paint.
> Their cries as we climbed into the town were insulting and not conciliatory.
> All their spears found were freshly poisoned.

Of the pagan casualties 4 only appear to have occurred in advance of the other 16 when they attempted to cut off the rear. It should be clearly understood that the latter action by the pagans was certainly offensive. They had an easy retreat to their rear. It was possibly the fact that they were not fired on when retiring which induced them to return to the attack. The Pero tribe were first visited by me in company with Mr Rendit in May 1909. He regarded them as a peculiarly low type of native. They have been visited several times since by me and although I have hitherto persuaded them to do the few things required of them yet they have not acted willingly. Last year they were told for the first time to pay tax (1911–1912) but neglected to do so until May when visited by Capt. Turner with an escort. On that occasion show of resistance was made by Filiya but eventually the nominal sum of £15 was collected from the whole group. The fact that Filiya were not punished for this show of resistance accounts no doubt in some measure for Gwandon's attitude this year.

17. Gwandon was also affected by the fact that a considerable number of Wurkunawa had migrated and settled among them to escape payment of tribute in Muri Province.

18. We remained among the Pero people until the 20th Feb. during which time the section was carefully counted, the tax £18.10.0 at 3d a householder collected, and some considerable work done on the rocky road between Gwandon and Bangwunji (Dadiya). When I left I was completely satisfied with the state of the tribe to hold out and certain that no more trouble will be experienced. I am doing some road [footpath] work among all these pagans as I pass through because nothing else brings us into such close personal contact with them because of the disciplinary effect of such work. I lay great stress on the civilizing influence of roads. Moreover the use of such tools as crowbars and pick axes, of which I have a private supply, is an education in itself.

20. The Sarkin Dadiya, released through the kindness of H.E. [His Excellency The Governor], met me in Filiya on his way home. Since when he has returned to his old position.

21. I expect to be about a week among the people of Dadiya

after which Cham and Waja will be visited. Some trouble has arisen in Cham as between pagan and Fulani.

T F Carlyle

The circumstances described in this report were commented on by the Deputy Governor of Northern Nigeria (Temple). But it was not only the death of 16 pagans which attracted comment.

18/5/13 Chief Secretary to Resident, Central Province, Naraguta

With reference to para.19 of Mr Carlyle's report on his tour among the pagan tribes of Gombe Division No. 145/1913 of the 22nd February 1913, which formed an enclosure to your letter 'on Tour' of the 2nd April 1913, H.E. the Deputy Governor comments as follows: 'What does Mr Carlyle mean by a private supply of picks and crowbars?'

T T Hopkins for acting Chief Secretary to the Govt.

2/8/13 T F Carlyle to the Resident, Central Province, Naraguta

My statement was as follows: 'The use of such tools as crowbars and pickaxes, of which I have a private supply, is an education in itself.'

The words in parentheses 'of which I have a private supply' were meant to control the word pickaxes only. The 2 crowbars, I had and have, are government property.

My intention was to prevent any question arising as to whether such pickaxes were government property and if so why they were not on charge. My meaning was that the pickaxes were my private property. As a matter of detail they were tools 14 in all, worn but useful which I acquired for a commercial consideration from a Nigerian mining company.

T F Carlyle

25/4/13 From the Resident, Central Province, Naraguta to the Resident, Gombe Division

The following enquiry has been telegraphed to me by the Deputy Governor:

Carlyle's report on Gwandon patrol x Are you satisfied that sixteen natives were actually killed.

Please reconsider and wire me (I note that you have expressed in your report your belief that the figures are correct: paragraph 12).

Carlyle confirmed on the 3/5/13 that sixteen natives were killed but Temple asked him, through the Resident, 'for a full and detailed report not a general statement such as he has made'. The report was duly submitted as follows:

5/6/13 From T F Carlyle, Resident iii, i/c Gombe Division to the Resident, Central Province, Naraguta.

I reply to the Deputy Governor's telegram No. 4706 I regret that I am not clear as to the nature of the details required beyond general evidence of the number killed and wounded it did not occur to me that other information would be sought.

2. Before explaining the nature of the evidence I obtained, I wish to make the position clear. First I have a decided opinion that the pagan resents such enquiries. I do not suggest that the Tangales like the Longudawa, eat their own dead; but the fact remains that any information in regard to the same is given grudgingly. The pagan's care to carry away his dead confirms this and I am certain, even after having made submission, he would evade any demand to produce the bodies. Again the pagan's attitude, when he comes in, is that he has to come to 'bury the hatchet': he wishes the matter to be wiped out and resents later

allusions to it. One would be more guarded in a case such as this where time was necessarily limited and my chief objects were to collect tribute and have the people pacified.

3. The affair happened on the morning of the 12th February. On return to camp I sent Sarkin Filiya to Sarkin Gwandon to tell the latter to come in and submit, and to bring me the numbers of the killed and wounded. Sarkin Gwandon came in that evening and, having given me the numbers as I reported them, made his submission and went. Sarkin Filiya said he had asked the people of Gwandon and he understood the numbers as given by Sarkin Gwandon were correct.

4. The next 2 days I counted Filiya. Sarkin Gwandon came in each day with supplies. He mentioned that most of the people were still in the bush, but his men had buried the dead and were back in the town during the day.

5. The third day I went to Gwandon to make a census and was met by Sarkin Gwandon and a few of his older followers. We started our count from the Sarki's compound. The latter said that one of his sons had died. I asked, 'In the fight?' He said 'yes'. This, Courier Dummi then told me, was the young man whose body I had seen during the affair on a rock adjacent. Few men were present. Judging they were still nervous I told the Sarki that I was going back to superintend the work being done by Filiya on the Kashe road and he had better call them. Then I left telling Malam Babelle to carry on the work and not to include the killed in the count but to find out about the wounded. When the Malam gave me his figures the next day he said he had accounted for the sixteen men killed and the 4 wounded and that all the latter were at Fukatuk.

6. The day following I went to Fukatuk, Yemba and Gondalu, hamlets of Gwondon. In Fukatuk I found 2 wounded men and in Yemba the other two. One only had other than a flesh wound. His elbow being broken.

9. The next day (the 18th Feb.) I moved with the escort to Kushe of the same group.

T F Carlyle, Lafia (Touring Camp)

Carlyle continued this patrol, as intimated in his first patrol report, paragraph 21, into the other districts of Tangale-Waja. Here is the remainder of his 1913 patrol report. The interesting fact is that during 1957/1958/1959 I trekked more than once to all the villages mentioned in both these reports. Very few could be reached by road and then only in the dry season. Many of my experiences were similar to those of Carlyle, except that political party and mission politics had by then infected the people.

15/5/13 Notes for Carlyle's 1913 patrol report.

Little trouble was experienced in Dadiya – the first count of population made by Malam Babelle and the courier was a poor one and a recount was made in which I joined. I cut a good road up the pass, but the descent though negotiable by horses is rough. Maidaikin Bangwanji was made a prisoner for the murder of his wife on the excuse of witchcraft. Evidence was not conclusive so he was sent back from Gombe.

Mwana – behaved very well. A soldier was convicted of receiving goods stolen from them. The town is very full of syphilis in advanced stages. There is a small *angwa* of tax evaders on the road to Wufa which we visited.

In Cham – the western most *angwa* loosed bees on to me when I started counting. They paid 3/4 of their tax and refused to pay more.

Four Fulani had been burnt to death. 2 men were produced who admitted they had burnt the bush near the Fulani camp. [Note: the Fulani encampment near Cham which is a permanent one is there to this day] I could not ascertain how far their admission was true or false. They said they were searching for rats. I could not let them go and I brought them into Gombe. One died soon after in prison from sickness. I let the other out in my compound. He ran a few days after.

Sarkin Kundio – new Sarki appointed. Taliko having died at Kano Durbar. New Sarki, Karen Taliko.

Jesse – Gave no trouble. Some young bloods were seen around (in my temporary absence) during the 2nd days counting. These people and Cham are rich in stock, Jessawa are very wealthy and have cattle. I saw some in the town. They have not paid *Jangali*.

Nyuwar – were very satisfactory and their road work excellent.

Waja – made a careful count of the hill tribes. Malam Babelle and Sarkin Kudu completed the count. Population more than doubled.

Wala Longuda – visited with 9 soldiers, people all away: no effort to pay tax. Burnt. Population about 60 to 70 households. People later came in to Sarkin Kudu to repent. Wala to be included in Waja as many of them are Bango. Sarkin Yaki will get a count.

Tula – camped at Wange. Sarkin Tula Panda has made a very excellent road through his town which avoids the awful road of old.

Ture – We made a night march on to Ture to catch Zarama Ture who had been playing pranks. One of his compound nearly broke Sarkin Ture's arm. Just missed Zarama. Sat down in his compound and thoroughly destroyed it. Called [Tula] Wange, Awok and Kaltungo out to search for him but no success. Later he came in to Gombe but could not bring Sarkin Ture's assailant who he said was hiding in Kama. This man (Ladipo) must be caught. Later heard he had been hiding in Wange farms towards Dadiya.

Took Sarkin Dadiya and Galadima Dadiya into Gombe via Nafada as they had been playing the fool again.

Took Sarkin Tangalto and deputy same way.

Tried to get him to bring in Sarkin Filiya and Gwandon but he reported they would not come.

[*Later*] Ladipo: Brought before me for trial. Sarkin Ture and witnesses having come to give evidence. This man is already extremely emaciated as the result of his fortnight's incarceration and if I jug him he will not last a month. He is too weak for that. He seems repentant. The Sarkin Ture put in a plea for him. Ladipo understands he is acquitted purely as a result of Sarkin Ture's intervention on his behalf.

T F Carlyle

Appendix IV

A Historical Note on Uthman Dan Fodio

In 1804, a Fulani religious teacher and writer, Uthman Dan Fodio, was living in Gobir town in today's Northern Nigeria. A teacher of the Maliki school of Islamic law, he had many followers who were motivated by his deep learning and reformist ideas. After increasing repression by the Hausa authorities, he led his followers into exile and started a political and social revolution which spread from Gobir throughout the north.

He was proclaimed 'Commander of the Faithful' by his followers, and this turned him into a political as well as a religious leader, giving him the authority to declare and pursue a *Jihad* or holy war, raise an army and become its commander. As a result of this proclamation, a widespread uprising began in the Hausa Emirates. This revolt in the north was largely composed of Fulani warriors, who held a powerful military advantage with their superior horsemanship. It was also widely supported by the Hausa tribesmen who were over-taxed and oppressed by their tribal rulers. The *Jihad* started in Gobir in 1804, and after four years of war, Uthman Dan Fodio found himself in command of a Fulani empire which was at the time the largest state in Africa.

After his death in 1817, his son, Muhammed Bello, became the ruler of what was called the Sokoto caliphate. Uthman's brother Abdullahi was given the title Emir of Gwandu and was placed in charge of the Western Emirates, Nupe and Ilorin. All the former Hausa states, parts of Nupe, Ilorin and Fulani outposts in

Bauchi and Adamawa were all ruled by a single politico-religious system. From the time of Uthman Dan Fodio there were 12 Fulani Emirs in the north. They remained until the British conquest at the beginning of the 20th century.

Uthman Dan Fodio wrote more than a hundred books concerning religion, government and Islamic culture and criticised existing African Muslim elites for what he saw as their greed, paganism, or violation of the standards of Shari'a law. He encouraged literacy and scholarship, and several of his sons and daughters emerged as scholars and writers. His writings and sayings continue to be much quoted today, and he is often affectionately referred to as Shehu in Northern Nigeria.

Appendix V

A historical note on the history of the Fulani ruling family in Banyo (now in the Cameroon Republic), its subsidiary fiefdom ruled from Gashaka and the subsequent Fulani, German and British administrations in Gashaka and Mambilla districts.

During the jihad of Uthman Dan Fodio in the early half of the 19th century, the Fulani Wolarbe clan moved southwards from the Lake Chad area under the chieftainship of Haman Joda and Samatu. In about 1835, Mohammadu Gabdo (Dandi), son of Samatu, attacked and captured Kwancha in what is now the Cameroon Republic. He then founded an empire comprising Kwancha, Banyo (in present day Cameroon) and Gashaka (formerly in British Cameroon and now in Nigeria). Towards the end of his reign he moved his headquarters from Kwancha to Gashaka. On his death in 1873, his three sons Usumanu, Bakari and Sambo who had been the three District Heads respectively of Banyo, Kwancha and Gashaka went to the Lamido (Emir) of Adamawa in Yola to ask for a ruling on the succession to their father's territory and Usumanu was appointed. But Sambo disagreed with the judgement and on his return to Gashaka set himself up as the independent ruler of Gashaka.

When Usumanu tried to enter Gashaka, Sambo refused him entry and so Usumanu set himself up in an independent camp outside the town. He occupied this for seven years before he finally accepted the situation and withdrew to Kwancha.

The first Europeans entered the area between 1880 and 1898,

217

and in 1885 Mr Moseley representing the Royal Niger Company visited Jamtari. Four years later a German, Herr Zindraff, visited Gashaka and other German explorers also visited the town.

In 1898 the inhabitants of Serti were alleged to have attacked a passing caravan and a Captain Parker led an expedition against them. Shortly afterwards, the ambitious Sambo decided to extend his authority and marched on Banyo. He was however defeated by Usumanu's son Umaru, subsequently captured and sent into exile in Madagali in the far north. The area over which Sambo ruled between 1873 and 1898 was never exactly established but did include some of the villages that lie among the western foothills of the Mambilla plateau.

During the German administration from 1901 to 1916, both Gashaka and Mambilla had been placed in Banyo Division and a customs post established on the border with Nigeria at Garbabi. In July 1916, during the First World War, the British captured Garbabi and Jamtari from the Germans and on 18th August captured Gashaka. Shortly afterwards Banyo was also captured.

Although Sambo's territorial acquisitions had not been great, his prestige was such that when the territory was placed under British sovereignty his son Halidu was acknowledged without question as the ruler of Gashaka. By this time, Umaru was ruling from Banyo and Halidu accepted his authority on his appointment in 1916. Thus the earlier judgement of the Lamido of Adamawa was confirmed a generation later.

The British subsequently handed over Banyo and Kwancha to the French but retained Gashaka under their authority. The former Fulani empire was therefore divided by the two colonial powers. Halidu died in 1918 and was succeeded by his brother Yakuba. He died in 1920 to be succeed by another brother, Mansuru, who was met by Migeod as mentioned in his book quoted in Appendix Six

In January 1924 the Kaka area south of Mambilla, which had previously fallen under the authority of Banyo, was transferred by the British from the Northern to the Southern administration in Bamenda Division, thereby further sub-dividing the former Fulani empire.

The Chief of Kabri had been recognised by the Germans as the premier Mambilla chief on the plateau and under him plans had been drawn up for a system of tax collection, but it was never undertaken owing to their defeat in the war.

The first British administrator to visit the plateau was Major Freemantle in December 1916, and he initiated another system of taxation. But it was not until 1924, when Captain Izard visited Mambilla, that a census was undertaken. This showed a population of roughly 4,000, which casts doubt on Migeod's assertion that the Germans had slaughtered 2,000 Mambilla when they first entered the area. Tales of such a slaughter would certainly have been handed down verbally over the years and yet in four years on Mambilla I never heard mention of such a figure. This population of 4,000 had grown to 88,000 by 1963.

Mansuru was deposed in 1929 and succeeded by another brother, Mohammadu Barewa, who himself was deposed in 1934. His successor, Marafa, was deposed three years later on charges of corruption and was succeeded by Dahiru with the title Dan Lawan. Dan Lawan was a direct appointee of the Lamido and not heir to Dandi's dynastic succession. In this respect it should be noted that since the British occupation and the splitting up of the Banyo empire, Gashaka and Mambilla had been placed under the Lamido of Adamawa at Yola and these appointments were confirmed by him. In 1939 Mansuru attempted a comeback but was quickly arrested. Dan Lawan was himself removed in 1952 and replaced by Mukkadas who I met coming down from the plateau on the first day that I ascended.

The continuation of the saga of the Banyo dynasty has been related in earlier chapters, and today independent District Heads rule Gashaka and Mambilla free from the Lamido's authority with the present Mambilla District Head, Mansuru, being a descendant of Sambo. Because of his untimely death, Audu Baju was able neither to sustain the brief Mambilla sovereignty nor to found a Mambilla ruling dynasty.

Appendix VI

A general note on the cattle-owning Fulani on the Mambilla plateau

The Fulani throughout Northern Nigeria are divided into the categories of settled and nomadic. The nomadic Fulani refer to the settled Fulani as 'Huya'en' (from the nomad Fulani word for house – *huyaru*), and they seldom refer to themselves by the name by which they are commonly called by outsiders, 'Mbororo'en', but either by their clan name or by the term 'Fulbe Ladde' or 'Fulbe Na'i'.

The distinction is however becoming more and more blurred as the nomadic Fulani become more settled and adopt the habits of their settled cousins.

The term 'Ardo' is an ambiguous one. On the one hand it means the traditional leader of a clan or section of a clan; on the other, the officially recognised collector of taxes. A newly appointed Ardo was given a turban and a gown by the District Head of Mambilla and was expected to be responsible for the grazing area assigned to him and to be a link with his people and the government. It is difficult to determine the headship of most clans. Nomadic Fulani custom has it that a successful man with a good herd of cattle and some sons and nephews assumes or purchases the title from another Ardo. Once obtained it becomes hereditary – rather like an hereditary English peerage. Thus some clans have one Ardo and others more than one. But on Mambilla a newly appointed incumbent had to have his position confirmed by the Native Authority.

The nomadic Fulani on Mambilla, by moving up into a *cul de sac* rapidly lost many of the characteristics of their brethren on the plains below. Their houses became permanent constructions of mud and thatch, instead of traditional *bukkoki* of grass and leaves or a simple corn stalk shelter. They could not migrate but had to remain settled in their allotted grazing area. This enforced settlement encouraged the younger generation to adopt the habits and tastes of the settled Fulani and Hausa communities nearby. For example the initiation ceremony of *sharo*, involving the beating of a youth on the chest with a stick, was unheard of on Mambilla. When questioned as to why they had abandoned this practice the reply was that 'It hurt too much!' When I was on Mambilla they did however try to keep the blood pure by avoiding inter-marriage with other clans or with Hausa/Mambilla tribesmen. At Nguroje, the hair of the Bawanko'en was noticeably straight. At Mayo Ndaga, the girls of the Karwanko'en were very light skinned. However, with the arrival of the road and the influx of many foreign elements on to the plateau I am sure that these racial characteristics have long-since been broken down.

The origin of the Fulani has caused endless speculation, and theories trying to establish their migration from Egypt and even India have been put forward. My own view, and that of many of the Fulani themselves, is that they originated in present day Mali near to Futa Toro. But the speculation will continue and it is unlikely that sufficient proof can be brought forward to prove conclusively any of the propounded theories.

The following table shows the Fulani clans on Mambilla at the time of my stay there.

	Name of Clan	Colour of Cattle (Red – Rahaji; White – Yakanaji)
1	Autanko'en (Gisanko'en)	red
2	Ba'en	white
3	Barbanko'en	red
4	Bawanko'en	red
5	Butanko'en	white
6	Daneji	white
7	Dauranko'en (Natirbe)	white
8	Faranko'en	red
9	Gamadanko'en	red
10	Gamanko'en (Galanko'en)	white
11	Geroji	red
12	Joranko'en	white
13	Karwanko'en	white
14	Mazanko'en	red
15	Rahaji (Sulibanko'en)	red
16	Sadanko'en	white
17	Sisilbe	white
18	Siwalbe (Salanko'en)	white
19	Wewebbe (Iyasanko'en)	white

Appendix VII

Writings of Mr Migeod, a traveller on Mambilla and in Gashaka during the 1920s who offers interesting observations of Mambilla tribal customs at that time.

In 1923, F W H Migeod trekked from Victoria in the then British Cameroons to Yola in Adamawa Province, Northern Nigeria, where his brother, Charles Migeod, was the Resident. He travelled across Mambilla by way of Mbang, Tamnya, Mbamga, Vokkude and Warwar. He crossed the River Donga en route to Titong and reached Mayo Ndaga (then called Hama Joda) via Kumo. He descended the plateau following the path from Dundere to Sabere and on to Yakuba, Gashaka and Serti (the last named route being the reverse of my trek back from Filinga plateau). He published an account of this journey in 1925 under the title *Through British Cameroons* (Heath Cranton), and his observations on Mambilla and Gashaka make interesting reading nearly 70 years on.

For example, when the boundary between the Northern half and the Southern half of the Cameroons was demarcated, the Kaka territory was in dispute. The District Officer Yola 'brought with him the Chief of Gashaka, a Fula, with the idea of making the Mbem and other Kaka tribes accept him as their Head Chief'. However, this negotiation clearly failed as the bulk of the Kaka were placed under the Southern administration. But even the name Kaka is questioned. Migeod concludes that it describes an area of country, not a tribe, and that the name Kaka was given to the area by the Fulani who found the inhabitants to have strong fighting characteristics. Kaka means (according to Mr Migeod) 'the nasty fighting people'.

He observes that in Mbem he was told that the Mambilla used to sell corpses for food and that the Mambilla have their own ten-day week (which they do). At Tamnya he discovered that the village name (Tamnia) came from the current Mambilla chief of that name and that the people called it Ngokh. He comments somewhat scathingly on the properties of *yom* (the valuable Mambilla source of fuel and green manure) and discovers that the men and the women only wear loin cloths (men) and leaves or beads (women).

'As for the dress of men, it was merely a piece of blue cloth between the legs; but instead of any rag serving, some care was given to give it a thickened edge.'

I only once saw old women dressed in beads and nothing more, but I had always been told that this was their traditional dress, despite the cold.

Of a conversation with the Chief of Kumo, Migeod writes: 'The Chief Ngebana – or, rather, his linguist – gave me a lot of information. They began by saying the Mambilla were all one, but later modified it by saying only Kabri, Titong and Kumo talked the same. They said that they moved here from Benekerkel, when the village got too small for them. Mambilla is not a name of their own. Like the Kaka it was given them by the Fulani ...

'There are no country cattle, and never had been, only sheep and goats. What cattle there are were brought by the Fulani. There is no cotton grown nor spun. Also there is no iron ... In burial, bodies of both men and women alike, and the chief also, are buried in a niche off the grave. The body sits up and the niche is closed with mats, etc. The head is not cut off but the belly is opened and examined. Stones are preserved to represent the deceased's head, and food is poured on them.'

Migeod also alleges that the Germans had to kill more than 2,000 Mambilla before they managed to subjugate them. This is something that I have never heard and if true it must have made substantial inroads into the overall numbers of the tribe.

He confirms my understanding that the plateau was formerly uninhabited and that the Mambilla came on to it from the Banyo region in the 19th century – no doubt hotly pursued by Fulani slave raiders. He notes that the plateau is mainly treeless with the exception of the lush valleys (*kurmis*). This is an interesting observation in view of the lack of trees and severe erosion of today. It is clear that whatever other damage the superfluity of cattle on Mambilla has caused they are not responsible for the loss of tree cover.

In a parallel situation to what happened in the early 1960s, the Mambilla paramount chief had recently been deposed and a Fulani chief nominated by Mansuru, the Chief of Gashaka, had been set in authority over the Mambilla. This was one Hama Joda whose district headquarters was, in those days, in Jalingo (Mayo Ndaga). In spite of his aversion both to the Fulani and to Islam, Migeod rather liked Hama Joda until he was approached by Mambilla farmers aggrieved by damage to their crops by marauding Fulani cattle. He observes how the Fulani take no notice of such complaints: '… as the country has been put under Fulani rulers there is no redress against them as they themselves are the court of appeal.'

When Hama Joda tried to make his journey to Dundere somewhat shorter he commented: 'A short-cut had been made (for me) through a corn field, which I thought quite wrong, but a Fulani chief is indifferent to the views of his pagan subjects or slaves.'

Mansuru had quickly fallen into dispute with his appointee, Hama Joda, and seemed to rue his recent appointment: 'Hama Joda, he [Mansuru] said, was nobody till two years before, when he came out of Banyo, having been a Constable or Messenger in the German days. I learnt later how Hama Joda wants all the country and wants to take his [Mansuru's] place.'

Truly, nothing changes.

Appendix VIII

Finally, I end with stories from Genesis in Pidgin English. Pidgin English was spoken on Mambilla but the homeland of this quaint version of English was Bamenda further to the south, which suffered from much greater missionary influence. This highly individual translation was found in the papers of a former District Officer who served in the area. Incidentally, the Pidgin English word for a Muslim is a 'Knockhead'. I am sure the reader understands why if he has observed a Muslim at prayer.

Genesis

For de first time, noting been be – only de Lawd, He be.
An' de Lawd, He done go work hard for make dis ting dey call um Earth. For six day de Lord He work an' He done make all ting – everyt'ing He go put for Earth. Plenty beef, plenty guinea corn, plenty mango, plenty groundnut – eveyt'ing. An' for de wata He put plenty fish, an' for de air, He put plenty kinda bird.

After six day de Lawd he done go sleep. An' when He sleep palaver start for dis place dey call um Heaven. Dis Heaven be place where we go live after we done die, if we no be so-so bad for dis Earth. De Angel dey live for Heaven an' play de banjo and get plenty fine chop and plenty palm-wine.

De headman of dem Angel, dey call 'um Gabriel. When dis palaver start for Heaven, there be plenty humbug by bad angel, dey call 'um Lucifer. An' Gabriel go catch Lucifer and go beat 'um An' palaver stop one-time.

An' de Lawd tell Gabriel he be good man too much, an' He

go dash Gabriel one trumpet. An' Gabriel he get licence for play trumpet and hit drum for Heaven. An' Lucifer go for Hellfire, where he be headman now.

After de Lawd go lookum dis ting dey call 'um Earth, He savvy dat no man be for seat. So de Lawd take small piece Earth an' He go breathe – an' man dey.

An' de Lawd He go call dis man Hadam. De Lawd He say, 'Hadam.' An Hadam he say, 'Yes sah.' De Lawd He say, 'Hadam, you see dis garden? Dey call 'um Paradise. Everyt'ing for dis garden be for you – but dem mango tree dat be for middle of garden, dat no be for you. Dat tree be white man chop, dat no be black man chop. You no go chop 'um, or you get plenty pain for belly. You savvy?'

An' Hadam he say, 'Yes sah, Lawd. I savvy.'

De Lawd He done go back for Heaven to hear Gabriel play de trumpet. An' Hadam he go walka walka for garden, where everyt'ing be fine too much. Byem-bye de Lawd He come back for Earth an' go lookum see Hadam. An' de Lawd say, 'Hadam everyt'ing be fine? You like 'um?' An Hadam he say, 'Yes sah, everyt'ing no be bad but …

An de Lawd say, 'Whassa matta Hadam? You done get small trouble?' An' Hadam he say, ' No, Lawd, I no get trouble, Sah – I no get woman.'

An de Lawd He say, 'Ah ha.'

Den de Lawd He make Hadam go sleep for one place, an' He go take small piece bone from Haddam side – dey call um Whish-bone. He go breathe – an' woman dey. An' de Lawd He go call dis woman, Heva.

De Lawd He go wake Hadam an' He say, 'Hadam, you see dis woman, Heva?' Hadam he say, 'Yes sah, Lawd. I see 'um. He be sweet pass stinkfish.' Den de Lawd go 'way up to Heaven an' Hadam an' Heva go walka for garden where dey go play plenty.

One day, when Hadam go 'way for catch fish, Heva done take small walk an' she meet Shanake. An' Shanake he say, 'Hello, Heva. An Heva she say, 'Hello, Shanake.'

An' Shanake he say, ' Whassa matter, Heva, Why you no go

chop dem fine, fine mango from tree for middle of garden?' An' Heva she say, 'A'a dat be white man chop, dat no be black man chop. Hadam done tell me we get plenty trouble, plenty pain for belly if we go chop um.'

An Shanake he say, 'Ah, Hadam be bloo' fool. Dat chop be good chop for black man pass all. You chop 'um, you like 'um.' An' Heva she done chop 'um an' she done like 'um too much. She put dem mango for Hadam groundnut stew – then there be plenty trouble for Paradise one time.

Hadam and Heva dey done savvy dey be naked, dey no get cloth, so dey go put 'um hat for head. Byem-bye one man dey call 'um Noah, he Headman for one big boat, an' he done take Heva for sail on lagoon an' dey make plenty humbug for Hadam.

Den de Lawd he done come back for Earth an' He go call, 'Hadam.' But Hadam go fear de Lawd and done go for bush one time. Again de Lawd call, 'Hadam.' An' Hadam he say for small voice, 'Yes sah, Lawd.' An' de Lawd say, 'Close me Hadam, close me.' An' Hadam close de Lawd.

De Lawd say, ' Whassa matta, Hadam? Why you go for bush?' An' Hadam say, 'I no get cloth, Lawd, so I know want that you done see me naked.' An' de Lawd he be vex too much. 'What ting dis who tell you you be naked?' He say, 'Aha, you done chop dem mango for tree for middle garden.' An' Hadam say, 'I no go chop um, Lawd. De woman you done make for me she go put 'um for groundnut stew.'

Den de Lawd made plenty palaver an' he done drove Hadam and Heva from Paradise.

In retrospect, even through a tint of rose, Mambilla was my paradise lost.

Glossary

Adamawa A former province in Northern Nigeria ruled over by a Fulani Emir known as the Lamido whose headquarters were in Yola

Ardo (Ardo'en) Fulani Chief or clan head

Arnardo (Arnardo'en) A pagan chief under Fulani jurisdiction. From the Hausa *arna* meaning 'pagan'

Barriki European living quarters

Durbar An Indian word meaning an Indian ruler's court. In Nigeria, a ceremonial gathering of Emirs, Chiefs and the people under their jurisdiction.

Fulani A West African people, predominantly Muslim, composed of many clans some of whom are nomadic cattle owners

Hausa A West African Muslim people who live predominantly in Northern Nigeria and whose language is West Africa's *linqua franca*

Kanuri A West African Muslim people who live mainly in north-east Nigeria and whose traditional ruler is known as the Shehu. The Kanuri Shehu was formerly based in Kukawa in Borno Province. His palace is now in Maiduguri where Boko Haram originated.

Sarki Emir or Chief

Sarkin Barriki Resthouse caretaker

Sarkin Tsafi Witch doctor

European Administrative Hierarchy

Resident The Resident was in charge of a Province of which there were 12 in Northern Nigeria during my time.

Senior District Officer (SDO), District Officer (DO) In charge of a Division within the Province

Assistant District Officer (ADO) In charge of a part of the Division under the District Officer

District A local government area under the control of the Native Authority (local government), and usually with a District Head as senior official answerable to the Native Authority

Division The 12 provinces of Northern Nigeria were divided into divisions, which often embraced more than one Native Authority.

Native Authority Similar to a local government in the United Kingdom

Native Authority Police A Native Authority police force armed only with truncheons

Nigeria Police A Federal Government police force which was permitted to bear firearms

Public Works Department (PWD) A government department responsible for the construction and maintenance of government buildings and also for the maintenance and building of roads

African Administrative Hierarchy

Emir Head of one of the 12 Emirates in place when the British colonised Northern Nigeria. Formerly Hausa they were replaced by Fulani Emirs during the Jihad of Uthman dan Fodio (see footnote 2 on p. 10; p. 14ff)

District Head Head of a district under the Emir

Village Head Head of a village administrative area under the District Head

Hamlet Head Head of a hamlet under the Village Head

In Adamawa Province

Lamido Equivalent to an Emir. The traditional title of the Fulani ruler of Adamawa province

Ardo A Fulani clan headman

Arnardo A 'pagan' Village Head under the Lamido's jurisdiction

In Borno Province

Shehu Equivalent to an Emir. The traditional title of the Kanuri ruler of Borno Province

Kacalla A Village Head of the Kanuri tribe

Note: The first Governor of Northern Nigeria, Lord Lugard, instituted a system of Indirect Rule whereby the British administration ruled through the existing African structures which were in place when they colonised the north. An effective African administration was already in place and had been for many centuries before the arrival of the British. The British abolished some of the least desirable practices such as slavery and the more extreme elements of Shari'a law such as stoning to death for adultery.

Acknowledgements

Abubakar Jauro's (Bobboi's) visit to my home in Kent inspired me to publish this book. Without his enthusiasm and long-term friendship, it would not be in your hands. Deep thanks are due to Kathryn Rae, Derek Mountain, Bobboi, Roddy Dunnett and Jane McMorland Hunter who read through the typescript and gave me invaluable advice. Amanda Helm of Helm Information advised soundly on all technical aspects of publication. I would like to thank the family of the late Sir Hanns Vischer (Dan Hausa) who gave me permission to use two of his illustrations on the cover. Some of the photographs reproduced here were retrieved by me from a waste dump when NORLA (the Northern Nigeria Literacy Agency) was disbanded in the 1960s, the rest are my own.

But my biggest 'thank you' goes to Penny Mountain who edited a muddled typescript, full of inconsistencies, and turned it into a very well-edited end product. She also battled with my stubbornness and political incorrectness as well – no mean feat.

I salute my predecessors in the Colonial Administration in Northern Nigeria. I have drawn on a number of their reports and fully realise how much tougher the life of a bush DO was in the opening decades of the 20th century. Battling with constant bouts of fever, they are the unsung heroes of Northern Nigeria who brought peace in the form of *Pax Britannica* to a turbulent land.

> *'Who'll shake his hand?'*
> *'I,' said the Fever,*
> *'And I'm no deceiver,*
> *I'll shake his hand!'*
> Rudyard Kipling

And a final salute to the people of Northern Nigeria, especially the people on the Mambilla plateau, who through their loyalty, steadfastness and sense of humour, provided me with some of the happiest years of my life.

Zan ci gaba da tunawa da su, har karshen duniya.

Bibliography

I have consulted and quoted from the following books:

A Handbook of Health in the Tropics (1952). H M Stationery Office, London.

Hastings, A C G (1925). *Nigerian Days*. John Lane The Bodley Head, London.

Meek, C K (1931). *Tribal Studies in Northern Nigeria* (Volumes 1 and 2*)*. Kegan Paul, Trench, Trubner, London.

Migeod, F W H (1925). *Through British Cameroons*. Heath Cranton, London

Index

General

People
African names – in written order
Other names – surname first

Tribes

Places